The Essential Guide to Secondary Mathematics

Combining research-based theory with fresh, practical guidance for the classroom, *The Essential Guide to Secondary Mathematics* is a stimulating new resource for all student and practising teachers looking for new ideas and inspiration. With an emphasis on exciting your mathematical and pedagogical passions, it focuses on the dynamics of the classroom and the process of designing and using rich mathematical tasks.

Written by a highly experienced mathematics teacher who understands the realities of the secondary classroom, this book combines insights from the latest research into mathematical learning with useful strategies and ideas for engaging teaching. The text is punctuated by frequent tasks, some mathematical and others more reflective, which are designed to encourage independent thinking. Key topics covered include:

- preparing yourself: thinking about mathematics and pedagogy, taking care of your health and dealing with stress
- different styles of learning and teaching mathematics
- ideas for lessons: what does it take to turn an idea into a lesson?
- tasks, timings and resources
- equality and dealing positively with difference
- mathematical starters, fillers and finishers: achieving variety
- the mathematical classroom community: seating layouts, displays and practical considerations
- assessment: effective strategies for responding to learners' mathematics, and writing reports.

The Essential Guide to Secondary Mathematics will be a valuable resource both for beginning teachers interested in developing their understanding and for experienced teachers looking to re-evaluate their practice. Aiming to develop all aspects of your mathematics teaching, this book will help you to devise, adapt and implement ideas for successful and enjoyable teaching and learning.

Colin Foster teaches secondary mathematics at King Henry VIII School, Coventry, UK, and is the author of a wide range of books and articles about teaching mathematics. He is a former co-editor of the journal *Mathematics Teaching*, a chartered mathematics teacher and a member of the Association of Teachers of Mathematics and the Mathematical Association.

The Essential Guide to Secondary Mathematics

Successful and enjoyable teaching and learning

Colin Foster

Routledge
Taylor & Francis Group

LONDON AND NEW YORK

First published 2013
by Routledge
2 Park Square, Milton Park, Abingdon, Oxon OX14 4RN

Simultaneously published in the USA and Canada
by Routledge
711 Third Avenue, New York, NY 10017

Routledge is an imprint of the Taylor & Francis Group, an informa business

British Library Cataloguing in Publication Data
A catalogue record for this book is available from the British Library

Library of Congress Cataloging in Publication Data
Foster, Colin, 1973-
The essential guide to secondary mathematics : successful and enjoyable teaching
and learning / Colin Foster.
    p. cm.
Includes index.
ISBN 978-0-415-52770-5 (hardback)—ISBN 978-0-415-52771-2—
ISBN 978-0-203-11883-2 1. Mathematics—Study and teaching (Secondary)
2. Effective teaching. I. Title.
QA11.2.F674 2012
510.71'2—dc23   2012008150

ISBN: 978-0-415-52770-5 (hbk)
ISBN: 978-0-415-52771-2 (pbk)
ISBN: 978-0-203-11883-2 (ebk)

Typeset in Bembo
by Cenveo Publisher Services

MIX
Paper from
responsible sources
FSC® C004839
www.fsc.org

Printed and bound in Great Britain by the MPG Books Group

Contents

Illustrations

Figures

Table

Tasks

Chapter 3

Chapter 4

Chapter 5

Chapter 6

Acknowledgments

I would like to thank the many colleagues that I have worked with over the years for all their stimulating thoughts, provocative challenges and generosity of time. I would particularly like to thank John Mason, Anne Watson and Malcolm Swan for the many *Institutes of Mathematics Pedagogy* that they have organized, and for the insights into mathematics and mathematics education that have arisen from the participants there. I would also like to thank the members of the *Association of Teachers of Mathematics* whose ideas and comments at numerous annual conferences have informed my thinking in so many ways. The team at Routledge have worked extremely hard to bring this book together and I am very grateful to them. Most of all, I thank my wife, Sharifah, for her unfailing support at all times.

Introduction

This book is not just for those who are beginning as mathematics teachers; it is intended just as much for those with more experience. It deliberately avoids dwelling on the intricacies of the particular requirements for passing an initial teacher education course or acquiring newly-qualified-teacher status. Instead, it aims to be about mathematics and the learning of mathematics as ends in themselves. Each chapter is punctuated at intervals with *Tasks*, some purely mathematical and others more reflective. Some of the mathematical tasks could be used in secondary mathematics classrooms, but they are primarily intended for the reader to engage with. By working regularly on mathematics as you go through the book, you will find that many of the issues discussed will be brought into sharper focus. The reflective tasks are intended to give you the opportunity to ponder what you think about a particular issue. There are rarely simple answers and you will certainly take a different view from me on some of the issues. Some of the tasks are intended to be provocative and destabilizing; some you may find unhelpful—in which case, please just move on to whatever comes next.

No book can tell anyone how to teach mathematics any more than any colleague or mentor can. Every mathematics teacher must find their own way to bring to life the beliefs that they hold about mathematics, about education and about human beings. So this book doesn't attempt to force a particular viewpoint on you, although neither does it seek to conceal my own views. Different perspectives are offered and questions asked, allowing you space to find your own position. I assume that every mathematics teacher, no matter how long in the tooth, can find ways in which they might develop their practice in the classroom. It is a truism to say that to be a teacher is to be a learner too. This book is a tool for mathematics teachers who wish to change and become better at the job that they do. I hope that beginning teachers will return to it at later stages in their career and that it will be of interest to teachers with experience in another subject area (or a different age range) who will be taking on some secondary mathematics classes and might find some differences from what they are used to doing.

Pressures on the mathematics teacher are increasing all the time, with ever more detailed and prescriptive 'guidance'/'support'/interference from those who may not always seem to understand the reality 'on the ground'. It is important for mathematics teachers to have the knowledge and confidence to work with young learners of mathematics in ways that they judge to be appropriate for their situation. All mathematics teachers should be well informed about different viewpoints and possible ways of working, but no one else can know your class as you do. As mathematics teachers, we have the opportunity and responsibility to offer mathematical tasks that will promote our learners' development in, and love for, mathematics, and to support them as they work on such tasks. This book aims to help us in that important work.

Colin Foster
January 2012

Chapter 1

The mathematics teacher

I don't understand why anyone would want to be a maths teacher!

Parent at parents' evening

Since this is a book about mathematics teaching, let's begin with some mathematics.

Task Paint

A painter mixes 5 litres of white paint with 3 litres of blue paint.
Then they realize that they meant to do it the other way round.
What is the least wasteful way now of getting the desired colour in sufficient quantity?

Did you try this task? Throughout this book, there will be different kinds of tasks, some mathematical and some not. Perhaps you have seen it (or a clone of it) before, or used it with learners, maybe recently. The tasks in this book will inevitably be 'hit and miss' to some extent; as the reader, you should *use* this book rather than *submit* to it. If you don't find something useful, move on to the next part. Sometimes I find that I am in the mood for working on mathematics; other times I am not. Some tasks immediately grab me; others don't. Of course, such variations in motivation will be true of the learners we work with as well as of ourselves (Middleton and Spanias, 1999). You will find comments on the mathematical tasks at the end of each chapter.

1.1 Motivation

Mathematics is the queen of the sciences.

Carl Friedrich Gauss

Here is a different kind of task.

Task Why teach mathematics?

Why are you reading this book?
What is your interest in mathematics teaching?
How did you get to this point?

Mathematics teachers come from a variety of backgrounds (Richardson and Watt, 2005). You may be completely new to teaching, or you might be moving to mathematics teaching from teaching something else. Or you might have lots of experience as a mathematics teacher but want to re-think what you do and come at your work in a fresh way. Some mathematics teachers have had a previous career, either in a mathematics-related area or in something else. Some mathematics teachers have mathematics degrees, some have degrees in closely related subjects and some don't. Whatever your particular background, experiences and interests, these will be your strengths and will help to inform the kind of mathematics teacher that you become. It is sensible to view your past positively, since you can't change it, and to draw on whatever advantages it may give you.

People have all sorts of reasons for becoming mathematics teachers (Hutchings, 1996). Sometimes it runs in families (Watt *et al.*, 2007), and even though someone's parents may well have advised them against going into the teaching profession, they did nonetheless. Well-qualified mathematicians are much in demand in a range of occupations, so mathematics teaching is often a conscious choice to accept a significantly lower salary than might be available elsewhere. For some, the termly rhythm and daily hours of the teaching life fit in well with family commitments. For whatever reasons, teaching exerts a powerful draw on many people, often from a young age, at the same time as being widely recognized as a demanding and difficult job.

Task Alternatives

I admire people who teach maths, but I couldn't do it myself. I couldn't stand teaching the same things over and over again.

                                                                      Research mathematician

What do you think you would be if you *weren't* a mathematics teacher?

Some mathematics teachers cannot imagine being anything else: they don't know what they would do in a world in which mathematics teachers were not required! On the other hand, if you have had a previous career, then this could be your answer. Or perhaps you have a future aspiration and mathematics teaching is something you are doing in between other things. If you weren't a mathematics teacher, maybe you would do something completely unrelated to mathematics or teaching. However, many mathematics teachers, when asked this question, talk either about something mathematical or something educational.

Mathematics Teacher *or* Mathematics Teacher

Some mathematics teachers see themselves firstly as mathematicians. Perhaps they enjoyed their mathematics degree a great deal and considered research in a university or working in a highly mathematical field afterwards. School teaching may have been what they always imagined themselves doing, or may have arisen as a backup option when their real ambition didn't materialize. They have a love for mathematics that they want to share with those they teach. They may particularly enjoy teaching students who are preparing to study mathematics at university.	Some mathematics teachers see themselves first and foremost as teachers. Perhaps they considered being a primary school teacher, attracted by the idea of being a generalist and teaching a range of subjects. When someone asks them, 'What do you teach?' they like to say, 'Children' rather than 'Maths'. If they weren't mathematics teachers, they would teach something else, either in a school or elsewhere. They enjoy working with people, especially youngsters. They may enjoy teaching the younger years at least as much as, if not more than, older learners.

Figure 1.1 Some stereotypes of mathematics teachers

Figure 1.1 characterizes mathematics teachers as firstly teachers or as firstly mathematicians. Of course, these portraits are stereotypes, and many mathematics teachers will position themselves somewhere between these extremes, but these descriptions may help you to locate your chief motivations in being a mathematics teacher. Understanding this may help you to grow into the sort of mathematics teacher that reflects who you really are.

> # Task Stereotypes
>
> *You can tell an extrovert mathematician because when you're talking to them they look at your toes rather than theirs.*
>
> Old joke
>
> What different difficulties might each of the two stereotypical mathematics teachers portrayed in Figure 1.1 experience in school?
> Do you find yourself identifying more closely with one than with the other?

For evidence that mathematicians have something of an image problem in Western society today, you need look no further than popular books and films. Rensaa (2006: 2) comments that 'a widespread public image of mathematics is that it is difficult, cold, abstract and in many cultures, largely masculine'. Mendick (2002: 44) concludes that 'The dominant discourse around mathematicians in popular culture depicts them as boring, obsessed with the irrelevant, socially incompetent, male, and unsuccessfully heterosexual'. A study in which children were asked to 'draw a mathematician at work' predictably led to a lot of badly-dressed bald white men in glasses (Picker and Berry, 2000). (Although such depictions were highly stereotypical, many of their drawings do look rather like people I know!)

Such a character might be expected to be poorly adapted for life in a classroom, and many beginning mathematics teachers do experience something of a culture shock if they move directly from being an undergraduate mathematics student to teaching ratio to a class of 11-year-olds. Those with a more introverted personality can initially find it difficult to establish a comfortable classroom manner, yet in the end frequently make popular and effective teachers. To be a successful teacher, it is not necessary to try to be like the most outgoing person you know – great teachers come in all types and it is healthy for learners to work with a wide variety of different kinds of adults in school. Learners' prejudices can become self-perpetuating if only certain types of children think that working with mathematics could be for them. Ideally, within a mathematics department a variety of different types of teachers, male and female, from different backgrounds and with different personalities, will provide role models for many different learners.

At the other end of the spectrum, some teachers seem comfortable in the classroom from the very beginning but lack confidence over their mathematical knowledge. Sometimes teachers are just rusty if they haven't used some of their mathematics for some years, and they will find it coming back as they go on. Others may need to address their subject knowledge more explicitly, particularly if they are teaching older learners for the first time. Even mathematicians who have been successful in obtaining a university mathematics degree sometimes later say that they don't feel that they really understood many basic things thoroughly until they began teaching them and dealing with learners' questions and ideas. Preparing to teach something can be an effective way to learn (or re-learn) it. If you know that you have mathematical weaknesses that could harm your teaching, it is best to be honest about it and begin to address them, perhaps with support from a knowledgeable colleague.

1.2 Mathematics as a subject

> Mathematics, rightly viewed, possesses not only truth, but supreme beauty.
>
> Bertrand Russell

It is one thing to enjoy mathematics yourself, as an interest to read books about it, solve puzzles, talk about it, watch television documentaries about it, or use it in your life or work. It is quite another thing to *impose* mathematics on other people who may not feel the same way about it or think that they need it or can do it. Do mathematics teachers have the right to do that? Mathematics teachers who feel uneasy about this can find it difficult in the classroom when learners do not respond as enthusiastically as they might wish.

Task   Maze

```
              S
          S   H   S
      S   H   T   H   S
  S   H   T   A   T   H   S
S H T A M A T H S
  S   H   T   A   T   H   S
      S   H   T   H   S
          S   H   S
              S
```

Moving from letter to letter, in how many ways can you spell MATHS?
Are you sure that you have found all the possible ways?
Can you be certain that you didn't miss any? How?
What happens with other words?

Did you do this task? If you did, did you find it fun? Did you think to try *palindromic* words as well? Do you think that you learned anything from doing it? Is it the sort of task that you would use with learners? For some people, puzzles such as this are enjoyable and interesting in their own right: there is a self-imposed challenge in using your powers to solve something, which many people relish. A lot of mathematics teachers enjoy crosswords or Sudoku puzzles, but no one thinks that these things have worldly importance. Unless it is for a competition, once you complete the puzzle, it probably goes straight in the bin – the final answer is of no importance; only the experience of the doing. But not all learners will be excited about working on puzzles.

Task Why learn mathematics?

Why do we have to learn this? When will we ever actually use this?
Learners of mathematics

Why do you think mathematics is worth learning?
Do you believe in compulsory mathematics education? If so, up to what age? Why?

It can be very helpful to think about what you believe about these issues before you go into the mathematics classroom (Noyes, 2007). Of course, there are no right or wrong answers, but knowing what you think can give you the confidence to engage with some of the sorts of things that learners may say (Ernest, 2000; Heymann, 2003). For some, mathematics possesses intrinsic interest, doing mathematics is fun and no further justification is needed. Many mathematics teachers may feel that way, but inevitably when you are teaching a compulsory subject not all learners will share your perspective. You might hope to change learners' minds about this over a period of time, but in the meantime it may be more realistic to accept that some learners will, at best, see mathematics as a means to an end (a service subject) and, at worst, as an unwarranted intrusion into their lives! Even some who do well in mathematics (as measured by test results) may harbour negative perceptions of the subject. Noddings (2003: 202) comments that 'Huge numbers of ... "successful" students finish their schooling with a fear and loathing of mathematics that will last a lifetime'.

Task Responses

You might like to think about the following responses that a mathematics teacher might make and the assumptions that lie behind each.
What are the possible benefits of responding in each of these ways? What are the dangers?

- Maths is useful in all sorts of everyday situations, such as home DIY or managing your money. If you don't understand maths, you'll get taken advantage of in life – you won't be able to check your payslip or get a good financial deal; you'll be conned whenever you buy anything!

- The world is getting more and more technological and more and more people need more and more maths in all sorts of jobs these days. Employers consistently say that they want numerate people.
- OK, you may not use this particular bit of maths in the future, but it's all good exercise for your brain, making you think, strengthening all those brain cells in there! And you're going to use your brain in the future, whatever you end up doing!
- You don't come to school mainly to get vocational training for your future career. This is your *general* education – it makes you more human to learn about a range of things, many of which you probably won't be doing yourself in the future. It's about understanding the world around you and finding out what you like and what other people do.
- Because it's fun! Even if you're not enjoying this, stick with it and I think that by the end of term you'll be liking maths at least a little bit more than you are at the moment.

1.2.1 Utility for life

Arguments based on the usefulness of mathematics in everyday life depend on what someone else envisages as 'everyday life'. Many learners don't live in houses that their families own, so the opportunities (or money) for home DIY may be considerably more limited than they might be for the typically middle-class mathematics teacher. At the other extreme, learners from wealthier backgrounds might not readily envisage themselves buying and sawing up wood: they would get a carpenter to do it. Another problem is that the mathematics of everyday life tends to focus on money, length/area/volume calculations and probability. So it is harder to use this sort of argument if your lesson is on a pure mathematics topic such as the irrationality of $\sqrt{2}$. Some mathematics educators have argued that real mathematics is not actually very useful in ordinary life (Andrews, 1998), while others have strongly disagreed (Huckstep, 2003). Noddings (2003), for instance, believes that algebra and geometry as currently offered in schools are much less vital to the majority of learners (or for society) than, say, learning about parenting and interpersonal relations. Spencer (1910: 30) suggests that an archaeologist from the future examining our school books and examination papers would conclude that this must have been a curriculum for people who were not going to have children, since there was no mention of them.

1.2.2 Utility for careers

Again, if the learner replies that they are going to be a pop singer, it may be hard to convince them why mathematics (beyond counting their money) is likely to be essential to them. Many learners may anticipate lengthy periods of unemployment and are unlikely to be swayed by possible benefits that might seem to be a long way off. Learners who 'know' that they are going to be an accountant or an engineer, for instance, might be more inclined to appreciate the importance of the subject for their future. However, that does not necessarily mean that they will enjoy today's lesson any more – they might just be more willing to 'suffer' it, which is hardly ideal. There are serious problems with an over-emphasis on the economic benefits of education; for example, Noddings (2003: 4) remarks that 'It is as though our society has simply decided that the purpose of schooling is economic – to improve the financial condition of individuals and to advance the prosperity of the nation'. For many mathematics teachers, this is not what it is all about.

1.2.3 Brain training

Mathematics may be one way of 'exercising' the brain, but it is by no means the only one; learners may prefer to exercise other parts of the brain in other ways. Also, like the previous two responses, this seems to regard mathematics as merely a means to an end, possibly devaluing it as a subject in its own right. After all, memorizing the telephone directory would be a mental challenge, but the benefit would hardly be worth the effort. There must be more to learning mathematics than getting a mental workout.

1.2.4 Learning for a better society

If the learner has a very different philosophy of life, this response may fall on deaf ears, but it is hard to argue with the view that education should be enriching and empowering. It is only by tasting a wide range of disciplines that learners can discover where their particular interests may lie. Understanding what people very different from ourselves are doing in their lives helps to make a cohesive democratic society (Povey, 2003), and, according to Russell (2009: 113–4), 'The defence of the state in all civilised countries is quite as much in the hands of teachers as in those of the armed forces. ... Teachers are more than any other class the guardians of civilisation'.

1.2.5 Enjoyment

It is hard to argue against pleasure! Not everyone enjoys mathematics but many learners do, at least some of the time, or can do if given more positive experiences of it. Even if they are not spectacularly successful in traditional examinations, many learners obtain a lot of satisfaction from solving problems and getting definite solutions. The coherence and power of mathematics appeals to many learners, even if they may not always wish to admit it in front of their peers. Some learners begin to enjoy a subject only when they have reached a certain stage in it, so it may be necessary to persevere with some things for a little while before the enjoyment comes. Subsequent chapters will suggest ways of promoting enjoyment in the learning of mathematics.

Of course, there may be an agenda behind the question. It is wise to take learners' questions seriously but to be aware that a question like this can sometimes be equivalent to a statement, and that the learner may not really want an answer. Such a question may reveal a healthy scepticism regarding the education process; during their teenage years, many learners experience a great desire to leave school and make their own way in life, and questioning the curriculum and those who run it may be part of that. Sometimes a particularly difficult or unstimulating mathematical task may provoke learners into asking 'why' out of frustration, or it may arise out of an extended period of disillusionment with the subject. Acknowledging these feelings may be more helpful than giving clever answers.

Task Responding

How can it be that mathematics, being after all a product of human thought which is independent of experience, is so admirably appropriate to the objects of reality?

Albert Einstein

Can you think of other types of response than the five given?
Which sort of response resonates most strongly with you? Why do you think that is?
What sort of approach would/do you use in the classroom?

Pre-prepared answers that are trotted out thoughtlessly are unlikely to be helpful, and getting to know your learners so that you can relate what you say to their perspectives and interests is vital. You may not be able to convince everyone that mathematics is as important as you think it is, and it may be wise to see their view of mathematics as a 'work in progress'.

1.3 Your perspective

> I love it when something clicks mathematically for a pupil and it's as if a light has come on.
>
> Mathematics teacher

The discussion above presupposes that 'mathematics' as taught in schools corresponds to 'mathematics' as otherwise understood, but that is not necessarily the case. There has always been lively discussion over what should go into the school mathematics curriculum (Robitaille and Dirks, 1982; Noss, 1994). There are many competing interests, from the academic demands of universities (both for mathematics courses and for courses that *use* some mathematics) to the wide-ranging perspectives of industry, to those who think that education should be an end in itself, not something that panders to changing economic and technological requirements. The debate sometimes polarizes into traditionalist advocates of *back to basics* on the one hand, with an emphasis on mental numeracy and old-fashioned pencil-and-paper calculations, and *progressives* on the other, who seek to draw on more modern developments in mathematics that are seen as relating more closely to the needs of today's society, including appropriate utilization of modern technology (O'Brien, 2007). The *new maths* movement had its heyday in the 1960s, but has received criticism (Kline, 1976). There are equally heated debates over mathematics *pedagogy* (how the subject is taught), and many of these issues will be encountered in later chapters.

Task Discovered or invented?

Mathematics is the language with which God has written the universe.

Galileo Galilei

Do you think that mathematics is discovered or invented? Why?
Can we know that mathematics is true?

You may not find it easy to decide, but your views on this are likely to influence how you teach, and it is worth considering what you believe (Mazur, 2008; Beswick, 2007; Sarukkai, 2005; Hamming, 1980). It can also be an interesting issue to raise with learners (Rowlands and Davies, 2006), for instance by asking what they think mathematics could be like in another part of the universe (Hamming, 1998). Many mathematics teachers seem to take an *absolutist* perspective on the subject, believing that mathematical claims, once proved, are perfectly and completely true forever, independent of the opinions of human beings (Rowlands *et al.*, 2001). The opposite *fallibilist* view (Ernest, 1999) stresses that mathematics is a human enterprise, where mistakes can be made from time to time, so ultimately all results are open to revision. The proof of some theorems requires extremely detailed checking by numerous mathematicians (Singh, 2002) or the verification of thousands of special cases, which is sometimes feasible only by computer (Wilson, 2002). In cases such as these, how many people can really claim to 'know' for themselves that those theorems are true?

It is often assumed that mathematics teachers who take an absolutist perspective will tend to see the subject as an unchanging body of knowledge which must be 'passed on' to their learners, leading to dull chalk-and-talk *delivery* teaching approaches and an absence of creative thinking (Povey, 2002), although this link has been challenged (Rowlands *et al.*, 2011). Certainly, there are as many perspectives on mathematics teaching as there are mathematics teachers, as the following task may reveal.

Task Metaphors

It's like keeeping a whole load of plates spinning constantly.

Mathematics teacher

What other metaphors for mathematics teaching can you think of?
Are they for teaching generally or more specific to mathematics?
Which metaphors do you identify most closely with? Why do you think that might be?

When considering how to view the practice of teaching, stark contrasts are sometimes offered, such as 'a sage on the stage or a guide on the side' (King, 1993). Either you are going to stand at the front of the classroom and broadcast your wisdom, while learners listen meekly and take notes, or you are going to sit in the passenger seat and watch passively while the learners take complete control of every decision. More commonly, some middle ground is found between these extremes.

Some people think of teaching primarily as one of the *caring* professions, like social work or counselling. Others think medically, drawing parallels with a doctor or psychiatrist, where diagnoses of difficulties are made and treatments prescribed. Some might focus primarily on management issues ('crowd control') and think of police officers, bouncers, prison officers, babysitters or even zoo keepers! Others might think of a life coach or relate teaching mathematics to working on mathematical problems in academia or industry. Metaphors emphasize one aspect to the detriment of all others, and this is their advantage as well as their drawback. The language that you use in relation to teaching mathematics can become habitual and affect the direction that your teaching takes, so it is sensible from time to time to review whether the way you talk about your work supports what you want to achieve or frustrates it. Some of the subsequent chapters will take up some of these ideas.

Task Joys

Teaching maths can be difficult, but there are always surprises to keep you on your toes!

Mathematics teacher

What are some of the joys of teaching mathematics that are most important for you?
(You might need to anticipate if you have not done much mathematics teaching yet.)

Many teachers report high levels of satisfaction with their profession (Chapman and Lowther, 1982). The enthusiasm of young people and their wide-eyed interest in the world around them can be very touching. Seeing 'lights come on' as a learner understands a mathematical idea for the first time is extremely rewarding, as is watching as learners take control of some mathematics, perhaps making conjectures or proving something for themselves. Being involved at such an important stage in other human beings' lives and being present when important ideas are taking root can feel like a privilege. There is much pleasure in seeing young people mature – in many social ways, but also mathematically, progressing and growing in confidence. Being paid to work on mathematics is enough for some mathematics teachers, and of course some teachers just enjoy having a captive audience (at least some of the time)!

For most mathematics teachers, teaching isn't just something they do during the day and then forget about; like any profession which involves working with people, it can become an identity and affect how you relate to people outside work. When off duty, mathematics teachers can find themselves thinking from an educational perspective about children (including their own) and looking for mathematics wherever they go. Many teachers find it hard to switch off during term time, and if you begin to feel trapped in your work–life (im-)balance, experiencing insomnia or anxiety, it is definitely time to seek help and not to accept this as normal (see chapter 3). All of your experiences will affect how you fill out your role as a teacher of mathematics. As a teacher, you bring to the classroom the totality of your life up to that point: your experiences, your attitudes, your beliefs. Nobody's background is intrinsically better than anyone else's, but it can be useful to think about how your 'mathematics teacher' side can benefit from everything else that is you.

The *Association of Teachers of Mathematics* (www.atm.org.uk) has four 'Guiding Principles', which can be a very good starting point for thinking about what it means to be involved in mathematics teaching. They are reproduced below for your consideration.

- The ability to operate mathematically is an aspect of human functioning which is as universal as language itself. Attention needs constantly to be drawn to this fact. Any possibility of intimidating with mathematical expertise is to be avoided.
- The power to learn rests with the learner. Teaching has a subordinate role. The teacher has a duty to seek out ways to engage the power of the learner.
- It is important to examine critically approaches to teaching and to explore new possibilities, whether deriving from research, from technological developments or from the imaginative and insightful ideas of others.
- Teaching and learning are cooperative activities. Encouraging a questioning approach and giving due attention to the ideas of others are attitudes to be encouraged. Influence is best sought by building networks of contacts in professional circles. (taken from www.atm.org.uk/about/)

Task   Summary task

People who become teachers haven't really grown up: they want to spend their whole lives going to school.
At least you get long holidays!
Those who can, do; those who can't, teach.

Parents

What motivates you to teach mathematics?
Write down some of the characteristics that you aspire to as a mathematics teacher.
Are there any things that you particularly want to *avoid*?

Comments on mathematical tasks

Task: Paint

Children in the twenty-first century are very used to clicking 'undo' and can be quite flummoxed by situations such as this, in which that is just not possible! There are many real-life modelling issues to contend with (see pages 47–51). Perhaps the painter could just live with the paler colour? Perhaps they cannot afford to buy more paint, or it is out of stock? But in the spirit of puzzles such as this, they will need to pour off $\frac{2}{5}$ of the mixture, to obtain a mixture containing 3 litres of white and 1.8 litres of blue. Then they need to supply another 3.2 litres of blue paint to make 8 litres of the right colour.

It is interesting to generalize to a starting point of w litres of white and b litres of blue and also to consider what happens if blue paint is more expensive than white (e.g., suppose it costs twice as much) – does it make a difference if we seek the *cheapest* solution rather than the one that is least wasteful of paint? What if white paint is more hazardous to dispose of?

Task: Maze

If you know about *Pascal's triangle*, that might help you. It is interesting to explore words of different lengths (maybe start with MA or MAT and work upwards – to MATHEMATICS, perhaps). Is it just the number of letters in the word that matters? A palindromic word such as LEVEL requires more thought. You might also try extending the idea to three dimensions.

Further reading

Holt, J. (1990) *How Children Fail*, London: Penguin.
Ollerton, M. (2009) *The Mathematics Teacher's Handbook*, London: Continuum.

Chapter 2

Developing as a mathematics teacher

> They say that the first 40 years are the most difficult; after that, it's fine.
>
> Mathematics teacher

You may be an experienced mathematics teacher already, or you may be just starting out. Whatever point you are at, developing in your role is important to any professional. Most teachers would say that they want to be a better teacher in a year's time than they are now. In this chapter, we will look at some ways to develop your practice as a mathematics teacher, and many of these themes will be developed further throughout the rest of the book.

2.1 Learning for yourself

> Everyone has been to school, so every person you meet thinks they automatically know how to teach.
>
> Mathematics teacher

Everyone brings experiences that are relevant to being a teacher of mathematics, the most important of which is that of being a learner of mathematics. No doctor can have personally suffered all of the illnesses that they will treat during their career, and no mathematics teacher will have experienced every possible difficulty with every possible part of the subject. However, every mathematics teacher will have learned for themselves everything that they will teach. You cannot be a mathematics teacher without also being a learner in at least three ways: a learner of mathematics, a learner of mathematics pedagogy and a learner of the learners that you teach.

2.1.1 A learner of mathematics

> A teacher who is not always thinking about solving problems – ones he does not know the answer to – is psychologically simply not prepared to teach problem solving to his students.
>
> Paul Halmos

With this in mind, here is another mathematical task to try (with comments, as usual, at the end of the chapter).

Task Dots

How many dots are there in this drawing?
Can you find out without counting them all?
Make another dotty picture and try to do the same.

Not surprisingly, if you are going to teach mathematics it is useful if you know something about the subject yourself (McNamara, 1991)! Teachers' mathematical knowledge (Shulman, 1986) cannot always be taken for granted (Rowland *et al.*, 2005); indeed, it may be that there is currently a crisis of *subject content knowledge* among mathematics teachers, and a particular shortage of mathematics specialists in primary schools (Goulding *et al.*, 2002). Not all secondary mathematics teachers are confident to teach all classes or all sixth-form options.

However, as well as having learned mathematics in the past, it is important that mathematics teachers continue to see themselves as mathematics *learners* throughout their working lives (and many will find time for even more recreational mathematics in retirement). Working with learners of mathematics on a daily basis can be an effective way of developing your subject knowledge, provided that you take advantage of the opportunities that arise. Learners have a habit of asking simple-sounding but deep questions about mathematics. It is common even for mathematics teachers who have strong mathematical backgrounds to be fazed sometimes by a mathematical question from a young learner.

Task Learning

I have never let my schooling interfere with my education.

Mark Twain

When did you last learn something mathematical?
What was it?
Was it planned or unplanned?
Were you alone? Did someone 'teach' you?

Any mathematics teacher will have learned their mathematics in a variety of ways, ranging perhaps from the traditional university degree to various courses and conferences, private reading and informal conversations. It is much too simplistic to judge someone's knowledge of mathematics merely on the basis of their formal qualifications: biographies of professional mathematicians reveal that many have had quite unconventional mathematical backgrounds (for example, see Kaluza, 2005). For suggestions on ways of developing your mathematical knowledge, see chapter 3.

Task Mathematical knowledge

When I taught Further Maths, I just kept a lesson or two ahead of the class, and it worked fine.

Mathematics teacher

How much mathematics do you think a teacher needs to know to teach pupils up to age 11, age 16 and age 18?

How important do you think that a mathematics degree is for a mathematics teacher?

Teachers are sometimes guilty of assuming that their particular background is best and are less accepting of the routes taken by their colleagues. It is helpful to see every mathematics teacher's subject knowledge as a 'work in progress' and to recognize that someone who knows less content might nonetheless have highly mathematical *habits* that enable them to solve problems unlike any that they have ever seen before or specifically learned to tackle. There are many ways to be a good mathematician and it is restrictive to apply inflexible criteria to all mathematics teachers.

There is no denying that subject knowledge does matter. Knowing things beyond the learners' *mathematical horizon* can be enriching in the classroom (Zazkis and Mamolo, 2011). For example, it may be helpful, when teaching that the angles in a triangle add up to 180°, to know a little about *spherical triangles*. It may help when teaching about corresponding angles to know about the *parallel postulate* and *elliptical* and *hyperbolic geometry* – not necessarily in detail, but knowing that they exist brings out the distinctiveness of Euclidean geometry more starkly (Mlodinow, 2001). It may be important when teaching equivalent fractions to know that not all decimals can be represented exactly as a fraction. If a learner asks why their calculator gives an error when they try to work out the square root of a negative number, it may be helpful to know about *imaginary numbers*. If you are teaching the *scalar product* to sixth formers, it may be helpful to know that there is also a *vector product*, which explains why it is preferable to use a dot rather than a cross for it. There is evidence that weaker subject knowledge tends to result in teachers being more *procedural* in the classroom, teaching learners to memorize rules rather than teaching for understanding (Goulding *et al.*, 2002).

> ## Task Questions
>
> How might you react to these questions from learners?
>
> Why isn't pi exactly 3?
> If you zoom in on a circle, is it really a straight line?
> Do parallel lines meet at infinity?
> Is infinity an actual number?

It is certainly possible to help someone with their mathematics even when you yourself do not know 'the answer'. This is normal behaviour for research mathematicians at coffee time. No one can know all mathematics or the answer to every question a learner (of any age) might ask. Mathematics is a rapidly changing field and it can be hard to keep up-to-date with which conjectures have become proofs and with different applications of the subject. When faced with your own ignorance, as we all are from time to time, it is good to make the most of this opportunity to recognize what it feels like *not* to know, as this can improve your ability to empathize with your learners. It is more important to *be mathematical* than to be a walking encyclopaedia; frequently, an answer to a specific question can be found on the internet (e.g., at www.wolframalpha.com). More often, the situation is well served by asking mathematical questions and *thinking out loud*. Many mathematics teachers will identify with the situation where they are standing at the board working on a problem and cannot immediately see what to do next. Or perhaps you realize that you must have made a mistake but cannot straightaway pinpoint it exactly. The uncertainty and confusion may last for just a few seconds (though it can feel like an eternity!) or it may take much longer to resolve.

Of course, if you have just 'proved' that 2 = 1, or otherwise realize that you have made a mistake, it is best to admit it without shame as one of those things that happens to everyone from time to time. If you act as though you have done something terrible, learners may mirror this response when they are stuck. In such situations, you have several options:

- *Talk about what you are thinking.*
  For example, 'OK, I can see I've gone wrong here because that can't be that because... So I'm looking back and I know this line is right because ... So I'm thinking maybe I made a mistake here because ...' Learners may find this more enlightening than the presentation of a polished solution. Such occasions are good opportunities to model *error-correction techniques* and how to deal with being stuck. Sometimes a line of algebra can be checked by trying a particular value, or using dimensions or a diagram can help. Sometimes reversing a process enables you to see what doesn't match up, or trying a different method or simplifying the problem. There will be more about *being mathematical* in chapter 3.
- *Sit down and let a learner take over.*
  This can work well if learners have already solved the problem that you are discussing—sometimes you may feel that everyone in the room except you knows how to do it!

- *Ask learners in pairs or groups to try to resolve the difficulty.*
  With the spotlight off you for a moment, it often takes only a short time to get to grips with it.
- *Return to it next lesson after having a think.*

Not every mathematics teacher is comfortable with being watched when they are stuck. Struggling in public can be hard, and some will be tempted to rub everything out straightaway and say that they will look at it later and discuss it in the next lesson. However, if you can handle it, the experience of *shared stuckness* can be very beneficial. Sometimes when learners describe how their mathematics teacher solves problems on the board they use words like 'magic'. Yet if you want to learn magic there can be an advantage in watching less good magicians, who make mistakes or do things slightly clumsily, rather than those with a faultless technique. The slightly less polished ones enable you to see what they are doing more easily, and perhaps you are slightly less in awe and more open to imagining doing the same things yourself. Of course, if you are regularly making numerous errors in the classroom, and being helped by the learners, then that is likely to become a barrier to their learning, and it will be important for you to seek support and work on boosting your subject knowledge.

Task Integration

For which values of p and q can you find the following integrals?

$$\int x^p (1+x)^q dx$$

$$\int x(1+x^p)^q dx$$

What methods of integration will work in each case? Why?

A task like this could be mathematically challenging for many practising mathematics teachers. Perhaps you do not teach calculus to the learners that you work with, but whatever mathematical level you teach at is likely to contain areas that make you pause for mathematical thought. These are good areas to try to develop. It doesn't have to be something particularly hard or impressive-sounding; it could be some content from the secondary curriculum. Because of their age or the country they grew up in, some mathematics teachers may never have studied topics such as transformation geometry, circle theorems, moving averages or some statistical tests, for instance. Perhaps you have never read Euclid but always wanted to? Perhaps you have heard about *Möbius bands* but would like to learn more about topology? Popular mathematics paperbacks can be a great way to start (e.g., Gardner, 2005; Stewart, 2010).

2.1.2 A learner of mathematics pedagogy

> Those who can, do; those who can't, teach; yet even those who can, can't always teach!
>
> Anon.

Not everyone appreciates that there is more to mathematics teaching than knowing the mathematics. *Pedagogy*, or 'the science of teaching' (Simon, 1981), involves understanding how learners learn. Sometimes parents assume that anyone with a knowledge of mathematics will make an effective teacher, and occasionally courses designed to help teachers to teach 'hard mathematics' (e.g., post-16) focus solely on the mathematical content, leaving teachers uncertain how to help learners engage with that content for themselves. Accepting the fuzziness of the social sciences can be hard for a mathematics teacher brought up on strict deductive logic.

Task Uncle

We know that he's struggling a bit with his maths at the moment, but his uncle has a maths degree, so he's going to help him with it.

Parent

What might be the possible benefits or disadvantages of this?

It would be dangerous to over-privilege the teaching profession by implying that no one could possibly be able to help a child with their learning unless they have a teaching qualification. Clearly, many people possess the patience, interest and understanding to assist a learner's mathematical development. A learner might relate well to a trusted member of the family who has the time to spend with them that their busy teacher might not appear to have (see chapter 14). But it is by no means guaranteed that any mathematician will make a good teacher, even if they can remember their elementary mathematics from years ago. Pedagogy is vital if teachers are to be effective (Gore *et al.*, 2006).

When reflecting on their own learning of mathematics at university, mathematics teachers sometimes report being very disappointed with the quality of their lecturers, even though they may have had outstanding subject knowledge. It is clearly not enough just to be able to do the sums yourself! An effective teacher will be aware of common difficulties and will have ideas of questions and tasks that may help learners to work things out for themselves. They will also know the sorts of ideas that are likely to be taught at particular ages. A learner who was meeting trigonometry for the first time in Year 9 was puzzled when his father tried to help him but assumed that the angles would be measured in radians rather than in degrees. Family members sometimes call on methods they recall (or partially recall) being taught when they were at school, and these may not match the child's experience. This might lead to a valuable widening of experience for the learner, but on the other hand could potentially lead to clashes.

Shulman (1986) refers to *pedagogical content knowledge* as that:

> which goes beyond knowledge of subject matter per se to the dimension of subject matter knowledge *for teaching* ... the most useful forms of representation ... the most

powerful analogies, illustrations, examples, explanations, and demonstrations – in a word, the ways of representing and formulating the subject that make it comprehensible to others.

(p. 9)

Every teacher, whether they regard themselves as a 'natural born teacher' or not (Grambs, 1952; Whitbecka, 2000), can improve in the ways they interact with learners and become more effective. It is the primary aim of this book to assist with this process.

Sometimes, very knowledgeable mathematics teachers can intimidate learners (and sometimes colleagues!) with what they know, and may find it harder to be sympathetic to difficulties that they cannot remember ever having had themselves. It may be the case that some mathematics teachers have grown to love the subject because they have learned that it is an arena in which they can show off. From an early age they may have derived pleasure from the kudos of being able to do a subject that is widely perceived as difficult. Some of the stereotypical traits of a mathematician include impatience and a desire for efficiency, which can lead to insensitivity when learners are taking their time over something or 'going all around the houses' to find a cumbersome solution. This is not inevitable, but it can be helpful to acknowledge the danger.

2.1.3 A learner of the learners that you teach

When you observe a maths lesson, watch the pupils *more than the teacher.*

Advice from a mathematics teacher

The most significant resource that you have at your disposal for developing as a mathematics teacher is the learners that you teach. Immersing yourself in the classroom, and training yourself to be attentive to what is happening, is one of the best ways to develop your practice. In chapter 10, we will consider specific strategies for becoming a better listener, with the development of the learner in mind, but here the focus is on the immediate benefits for the teacher. Learners are human beings, and getting to know them as people can be one of the most rewarding aspects of being a teacher.

Task Zero

At the end of a lesson, a learner stayed behind to ask a question:

> This is probably a really silly question, but I've never actually been sure: is zero actually a number?

How might you respond to this question?

Every mathematics teacher will have anecdotes of incidents that have happened in the classroom and that have stuck in their mind. Sometimes such stories can take on a normative role, being repeated so often that they become canonical and come to symbolize for that teacher some important aspects of learning mathematics. In discussion with colleagues, it becomes apparent where experiences overlap and where something seems to be unique and idiosyncratic. Both kinds of incident can be opportunities for learning if teachers take the time to reflect on them (see pages 22–23).

Task Learners

Think of a particular class that you teach.
What do you know about them as people?
What do you know about them mathematically?
What *don't* you know, and how could you find it out?
Might it help you to teach mathematics to them more effectively?

Mastering learners' names is an important part of relating to them as individuals, but it is only the start. Knowing how learners tend to think, what their interests and difficulties are and how to engage productively with them is vital. It is possible for teachers to assume that learners are just like themselves (or themselves at that age) and to suppose that what interests or appeals to the teacher will interest the learners, which may not always be the case! An opposite danger is *othering* the learners, regarding them as so different that they cannot possibly appreciate mathematics in the way that the teacher does. This can lead to a *dumbing down* of lesson content ('pearls before swine') which fails to take seriously learners' mathematical potential.

2.2 Being self-reflective

> I feel like I've got into a rut; my lessons are less interesting now than when I started teaching.
>
> Mathematics teacher

One of the dangers of experience is that we become a prisoner of our previous choices. Because we have got used to doing something in a certain way, it feels comfortable and right whenever we do it, and the more we acquiesce the more embedded that behaviour becomes, so that the idea of changing our practice is perceived as risky and threatening. Being more aware of the choices that you make *in the moment* can be a great way of recovering control and allowing your practice to develop in different directions. Schön (1983) describes the *reflective practitioner* as one who can think and act at the same time, and so deal professionally with new and difficult situations. Teachers frequently know more than they think they know; such *tacit knowledge*, acquired through experience, may be hard to put into words, but contributes to their behaviour in the classroom. The process of *reflection-in-action* seeks to make this knowledge explicit by *problematizing* things which had previously been taken for granted. One way to do this is by naming them (Pollard, 2006).

Task **Critical incident**

Think of a mathematical incident from a lesson that you have taught or observed.
It could be something said or done by the teacher or by a learner.
What is the most important feature of this incident for you? What do you think
  has made it stick in your mind?
What do you take away from this incident?

Mason's (2001) *discipline of noticing* involves developing one's sensitivity (*mindfulness*) so as to be aware of alternative possibilities when they are needed in practice. It can be very valuable to keep a *journal* (or use a voice recorder) to make what Mason calls *brief-but-vivid* descriptions of incidents or ideas that occur during mathematics lessons. It is easy to lose a thought or forget the details of a situation, and so miss an opportunity to reflect. Even a quick scribble made at the time can be sufficient to re-enter mentally, at a later moment, what it was that happened, and perhaps turn it into a piece of writing such as a blog. Mason advises distinguishing between an *account-of* an incident, which is objective and presents the facts (e.g., direct speech) in a neutral and unemotional manner, and an *account-for* the incident, which includes subjective judgements, justifications and attempts to explain what took place. By holding back initially on loaded language, alternative interpretations may be more easily considered and preconceived ideas challenged.

Task **Opportunity**

Have you ever realized in the classroom, just too late, that you have missed a
  great opportunity to do something?
What did it feel like?
Why do you think that you realized only *afterwards*?

Perhaps a learner makes an interesting comment and you say 'That's interesting' but are unsure how to develop it, and the moment slips away. Perhaps you interrupted a classroom discussion to say something and then reflected that if you had waited a little then a learner, rather than you, might have said something similar – or better. Being reflective involves developing your self-awareness to the point where it becomes *transformative*. When teachers can cultivate the ability to *think while acting*, they open up more opportunities to do something different. This involves developing an *internal supervisor* (Casement, 1990) who holds back from getting totally involved in what you are doing so as to retain a degree of objectivity. This *alter ego* can act as a *witness* to what is going on, noticing things and reporting back later, but can also intervene in the moment and change a particular course of action into a more useful one.

Task Triangle areas

A triangle has sides of length 4, 5 and *x*.
What is the maximum possible area of the triangle? Why?

Standing back and watching yourself at work can be an enlightening process. If you did this task, did you notice how you went about it? (There are some comments at the end of the chapter.) Noting explicitly what you are doing mathematically can open up different possibilities. Likewise, noticing an action in the classroom as you do it, and even before you do it, right down to the level of particular words and phrases and gestures, can enable you to take some control. The practice of talking about what is going on (*meta-commenting*), for instance in a blog or journal, focuses attention on the details of the situation.

2.3 Sharing experiences

> If you close your door, you keep *out* more than you keep *in*.
>
> Anon.

Despite working with people all day long, a teacher can sometimes find their profession a rather isolated one. Once you close your classroom door, you may feel cut off from other adults, and if things go wrong you may feel unable to talk to anyone about it – especially if they all seem incredibly busy, successful or weighed down with their own problems. However, as Pollard (2006: 21) comments, 'The value of engaging in reflective activity is almost always enhanced if it can be carried out in association with other colleagues'.

Task Contact time

What contacts do you typically have with colleagues during the day?
What opportunities are there to develop professionally from these?

All teachers need meaningful contact with colleagues during the working day, and that means more than formal meetings and the exchange of information about learners. Schools which invest in a large good-quality staffroom and entice teachers out of their departments at break time by providing decent cheap refreshments are very wise, because they encourage teachers to spend supportive time together. This can be a very pleasant way of developing your practice. There can be a great deal of common ground with colleagues who teach different subjects, and informal co-evaluation of lessons can easily take place over a cup of tea without either teacher recognizing what is happening. Of course, you cannot talk about mathematics education all day long, and it is very important to unwind and relax in between lessons. In schools where administrative demands are deliberately kept as low as possible and teachers' non-contact time is fiercely protected, teachers are more likely to be able to find the time to 'talk shop' as well as chat about life during their free time.

Many schools have systems to encourage colleagues to share resources. Sharing your ideas will help *you* as well as your colleagues: hoarding is harmful. If you try to cling to the materials that you have created and not let others use them, you are probably less likely to think of new ideas – a river that is dammed will turn stagnant. Magicians belong to a 'magic circle' in which they are sworn to secrecy, so that the details of their best tricks are not revealed to the public. Yet some members have deliberately sought to spill the beans on the grounds that it is good for everyone in the long run, because it forces magicians to innovate rather than recycling all the old ideas *ad nauseam*. It is now easy for mathematics teachers at different schools to share ideas through professional associations such as the *Association of Teachers of Mathematics* (www.atm.org.uk), the *Mathematical Association* (www.m-a.org.uk) and the online community at the *Times Educational Supplement* (www.tes.co.uk). The associations produce journals containing thought-provoking articles, and reading what others have written, and contributing yourself, is an excellent way to develop your thinking about mathematics teaching. The associations also run annual conferences, which are the highlight of the professional year for many mathematics teachers; they offer you the chance to 'recharge your batteries' and enjoy working on mathematics yourself and with interested colleagues and discussing what goes on in the classroom.

In your non-school life, try to notice when you learn something. If I have a cookery lesson or listen to a tour guide on holiday, I find myself being aware of how they do their job and interested in the learning process *per se*. If you have the opportunity to work with young people in a voluntary capacity, such as youth worker, or with a sports team, you may gain a great deal of understanding that will help within the school environment. You might watch some teenage television programmes, listen to popular music or look at magazines and computer games that appeal to that age group, if you haven't done so since you were their age. These things will not necessarily enter directly into your mathematics lessons – although sometimes you might be able to find connections – but if you are interested in working with young people then it is natural to want to understand as much as possible about how the world looks to them. If you are a form tutor, then it will be natural to talk to your learners about their lives and sometimes to watch them play a sports match or perform on stage or in a competition.

No one can tell you how to be a mathematics teacher, and you may find yourself disagreeing sometimes with colleagues that you respect greatly, because although what they do may work very well for them, it just doesn't for you. But it is sensible to hesitate before ruling out what anyone has to say. Whatever someone's experiences may be, try to find something to learn – even if it is why you *don't* want to take on a certain approach yourself. If you can observe and talk to as wide a range of mathematics teachers as possible, you will be able to maximize the diversity of your experiences. If you hear about teaching at another school that is quite different from what you are familiar with, try to get permission to spend a day or two there 'taking the temperature' – there may be ideas that you can take away, and maybe something that you can contribute to what they do.

> # Task Summary task
>
> *Common sense is the collection of prejudices acquired by age eighteen.*
>
> Albert Einstein
>
> Is there a particular area of mathematics that you would like to learn or re-learn? How could you do this?
>
> What are the chief ways in which you intend to develop as a mathematics teacher?
>
> What will help you to do that? What may hinder the process?
>
> What things will help you to make *different* 'mistakes' rather than the same ones over and over again?

Comments on mathematical tasks

Task: Dots

Most people can *subitize* (see at a glance how many there are) up to a small number of dots, but not this many. There are different ways of dividing up the dots to make them quicker to count, perhaps using your knowledge of *triangle numbers*, for instance. Generalizing will lead to different but equivalent algebraic expressions for the number of dots in the nth drawing. One elegant approach is to see the dots as three faces of a $5 \times 5 \times 5$ array of dots, the three faces meeting at the centre of the picture (Figure 2.1). Envisioning the visible dots as those on the surface means that there will be $5^3 - 4^3 = 61$, which is the 5th *centred hexagonal number* (or *hex number*).

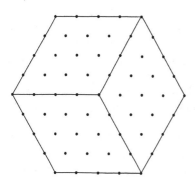

Figure 2.1 Dots on a cube

Task: Integration

One way to begin this task is with familiar 'special cases', such as $\int x(1+x^2)^q dx = \dfrac{(1+x^2)^{q+1}}{2(q+1)} + c$, where $q \neq -1$ (perhaps with q as a specific value). Several different methods of integration, such as substitution and integration by parts, may be used. Did you think about p and q not necessarily being positive and not necessarily being integers?

Task: Triangle areas

Did you reach for a trusty formula such as Area $= \frac{1}{2}ab\sin C$, setting $a = 4$, $b = 5$ and $C = 90°$, so as to maximize the area? Or did you think more visually? Perhaps you envisaged the angle between the two sides changing – were you sure straightaway that a right angle led to the maximum area? Or perhaps you worried about calculating the third side – maybe the values of 4 and 5 led you to think of a 3-4-5 right-angled triangle? Perhaps you inscribed your triangle in a circle?

Further reading

Gardner, M. (2005) *The Colossal Book of Short Puzzles and Problems*, London: W. W. Norton & Co.
Mason, J. (2001) *Researching Your Own Practice: the discipline of noticing*, London: RoutledgeFalmer.
Stewart, I. (2010) *Professor Stewart's Hoard of Mathematical Treasures*, London: Profile Books.

Part 1

Preparing to teach mathematics

Be prepared!

Scout motto

In this book, we are considering mathematics teaching under two related headings:

- *Preparing to teach mathematics* and
- *Teaching mathematics*.

This first part deals with *preparing*, by which I mean everything that happens *before* the mathematics lesson that is relevant to what happens *during* the lesson. This is much wider than the specific *planning* for that one particular lesson. Preparation underpins the whole process of planning and teaching (Figure A.1). Being well prepared to teach mathematics involves a more general state of readiness than merely having a lesson plan (on paper or in your head) for that one lesson. If you have some experience, you may find that when you are particularly pressed for time (due to life events as well as school pressure) you will rely more on your overall preparedness and less on specifics; at other times, when teaching a lesson that is well outside your comfort zone, you may be more dependent on particular details planned for one specific lesson. So this part of the book will look at some of the thoughts and experiences that can help a mathematics teacher to develop their all-round mathematical and pedagogical fitness, as well as at the specifics of getting ready for a particular mathematics lesson or sequence of lessons. Lesson plans should never be set in stone; the flexible mathematics teacher must be permitted to modify plans 'in flight' in order to respond to unanticipated developments. When this happens, it does not necessarily mean that there was anything wrong with the original plan, or with the learners! A good mathematics lesson will be a live, fluid situation.

Figure A.1 Preparation, planning and teaching a lesson

Lesson planning is often perceived as a solitary activity, but it does not have to be this way. Many mathematics departments have strong traditions of collaborative planning and, even where this is not the case, mathematics teachers can see themselves as operating as part of the wider mathematics education community, with online discussion forums and electronic and book resources, ideas and support available.

Chapter 3

Preparing yourself

We are what we repeatedly do. Excellence, then, is not an act, but a habit.

Aristotle

It is common for mathematics teachers to talk about preparing *lessons*, but prior to this it is important to begin with a teacher's most precious resource – themselves. How can a mathematics teacher be well-prepared, as a person and as a teacher, for life in the mathematics classroom? Preparing the *teacher* must come before preparing the *lesson* – and will continue after the lesson is finished and everyone has gone home.

Task **Sowing**

Sow a thought, and you reap an act;
Sow an act, and you reap a habit;
Sow a habit, and you reap a character;
Sow a character, and you reap a destiny.

Charles Reade

If this quote and the one at the top of the page have anything to say about mathematics teaching, what is it?
How do you feel about this perspective?

Both of these quotes speak of the importance of habits in controlling our actions. In any complicated human activity there is insufficient time to consider every detail of your behaviour explicitly. Many things have to operate 'below the surface' and flow out of habits that have been built up over a period of time. As Ulam (1991) explains:

> How terribly important habit is. ... Habits influence or perhaps can largely determine the choice of trains of thought in one's work. Once these are established (and in my opinion they may be established very quickly – sometimes after just a few trials), the "connections" or "programs" or "subroutines" become fixed.
>
> (p. 78)

Sometimes teachers are frustrated by what they see as their 'knee-jerk' reactions to classroom situations and wish that they could break out of a destructive cycle. Habits such as interrupting learners, hurrying them when they speak and giving swift evaluation of what they say can be hard to break out of when you decide that you wish to. Certain questions, such as 'Can you explain how you did it?' may be appropriate on occasion, but can end up so deeply ingrained into a mathematics teacher's practice that, in retrospect, they may sometimes seem unhelpful.

No one can give continuous deep consideration to every tiny aspect of their behaviour; we need habitual behaviours to free up our attention for other things, but we need to *train* our behaviour so that our habits when on 'auto-pilot' are in line with what we are trying to do. This is how all experts operate: if a basketball player tried to think about every little action needed to twist round and catch a ball in the air, he would probably fall over (Syed, 2011). We need to develop responses that are useful and then be confident to rely on the things that we have cultivated over time, and not fear them or become trapped by them. At the same time, we need to remain open to the possibility of modifying them in the future.

Task Habits

To do the same thing over and over again is not only boredom: it is to be controlled by, rather than to control, what you do.

Heraclitus

How much of what you do in the classroom do you regard as habitual and how much as conscious choice?
Do you think that this has changed since you began teaching?
What do you habitually do during a lesson when ...

- someone interrupts you?
- someone says something you were completely unprepared for?
- you realize that you are uncertain about some mathematics?
- someone comes into the classroom while a lesson is in progress?

When someone interrupts you, do you stop or do you continue? Do you instinctively talk louder, or do you hold back? When someone says something you had not anticipated, do you say, 'That's interesting' – has 'interesting' come to signal your own uncertainty of how to proceed? When you are 'caught out' mathematically, what does your body language do? Are you comfortable with being unsure? Could some of your reactions perhaps discourage your learners from asking 'awkward' questions or making comments that are a bit 'off the wall'? Is this something that you might like to work on?

Sometimes it is assumed that teachers have one fixed *teaching style* or way of working on a particular topic. When a colleague asks 'How do you teach negative numbers?', the question seems to imply that the teacher will have one fixed approach which they unfailingly employ, which may not be the case.

Every teacher has habitual behaviours. For example, I am conscious of stepping back when a child speaks quietly and I want the whole class to hear what they are saying, whereas in everyday life I would probably move closer in order to hear. I am sometimes aware of holding very still and speaking quietly when talking to a class that is boisterous and excitable (usually on days when it is windy outside), hoping that they will catch my calm rather than I catch their liveliness. I am aware that I sometimes smile and pause to think when someone says something I hadn't expected, but other times I probably look confused and frustrated that my train of thought has been derailed. When I am ready to speak and someone else speaks before me, I try to be glad because I have more time to improve what I might have said. If someone says exactly what I was going to say, I have tried to switch from feeling annoyed that they have beaten me to it to feeling satisfied and confirmed because another person had the same idea. Not all of these things have yet become completely habitual for me, and I don't always do them, but I *mostly* do them now, unless I choose to do something else – or am having a bad day!

However, these same habits can also enslave us, causing us to fall into the same patterns over and over again, slipping into the same traps, repeating the same old mistakes. So it matters what we repeatedly do over a period of time, not just because of the immediate consequences but because of how it changes us. A *behaviourist* would say that every time we do something and receive some kind of reward (even a very subtle one), it becomes more likely that we will do something similar in a similar situation in the future. This can happen unless we take time to reflect on how things are going and make conscious changes. Breaking out of a cycle of mutually reinforcing habits takes a deliberate act of the will, a decision not to be bound by your own previous actions.

3.1 You as a resource

> My life experience, not any university course, is what qualifies me to teach.
> Having kids is the best preparation I know for being a teacher!
>
> Mathematics teachers

Your life experiences, whatever they may be, are a very important part of what makes you *you*, and exploiting their potential for the classroom will make you a more effective teacher (Cosforda and Drapera, 2002). It is important that teachers do not give up on life outside school – your wider life is vital to you, and it will also help your teaching. The most important thing that you bring to any mathematics lesson is yourself. In this sense, the preparation for a lesson began the day you were born, so there is no such thing as an 'unprepared lesson'! In schools, 'preparation' is often taken to mean sitting down and writing a lesson plan, but there is much more to preparation than that. A living, breathing mathematics teacher in the classroom has plenty to offer even on those occasions where there is some mathematics that they don't know. They have learned to think mathematically and to respond in pedagogically sound ways.

Task Smallest number

In a moment, I'm going to invite everybody to write down a positive integer.

The winner will be the person who has written the smallest number that nobody else has written.

Think about which number you are going to write.

How would you plan for this opportunity?

This task invites learners to plan ahead – to consider what they will do when the time comes. Would your answer depend on how many people were in the room? Would it depend on who they happened to be? Do you think that there is an objectively 'best' solution to this problem? It is as much a psychological task as a mathematical one, and the same is true of planning a mathematics lesson.

Task Preparation

You know you're a real teacher when you mix up your timetable and the class that comes into the room isn't the one you were expecting, and you make up something on the spot and nobody notices!

A 'real' mathematics teacher

In what ways do you think that lesson preparation develops with experience?

The ways in which teachers prepare for mathematics lessons do seem to change with experience. Some teachers brag that they don't 'need' to prepare. Ulam (1991) thinks that lecturing mathematics does not require much preparation:

> In general, teaching mathematics is different from teaching other subjects. I feel, as do most mathematicians, that one can teach mathematics without much preparation, since it is a subject in which one thing leads to another, almost inevitably. In my own lectures to more advanced audiences, seminars, and societies, I discuss topics that currently occupy me; this is more of a stream of consciousness approach. I am told that I teach rather well.
>
> (p. 128)

Ulam appears to have found an approach which depends on the mathematical connections that he carries around with him all the time, coupled with attention to topics that are on his mind at the moment. This may have worked well for him at that time as a lecturer, but it is very doubtful that anyone could successfully carry this off in a school classroom today!

Some mathematics teachers' preparation focuses almost exclusively on the mathematics, with the result that if they are teaching a topic that they know well, have just taught, or are teaching a young year group, then they feel that they have little to prepare.

But this overlooks the human side of preparation, which involves considering the particular learners that you have to teach. Finding ways to engage them with the mathematical ideas will be the focus of future chapters.

Task Performance

Choose a performer that you admire – a sportsperson, a musician, an actor/actress, ...

Try to watch some backstage footage of them before they go on stage or find an interview in which they talk about how they prepare.

Do you think that there any similarities with teaching?

What goes through your mind as you walk down the corridor to your classroom just before the start of a lesson?

Of course, teaching is more than performing, but there may still be some interesting parallels.

3.2 Your thinking

> The essence of mathematics is its freedom.
>
> Georg Cantor

One aspect of your preparation of yourself is your thinking. This involves more than mathematics. Mathematics teachers may enjoy films, serious and non-serious books, television, theatre, blogs and talks on the web, along with discussions and debates from time to time. Any of these may have resonances with issues in education or may simply be interesting in their own right. More specifically, mathematics teachers need to be mathematicians, one definition of which is 'someone who does mathematics'.

Task Triangles

What is the same and what is different about these two shapes below?

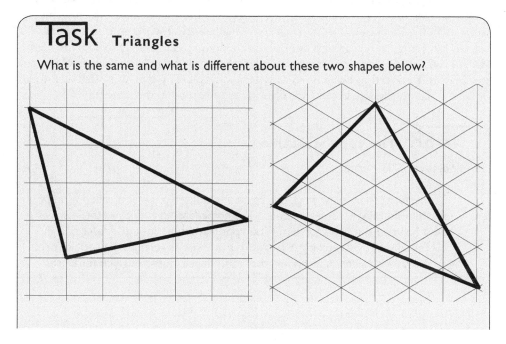

How would you work out

- their areas?
- their perimeters?
- their interior angles?

Can you find more than one approach?

Working on mathematics brings its own rewards, but one side effect is that mathematics teachers re-enter what it is like to *get stuck*. Mason *et al.* (2010: viii) advise that 'being stuck is an honourable state' and, of course, all mathematicians get stuck. For instance, Hofstadter (2000) quotes Farkas Bolyai, who wrote rather hysterically to his son seeking to discourage him from following in his footsteps and devoting fruitless years to attempting to prove Euclid's fifth postulate:

> I accomplished monstrous, enormous labors; my creations are far better than those of others and yet I have not achieved complete satisfaction. ... I have traveled past all reefs of this infernal Dead Sea and have always come back with broken mast and torn sail. ... I thoughtlessly risked my life and happiness.
>
> (p. 92)

On the other hand, if you never get stuck, you are probably not working on sufficiently difficult problems! There are many sources of good problems and you may need to experiment to find things that suit you. Some books provide specific guidance on how to solve mathematics problems (Pólya, 1990) and how to *think mathematically* through to a solution (Mason, 1999). Sometimes, when reading, I find something which seems ripe to be used in a lesson, but I need to do some mathematical work on it first myself. For example, I was recently reading a book about the history of geometry (Mlodinow, 2001) when I came across an interesting paragraph which I felt could be developed into a task (see below). I enjoyed working on this myself and was 'killing two birds with one stone', because I was preparing a lesson (actually a series of lessons) at the same time.

Task The rope stretcher

Mlodinow (2001) writes:

> To perform their surveying, the Egyptians utilized a person called a *harpedonopta*, literally, a 'rope stretcher'. The *harpedonopta* employed three slaves, who handled the rope for him. The rope had knots in it at prescribed distances so that by stretching it taut with the knots as vertices, you could form a triangle with sides of given lengths – and hence angles of given measures.
>
> (p. 7)

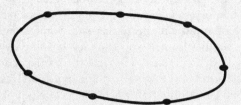

Suppose you have a loop containing 7 equally-spaced knots.
What triangles can you make? What are their side lengths and angles?
What happens if you have a different number of equally spaced knots?
What happens if the knots are not equally spaced?

I cannot imagine a music teacher who didn't listen to music for fun in their spare time. They probably also go to concerts (not just on school trips) and belong to orchestras or bands – they may even compose when they have time. Likewise, English teachers read novels and may write too (e.g., fan fiction). Most teachers are interested in their subject and wish they had more time to pursue it, so it is only natural if mathematics teachers do mathematics in their spare time (or at least while sitting at the back of a staff meeting!). However, a mathematics teacher is more than just a mathematician. Reflecting after a lesson need not take an enormous amount of time – formal lesson evaluations during teaching practice put many mathematics teachers off thinking critically about their teaching. But taking stock of previous lessons, thinking about individual learners and what they have said and done (not just behaviour problems, but mathematically), can be stimulating and enjoyable (see chapter 2).

Task Open day

At a school open day, we had laid out a variety of mathematical puzzles and I watched a young child doing one of them as his father stood beside him. The father appeared to become increasingly agitated as the child repeatedly put the pieces in the wrong places. He began to tell the child where to put the pieces, but the child ignored his advice. Eventually, he snatched the pieces from the child's hands and put them in the correct places and they left.

It appeared to me that his frustration (and embarrassment, perhaps, as I was watching) had built up to an intolerable level and he could no longer bear to see his child doing it wrongly.

Do you find it difficult when you see learners taking a long time to do something that seems straightforward to you or appear not to understand something that seems simple to you?

How do you feel when a learner solves a problem but you can see a much more elegant or efficient way?

Clearly, taking away the problem from the learner (literally in this case) removes the purpose of the task. The point is not to get the puzzle completed but for the learner to learn something – the task is just a means to that end. Sometimes learners in a classroom can be impatient with another learner who takes a long time over something that they have already 'completed'. Being interested in what the learner is doing, saying and thinking, and seeking to understand how they view things, is a good way to channel the energy that might otherwise build into frustration when you feel on top of the mathematics yourself. A violin teacher, for instance, who has a sensitive musical ear, and can make beautiful sounds with their instrument, spends day after day in a tiny room with children who scratch and scrape away at the strings, making a terrible noise. Somehow they learn to appreciate the sounds of the errors so as to help the children develop their skills.

3.3 Your energy

> I stayed up into the early hours last night preparing that observed lesson, and then I was so tired this morning I couldn't really concentrate when I had to do it!
>
> Tired mathematics teacher

Sometimes teachers prepare the details of a lesson meticulously but neglect to take care of themselves. The consequences of not eating properly or getting enough sleep are obvious, but problems can also result from a teacher's lack of a social life or from anxiety and guilt over feeling that they are neglecting their family. This can lead to resentment towards learners in the classroom or hostility towards colleagues. The most basic preparation any teacher needs is to take care of themselves. There is nothing selfish about focusing on one's own needs; it is often the best way to meet those of others. Classroom teaching is a tiring job, and balancing your energy during the day and in the evenings so that you are fresh, enthusiastic and 'ready for anything' is important. So preparation of self involves more than the cerebral; the affective side is essential too.

The increasing prevalence of stress in the teaching profession has been widely reported (Cooper and Travers, 1996). There is a culture in many schools in which teachers try to *cope* under enormous pressures and feel that to acknowledge that they have a problem would be to appear 'weak', which only makes matters worse. Teachers ascribe rising stress levels to, among other things, difficult learner behaviour, low social status, lack of parental support, poor pay and an excessive workload (Jarvis, 2002). Stress impacts hugely on teacher retention and makes many lives a misery. In some ways the mathematics teacher may be hit especially hard. The stereotypical temperament of a mathematician is introverted and perfectionist and they may cut themselves off from support and avoid talking about their problems. A mathematician expects every problem to have a solution and can be intolerant of ongoing difficulties that have no easy resolution. Stress can occur when reality doesn't match our expectations, so it is very important to be realistic and to ensure that you protect your health (including mental health) and general well-being. Sometimes the best way to prepare for a lesson may be to close your eyes for a few minutes in the staffroom or listen to some calming music. Nobody should regard a teacher doing that as if they are 'off task'!

It is important to take time off when you are feeling unwell; no one is indispensable. Schools need to have systems in place so that they can cope when a teacher is ill or has a family crisis. It should not be necessary to apologize for being under the weather – teachers are not superhuman! Everyone who works in a school will be familiar with the situation where a poorly colleague comes in all groggy and in a bad mood, spreads germs around the school, gets annoyed with the learners (grumpy teachers can very quickly do a lot of damage to their relationships with their classes) and then leaves part way through the day because it has all got too much. This then cascades through other colleagues who catch the bug and repeat the pattern. In particular, no teacher should be teaching with a sore throat – a teacher's voice is a key asset and needs rest in order to avoid serious damage.

Task Alcohol

When drawing a chemical structure, a line segment indicates a bond from one atom to another. A capital letter indicates the kind of atom; if there is none, then it is carbon. In an *aliphatic alcohol*, a hydroxyl group (–OH) is joined to a chain of carbon atoms in which there are no rings. Each carbon is bonded to four 'groups', which may be:

- another carbon atom,
- the hydroxyl group, or
- hydrogen atoms (which conventionally are not shown).

So there are two possible 3-carbon aliphatic alcohols:

n-propanol (propan-1-ol)   or   *iso*-propanol (propan-2-ol)

How many 4-carbon-containing aliphatic alcohols are there? Generalize.

It can be fun for learners to try to find all the possible alcohols and to attempt to generalize for similar molecular structures. Issues about the use and abuse of alcohol are certain to arise and can make for useful cross-curricular links.

Task Summary task

If you can't learn to do something well, learn to enjoy doing it poorly!

Proverb

In what ways do you think you can make the job of mathematics teaching fit your particular strengths and interests?

How can you protect yourself from being damaged by your chosen profession?

Comments on mathematical tasks

Task: Triangles

This can be interesting for learners who know about Pythagoras's theorem and trigonometry. One way to find the area of the first triangle is to surround it with a rectangle, work out its area and subtract the areas of the three right-angled triangles created around the edge (Figure 3.1). Alternatively, if you know *Pick's theorem* you could use that. A similar sort of approach with the second triangle would suggest surrounding it with an equilateral triangle (Figure 3.1 again). You might find the formula 'Area $= \frac{1}{2}ab\sin C$' useful. You could use Pick's theorem again for the area and the cosine rule to find the perimeter. Either the sine rule or trigonometry in right-angled triangles would give you the angles. You might be interested in seeing if you can generalize some of the results. For more details, see Litwiller and Duncan (1981).

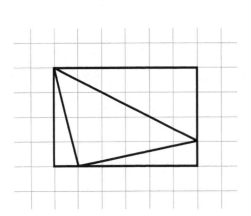 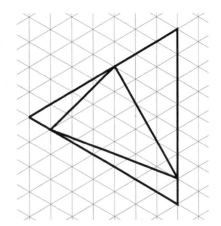

Figure 3.1 Finding areas

Task: Alcohol

There is one 2-carbon alcohol (Figure 3.2), four 4-carbon alcohols (Figure 3.3) and eight 5-carbon alcohols (Figure 3.4). The sequence 1, 2, 4, 8, ... may suggest that 16 should be the next term, but in fact there are *17* hexanols, as shown in Figure 3.5! The sequence then continues 39, 89, 211, 507, 1238, 3057, ... (sequence A000598 in *The On-Line Encyclopedia of Integer Sequences*: https://oeis.org/seis.html). (For other surprising sequences that begin 1, 2, 4, 8, ..., see page 161.)

Figure 3.2 Ethanol

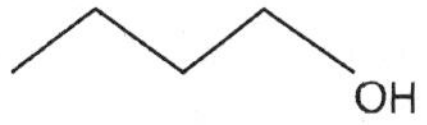

n-butanol (butan-1-ol)

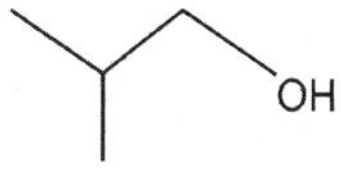

iso-butanol (2-methylpropan-1-ol)

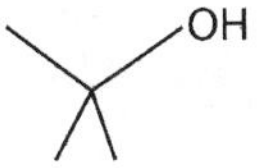

tert-butanol (2-methylpropan-2-ol)

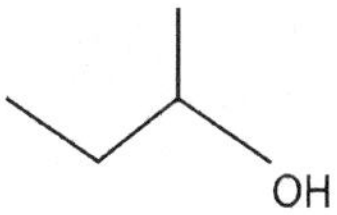

sec-butanol (butan-2-ol)

Figure 3.3 The four butanols

n-pentanol (pentan-1-ol)

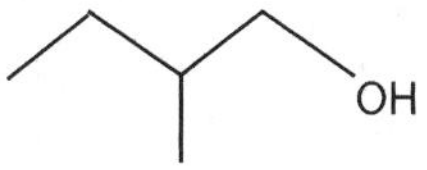

active amyl alcohol (2-methylbutan-1-ol)

neopentyl alcohol (2,2-dimethylpropan-1-ol)

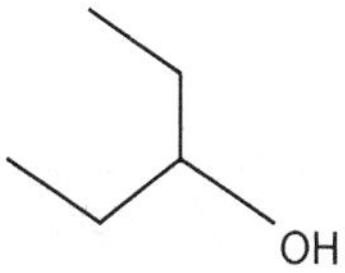

diethyl carbinol (pentan-3-ol)

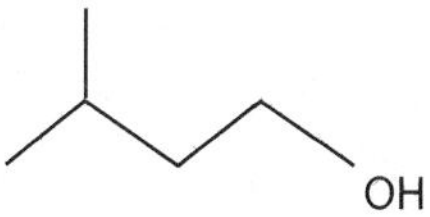

isopentyl alcohol (3-methylbutan-1-ol)

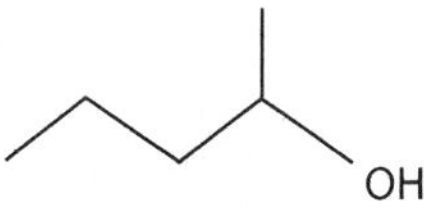

pentan-2-ol

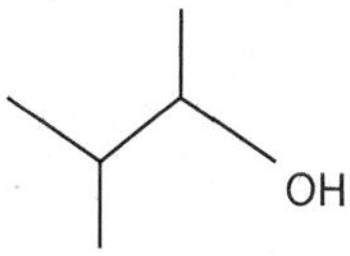

methyl isopropyl carbinol (3-methylbutan-2-ol)

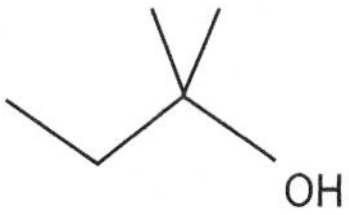

tertiary amyl alcohol (2-methylbutan-2-ol)

Figure 3.4 The eight pentanols

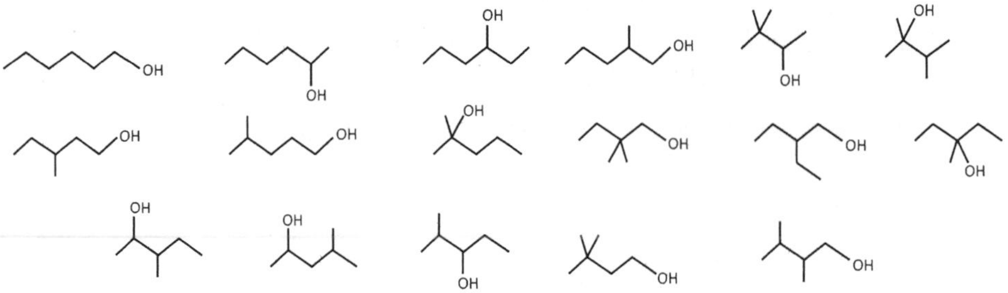

Figure 3.5 The *17* hexanols

Another interesting related example is that of the aliphatic alkanes, where there is one ethane, one propane, two butanes, three pentanes and five hexanes. The pattern 1, 1, 2, 3, 5, … might suggest the Fibonacci sequence, but in fact there are 9 heptanes (or 11, if you count the two stereoisomers each of 3-methylhexane and 2,3-dimethylpentane), rather than 8. The sequence then continues 18, 35, 75, 159, 355, 802, … (sequence A000602 in *The Online Encyclopedia of Integer Sequences*: https://oeis.org/seis.html). See also Greenwood (1977).

Further reading

Mason, J. (1999) *Learning and Doing Mathematics*, 2nd edn, York: QED.
Mason, J., Burton, L. and Stacey, K. (2010) *Thinking Mathematically*, 2nd edn, Harlow: Pearson Education Limited.
Pólya, G. (1990) *How to Solve It: a new aspect of mathematical method*, London: Penguin.

Chapter 4

Learning and teaching mathematics

> People often say: 'I teach them but they don't learn'. Well, if you know that, stop teaching. Not resign from your job: stop teaching in the way that doesn't reach people, and try to understand what there is to do ...
>
> Caleb Gattegno (Brown *et al.*, 1989: 12)

Any thoughts about *teaching* mathematics must begin with *learning* mathematics. All mathematics teachers begin as mathematics learners – and continue as mathematics learners, as we stressed in chapter 3. Teaching and learning are intimately entwined – you can certainly have learning without a teacher, but you cannot call something 'teaching' which does not lead to some learning (Figure 4.1). As Dewey (1991) said, back in the nineteenth century:

> Teaching and learning are correlative and corresponding processes, as much so as selling and buying. One might as well say he has sold when no one has bought, as to say that he has taught when no one has learned.
>
> (p. 29)

If your learners are not learning, then you are not teaching. Of course, learners are learning things all the time, but they may not be learning what you think or wish them to be learning.

Task Learning

Think about something you have learned recently: it could be mathematical or non-mathematical.
How did you learn it?
Was there a 'teacher'? If so, what did they do to help you learn?
If not, would you have liked one? Why? If so, what would you have liked them to do?

It is in the interests of teachers (and, of course, of people who write books about teaching!) to portray the teaching profession as vital, yet it is a fact that small children learn an

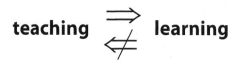

Figure 4.1 Teaching and learning

enormous amount in their early weeks and months without anyone teaching them as such (Holt, 1990): no one shows a child how to crawl. And in adult life many of us learn all manner of things, from how to be a parent to how to play a musical instrument to how to speak a foreign language to stamp collecting and cooking, without anyone ever teaching us explicitly. So how important is teaching, and what can we learn from how people learn things?

4.1 The value of theory

> Theory without practice is sterile; practice without theory is blind.
>
> Friedrich Engels (but attributed to various)

> Don't just do something; sit there!
>
> Anon.

Some people are naturally more contemplative, while others want to get up and get on with things. Some mathematics teachers like to analyse what happens in their classrooms, while others are impatient with such airy-fairy matters.

Task Theory

You learn to pass your teacher training course; then you learn to teach.
The stuff you read in books and talk about in university is all very well, but it's the classroom where you really learn!

Mathematics teachers

What is your attitude to learning to teach?
What relative importance do you give to theory and practice? Why?

Many mathematics teachers are sceptical of educational research, feeling that it complicates what is essentially a simple task. They may have reservations about the rigour of social science research in general, such as the statistical significance of results originating from small sample sizes or the subjective nature of some measures or styles of research. For those used to the hard sciences and notions of mathematical proof, the sensitivity of educational researchers' data to a myriad of complicated variables that are hard or impossible to control, and the tentative conclusions resulting, may make the whole process seem hardly worthwhile. However, *not* to study how people learn is hardly an option. The science of medicine is hugely complex, yet enormous progress has been made in establishing an evidence base for many treatments, although there is still a long way to go (Gawande, 2003). Research in education is further back still, yet books and journals make fascinating reading and help to ground the practice of teachers on the best available evidence.

No one can completely avoid theory; every mathematics teacher has ideas about how children learn. These may be a compilation of things they have read, experiences they have had (as learner as well as teacher), lessons from life (such as from being a parent) and things they have been told (or tell themselves), perhaps repeatedly. These *folk theories* are still theories; a teacher's collection of commonsense views forms their particular theory of education, and will lead to particular consequences in the classroom (Fox, 1983). Studying educational theory more formally will reinforce and challenge these views and help your own practice to be shaped not only by your own particular experiences but by the wider collected experiences and thoughts of others.

Politicians frequently disparage educational research. Ball (1997: 247) believes that education policy has sought to 'expunge' theory from teacher education: 'Theory is seen as both irrelevant and dangerous'. Drawing on Mahon (1992), he argues that theory is feared by those who wish to perpetuate the *status quo* because:

> Theory is a vehicle for 'thinking otherwise'; it is a platform for 'outrageous hypotheses' and for 'unleashing criticism'. ... The purpose of theory is to de-familiarise present practices and categories, to make them seem less self-evident and necessary, and to open up spaces for the invention of new forms of experience.
>
> (p. 249)

Those who have a vested interest in keeping things as they are will not want to promote research.

One way to respond to doubts about the value of educational theory is to get involved in action research yourself (McNiff, 2002), perhaps in conjunction with a local university education department. According to Johnston-Wilder (2010: 90), 'Action research is now seen by many as more efficient than "top-down" initiatives, in changing the practices of professionals who are both used to acting autonomously and are required to do so'. Mathematics teachers can be impatient with philosophy, wanting books and articles to give them ideas that they can take straight into the classroom and use immediately. In some ways, this parallels the behaviour of learners who sometimes just want to be shown 'how to do it; never mind why'. Many teacher educators strive to *educate* teachers in as wide a sense as possible, rather than merely *train* them (Maguire and Dillon, 1997). Beginning teachers often assume that they are going to be 'taught how to teach' and may be disillusioned when they are instead encouraged to work out a way for themselves.

When learners or those who have not thought much about teaching (e.g., many parents) need to teach somebody some mathematics, they often resort to *transmission teaching* (King, 1993). Bruner (2002: 14) describes this as 'a mold in which a single, presumably omniscient teacher explicitly tells or shows presumably unknowing learners something they presumably know nothing about'. According to McCallum *et al.* (2000: 275), 'In this model, the teacher is authoritarian pedagogue relaying knowledge, knowledge is adult-decided and the learner is seen as passive recipient; pupils are mostly engaged in seat work, drill and practice'. The result, as Noyes (2007: 11) describes it, is that 'Many children are trained to do mathematical calculations rather than being educated to think mathematically'. Ollerton (2009: 60) points out that 'If teaching were about passing on knowledge, we would end up in a downward spiral of knowledge; like "Chinese whispers" information becomes reduced, distorted and minimized'.

For many practising teachers, also, this can be the default when they are in a hurry and cannot think of a better way. The mathematics must be 'passed on' to the learners, and metaphors of *delivery* are common. Typically, the *chalk-and-talk* teacher stands at the board *broadcasting* to the room. Mathematics lessons which take a *back-to-basics* approach, in which the teacher does a lot of telling and the learners listen and copy things down into their books, have been characterized as *triple-X lessons*: *ex*planation, *ex*amples, *ex*ercises (Swain and Swan, 2007). With an emphasis on drill-and-practice, learners are expected to remember facts and procedures that are given to them. As far back as the turn of the twentieth century, Spencer (1910) condemned this approach in the strongest terms:

> To *tell* a child this and to *show* it the other, is not to teach it how to observe, but to make it a mere recipient of another's observations: a proceeding which weakens rather than strengthens its powers of self-instruction – which deprives it of the pleasures resulting from successful activity.
>
> (p. 102)

Such an approach to teaching mathematics can result in learners becoming *less* capable to tackle the unfamiliar and to think mathematically as they 'progress' through school.

4.2 Constructivism

> Knowledge arises neither from objects nor the child, but from interactions between the child and those objects.
>
> Jean Piaget

Constructivism has become the dominant epistemological viewpoint (the prevailing position on where knowledge comes from) in mathematics and science education (Ernest, 2011b). It assigns a much more active role to the learner than do the more traditional views of learning considered above. Piaget's idea of *genetic epistemology* asserts that children are biologically prepared to build up for themselves a picture of the world around them, with each child as a *lone scientist*. Just as organisms adapt to changes in their environment, human learning can be viewed as a process of *equilibration*, involving the *assimilation* of sense data into a *schema* (Skemp, 1971), alongside *accommodation* of the schema to fit the new information.

Radical constructivism (von Glasersfeld, 1995) considers that the meaning that each learner constructs is all that there is – there is no objective external mathematics. By contrast, *social constructivism* is less individualistic, emphasizing the role of other people and language in contributing to the learner's construction of knowledge (Ernest, 2011b). Acceptance of some form of constructivism has led to an emphasis on learners *exploring* mathematics for themselves by means of *open-ended investigative tasks* in which mathematical ideas can be *discovered*. Clearly, this is a dishonest process if learners are merely 'uncovering' what the teacher has just buried. Baxter and Williams (2010: 8) describe the *dilemma of telling* as 'how to facilitate students coming to certain understandings, without directly telling them what they need to know or to do'. Or, as Edwards and Mercer (1987: 126) put it, 'The teacher's dilemma is to have to inculcate knowledge while apparently eliciting it'.

Vygotsky (1978) used the term *zone of proximal development* (ZPD) to refer to the difference between what a learner can do unaided and what they can do with a teacher's assistance. He was frustrated with tests that took account only of what a child could do *alone*. He felt that two children who performed equally well in such a test might nevertheless be at significantly different developmental levels, if account was taken of what they could do with just a little help:

> If a child can do such-and-such independently, it means that the functions for such-and-such have matured in her. ... The zone of proximal development defines those functions that have not yet matured but are in the process of maturation, functions that will mature tomorrow but are currently in an embryonic state.
>
> (p. 86)

Two children might both be unable to swim unaided, but one might be able to swim quite well if given arm-bands, whereas the other still cannot. Or, in a mathematical context, two learners might both be unable to solve equations, but one might be able to with access to a calculator, whereas the other still might not.

For Vygotsky (1978), this distinction was crucial for teaching to be beneficial:

> [L]earning which is oriented toward developmental levels that have already been reached is ineffective from the viewpoint of a child's overall development. It does not aim for a new stage of the developmental process but rather lags behind this process. Thus, the notion of a zone of proximal development enables us to propound a new formula, namely that the only "good learning" is that which is in *advance* of development.
>
> (p. 89, italics added)

The ZPD bridges what the learner *can* do (and therefore does not need to do more of) and what they *cannot* (yet) do. It is important that help given in the ZPD does not create dependency – help is offered as a temporary measure, or *scaffolding*, which must be removed before the edifice is complete. Interestingly, Watson and Mason (2005) comment that:

> the scaffolding commonly used in many parts of the world consists of a collection of numerous wooden posts that are balanced on the concrete floor of the nth story of a building and used to wedge up the $(n + 1)$th floor. They are internal to the structure of the building.
>
> (p. 85)

This image, rather than the more conventional one of scaffolding pushing in from the outside, suggests that learners' internal capabilities may effectively scaffold their subsequent development. The practice of *scaffolding with fading* (Collins *et al.*, 1991) is consonant with the advice 'only do for people what they cannot yet do for themselves' (Mason, 2000: 101). (See page 132 for a discussion about the dangers of *funnelling*.)

Piaget's perspective that learners could only construct new knowledge when they had reached appropriate ages and stages has stood the test of time less well. Vygotsky (1978) comments that many people had previously assumed:

> that development is always a prerequisite for learning and that if a child's mental functions ... have not matured to the extent that he is capable of learning a particular subject then no instruction will prove useful. They especially feared premature instruction, the teaching of a subject before the child was ready for it. ... Because this approach is based on the premise that learning trails behind development ... it precludes the notion that learning may play a role in the course of the development.
>
> (p. 80)

Unless learners are given mathematical tasks that, to some extent, they 'are not ready for', then they will just be repeating things that they can already do.

Task Adding

Add up all the integers from 1 to 1000. How did you do it?

Add up all the even numbers from 1 to 1000. How did you do it?

Add up all the tenths from 1 to 1000 (i.e., 1 + 1.1 + 1.2 + 1.3 + ...). How did you do it?

Bruner's (1966) framework of *enactive–iconic–symbolic* indicates *three worlds* of experience. An *enactive* representation involves something physical that can be manipulated (a *kinesthetic* experience). For example, a learner might engage with triangle numbers by constructing 'staircases' from interlocking cubes: by building successive triangles, the learner might realize that one more cube is needed for each additional row (Figure 4.2). In the *iconic* world, the learner might make rough sketches of pyramids, in which not every cube was shown but the lengths of the rows were marked (Figure 4.3). Finally, in the *symbolic* representation, T_n could be used to represent the nth triangle number, and some algebra might show that adding on $n + 1$ gives the next triangle number, T_{n+1}:

$$T_n + (n+1) = \tfrac{1}{2}n(n+1) + (n+1) = \tfrac{1}{2}(n+1)(n+2) = T_{n+1}$$

A related framework is *manipulating – getting-a-sense-of – articulating* (Mason and Johnston-Wilder, 2006), in which stress is laid on the need for learners to be given time to form ideas before trying to crystallize them into words or symbols. In either of these schemes, transition from one stage to the next is not necessarily swift or straightforward.

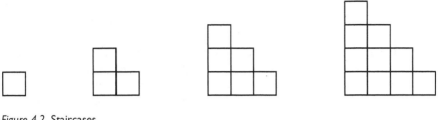

Figure 4.2 Staircases

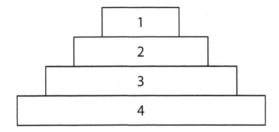

Figure 4.3 Pyramid

Task **Styles**

What we want is to see the child in pursuit of knowledge, and not knowledge in pursuit of the child.

George Bernard Shaw

What different teaching styles have you personally experienced as a learner of mathematics?
What do you think was most/least successful for you? Why?

4.3 Relevance

Real life is over-rated.

Cynical mathematics teacher

'Relevance' is increasingly seen as central to the teaching of mathematics. If only suitable contexts can be found to show learners how mathematics relates to their 'real world', it is thought, motivation will increase and learning will follow. However, *real* learning has to be to some extent beyond the learner's current horizon. Authentic geography lessons, for example, cannot be exclusively about the local area where the children live. Education seeks to *expand* learners' awarenesses, challenge their views of the world and give them insights into alternative possibilities. An excessively 'relevant' mathematics curriculum might end up focusing too much on *functional skills* such as calculating percentages and interpreting statistical data. It would be patronizing to suppose that these are all the mathematics that some learners will require.

When told about a mathematics lesson involving statistics 'relevant' to the learners in the class, Noyes (2007: 94) comments, 'Who would possibly want to know the mode shoe size for a class of 14-year-olds? ... I have seen too many lessons where pupils survey the distribution of pets, favourites, and so on of others in the group. So what!' By contrast, Noddings (2010) asks us to:

> Consider, for example, what a mathematics class might contribute to a unit on crime. Statistical information might be gathered on the location and number of crimes, on rates for various kinds of crime, on the ages of offenders, and on the cost to society; graphs and charts could be constructed. Data on changes in crime rates could be assembled. Intriguing questions could be asked: Were property crime rates lower when penalties were more severe – when, for example, even children were hanged as thieves? What does an average criminal case cost by way of lawyers' fees, police investigation, and court proceedings? Does it cost more to house a youth in a detention center or in an elite private school?
>
> (p. 139)

Noyes (2007: 96) offers an activity in which learners 'consider issues of global and national poverty and the relative difference between the rich and the poor'. He divides learners into six groups of size proportional to the populations of the six continents. He then distributes biscuits among the 'continents' in proportion to their relative shares of global wealth. The learners' objections of unfairness are striking!

Schooling is more than preparation for future jobs and life as a consumer (see chapter 1). A general education seeks to help learners understand what other people, different from themselves, might be absorbed with in their lives. It would be unthinkable to study music, for instance, without some awareness of major composers and the development of musical instruments in different parts of the world. Yet, in most mathematics schemes of work, learners are unlikely to gain more than a cursory sense of the fascinating history of the subject (Grugnetti and Rogers, 2000), despite the availability of some excellent resources (e.g., Ramsden, 2009). How will learners discover whether they want to use pure mathematics in the future if they do not experience much of it in school? *Realistic Mathematics Education*, developed at the Freudenthal Institute in The Netherlands, focuses on contexts for mathematics that are vivid and imaginable for learners (Hough and Gough, 2007). The attempt is not so much to find contexts that relate to situations that learners are already familiar with; rather, with ones within the *zone of proximal relevance* (Watson and Mason, 2005), which learners might *become* interested in and find illuminating.

Learners do not straightforwardly *transfer* what they learn in the mathematics classroom to situations outside it, any more than they bring in competence that they possess elsewhere. The theory of *situated cognition* (Lave, 1988) insists that mathematical behaviour is specific in nature to the situation in which it arises (e.g., school classroom or everyday life). Watson and Winbourne (2008: 4) comment that 'such perspectives offer promising ways to make sense of why people might not apply in one context what they had learnt in another'.

4.3.1 Pseudo-real life

It takes Leillah 25 seconds to run 100 metres. How long will it take her to run 500 metres?

When learners are given tasks such as working out how many rolls of carpet they would need in order to carpet their classroom, it is not always clear to what extent they are supposed to bring real-life considerations to bear. Too little reference to the real situation can provoke the teacher's ridicule ('Do you really think you can buy 2.4 rolls of carpet?'), but so can too much ('Well, obviously the floor is horizontal!'). Learners may know from practical experience that floors are not always horizontal and that off-cuts of carpet can often be bought in odd sizes. Williams *et al.* (2008: 155) 'wonder if the authenticity of the outside-school situation often survives the transfer into the classroom situation'. Many people have questioned the value of contexts that appear to be real-life but on closer examination are not really (Boaler, 1993; Ward-Penny, 2010). The issue does not go away as learners progress to mathematical modelling in the sixth form (Little, 2011a, 2011b).

Cooper and Harries (2003) have studied extensively what has now become an infamous mathematics question, in which children were asked how many journeys a lift would have to make to ferry 269 people up a building 14 at a time. Apparently the people in this question were happy to wait around for a considerable period, no one thinking to take the stairs or leave; nor did an extra person or two dare to squeeze into any of the journeys! It is doubtful that having only one lift for such a large building would even comply with health and safety legislation; nonetheless, after years of training on this kind of material, many children 'played the game', giving the answer '20', which was deemed 'correct'.

Such pseudo-real-life problems get mathematics education a bad name and seem to disadvantage particularly those learners who are already worst off (Cooper and Harries, 2005). When the key to success is to suspend reality, assume that people behave abnormally and rule out obvious alternative courses of action, thinking is reduced to the lowest possible level, resulting in learners being reluctant to bring what they *do* know from real life to bear on problems when that *is* what is wanted (Cooper and Harries, 2002). The structure of some questions perpetuates the idea that 'everything is linear', so that, presented with a recipe for making 10 cakes and asked to produce one for making 15 cakes, some learners will scale up the oven temperature by the same factor of 1.5.

Sometimes learners are expected to 'know' that it is 'better' to buy a larger packet of breakfast cereal if it is cheaper per gram. But the customer may not have enough ready cash to pay for the more economical but larger item. Affluent textbook writers may not hesitate to put it on their credit card, but for many people this is not financial reality. Perhaps the larger packet will go off before it is all used, or perhaps the 'best before' dates are different and the shop is trying to shift old stock by marking it down? Perhaps the smaller packets fit nicely in your cupboard, but the larger one will not go in? Perhaps you want to take one packet to work and leave the other one at home, so two small ones are better than one larger one? Perhaps the 'free' gifts in the smaller packets are better than those in the larger packet, or there is a different competition to enter on the back? There are many reasons why the 'sensible' choice could be different for different people and it is much more interesting to engage with complexity than to assume that life choices are always simple and obvious calculations.

Task Pseudo-real life

Look through the resources (worksheets, textbooks, examination papers) used in your school.
When and where are 'real-life' scenarios used?
How good do you think they are?

Some mathematics problems can inadvertently trivialize serious aspects of the real world. Disturbingly, Ariely (2010: 248) found that people find it hard to be empathetic and rational at the same time: '[I]t turned out to be extremely difficult for participants to think about calculation, statistical information, and numbers and to feel emotion at the same time.' More information about human need does not automatically lead to an increase in concern and action. Sudden disasters seem to lead to a greater charitable response than static or chronic states of need do (Small, 2010), and people's choices are not straightforward (Loewenstein and Small, 2007). Provocative statistics can lead to controversial issues, and finding ways to deal with these in the mathematics classroom requires care. Varma-Joshi (2007) offers a helpful approach:

> The pedagogy of teaching controversial issues is all-important. It is pointless and usually self defeating to lecture or moralise to students. Rather, they must be given the opportunity to debate in small safe groups, where each person's voice can be heard, including those of the minorities who may otherwise practise self-silencing, or be silenced by others.
>
> (p. 169)

4.3.2 'Pure' problems

Sometimes a problem that is really pure mathematics is 'dressed up' in real-world clothes – sometimes this just adds humour or makes the details easier to talk about. The 'context' is not there to motivate or introduce 'relevance', and in situations like this learners are normally quite tolerant of the unreal aspects, whether they comment on them or not.

Task Farmyard

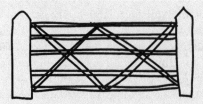

- A farmer asks her husband how many hens and how many rabbits there are in the yard. He says there are 53 heads and 142 legs. Can the farmer work it out?

- If it takes $1\frac{1}{2}$ chickens $1\frac{1}{2}$ days to lay $1\frac{1}{2}$ eggs, how long does it take 2 chickens to lay 4 eggs?

- It takes Moses 20 minutes to milk the cows by himself and it takes Qaylah 30 minutes to milk the cows by herself. If they both milk them together, how long will it take?

Would these tasks 'work' with your learners? Why / why not?
Would you be happy using them? Why / why not?

These problems are not intended to be an accurate portrayal of life on a modern farm; clearly, there is a playfulness about them. Moses and Qaylah may get in each other's way, knock over the pails of milk or chat so much that they take all morning to milk the cows. However, if translated into pure mathematical problems (e.g., 'I'm thinking of two integers …'), then these questions still possess some puzzling and interesting features; their relevance to a mathematics lesson does not depend on their connection with real life. Commenting on complaints that mathematics lessons are very often 'not about anything', Rowland (2000: xi) comments that 'mathematics is powerful *precisely because* it is not about anything in particular, enabling diversity of application and encouraging speculation beyond the realm of personal experience'.

Task Summary task

If we taught children to speak, they'd never learn.

Bill Hull

What views do you hold on the theoretical issues of this chapter?
How 'relevant' is relevance in your classroom? Why?

Comments on mathematical tasks

Task: Adding

The sum of the integers from 1 to 1000 (inclusive) is the 1000th triangle number, $\frac{1}{2} \times 1000 \times 1001 = 500\,500$. Did you assume that the sum of all the *even* numbers from 1 to 1000 (inclusive) was just half of this? It must be more than half, because each odd number is 1 less than each even number. So the odd numbers must add up to 500 less than the even numbers. So if the sum of the odd numbers is s, then the sum of the even numbers must be $s + 500$ and $s + (s + 500) = 500\,500$, so $s = 250\,000$, so $s + 500 = 250\,500$. Adding up all the tenths from 1 to 1000 inclusive requires a bit of care, but there are 9991 terms and the sum comes to $5\,000\,495.5$.

Task: Farmyard

The answers to the three problems are 18 rabbits and 35 hens; 3 days; and 12 minutes. Learners might like to try to list some of the assumptions that lie behind these answers, and perhaps try to put them in order of importance.

Further reading

Boaler, J. (1993) 'The role of contexts in the mathematics classroom: do they make mathematics more "real"?', *For the Learning of Mathematics*, 13(2), 12–17.

Ernest, P. (2011) *The Psychology of Learning Mathematics*, Saarbrucken, Germany: Lambert Academic Publishing.

Ward-Penny, R. (2010) 'Context or con? How might we better represent the "real-world" in the classroom?', *Mathematics in School*, 39(1), 10–12.

Chapter 5

Ideas for lessons

You ask me where I get my ideas ... they come unbidden.

Ludwig van Beethoven

A good mathematics lesson is usually built on at least one good idea. It could be a particular way of introducing or developing a specific topic; for example, teaching addition and subtraction of directed numbers (positive, negative, zero) by using learners to represent numbers and having them walk up and down a number line at the front of the classroom. Or it could be a specific mathematical problem which has a depth that you hope will draw learners into thinking about some particular aspect of mathematics. One way in which mathematics teachers develop experience is by accumulating and refining 'good ideas'.

5.1 The importance of ideas

The best way to have a good idea is to have lots of ideas.

Linus Pauling

Lesson planning begins with a mathematical idea, which might be arrived at either deliberately or by serendipity: creative ideas can come both ways. Sometimes the constraint of having to teach a particular topic nudges you into thinking of something that you might not have thought of otherwise. On the other hand, being open to possibilities can lead to stimulating ideas that are just too good not to incorporate into the mathematics curriculum somewhere.

5.1.1 Deliberate ideas

We have to reinvent the wheel every once in a while, not because we need a lot of wheels; but because we need a lot of inventors.

Bruce Joyce

Deliberate ideas happen when you have something specific that you need to teach to somebody soon.

> # Task Fractions
>
> I have to teach 'fractions' to Year 8 on Monday. What shall I do?
>
> What thoughts come to mind initially?
> Do different thoughts arise as you ponder for longer?

You might start by thinking about what you know about the class and what previous experiences of fractions they might have had. What sorts of lessons tend to work well with them? You might try to make links to some of their interests or to elements of a previous topic. To find further ideas, you might use the internet or books of lesson ideas, some of which are suggested at the end of this chapter. Some questions you might ask are:

- What difficulties and strengths are the learners likely to bring to this topic?
- What related experiences are learners likely to have had before?
- Can I exploit some of the learners' interests in the construction of the lesson?
- How will this lesson complement or contrast with things we have done recently?
- Does the scheme of work suggest anything interesting?
- What did I do last time I taught this topic? How did it go?
- What do my colleagues tend to do? (Have I asked them?)
- What ICT and other resources are available for this particular lesson?
- Are there good ideas in textbooks, books of lesson ideas, magazines, journals or on the internet?
- How much time can I spend on this topic?
- How much time have I got to prepare?!

It makes sense to benefit from ideas that are already 'out there' without abdicating complete responsibility to the author of a textbook scheme or resource. For Ollerton (2005: xiii), 'ownership is how a teacher adapts any ideas they pick up from various sources ... and makes them their own according to how they use them in their classrooms'.

5.1.2 Serendipitous ideas

> Originality is undetected plagiarism.
>
> William Ralph Inge

This way is much more fun, although it is not guaranteed to generate ideas that you can use immediately unless you have a very flexible structure to your teaching. Lesson ideas can come from all sorts of places. Once you get into the habit of looking for opportunities they begin to come more frequently. It is important to have some way of keeping the ideas that occur to you until you have a suitable opportunity to use them with learners. However, if you are particularly excited about an idea, or it is topical, that might be reason enough to suspend the usual ordering of topics and give the learners a bit of surprise. If you are enthusiastic about some mathematics, learners may find it interesting too – but not necessarily!

Here are some ideas that came to me recently and that I was able to use in mathematics lessons:

- When I was ordering pizza, I noticed that the pizza company divided larger pizzas into more slices than smaller pizzas. This set me wondering whether a slice of an extra-large pizza was bigger or smaller than a slice of a medium pizza. I realized that I could use this with learners as a way of working on areas of circles, sequences and linear and area scale factors.

- In a lesson I asked learners to draw a circle of radius 5 cm and to use compasses to mark off points at 5 cm intervals around the circumference to create a regular hexagon. After experimenting for a few minutes, one learner said that if you made marks every 6 cm instead, you obtained a regular pentagon. His construction was not exact, but close, and I thought that this would be an interesting situation for older learners, who knew about trigonometry, to analyse and work out percentage errors.

- My wife bought a clock for our living room which had no numbers around the edge and no manufacturer's name in the centre. So if you ignored the hands then it had perfect 12-fold symmetry. As I fixed it to the wall, I wondered whether anyone would be able to tell if I rotated it a multiple of 30°. Could I move on the hands to make it tell the time normally? What if I looked at a snapshot of the clock in a mirror? Could you tell a reflected clock from an unreflected clock in a photograph? This led to some work on symmetry and angles.

- In Bristol, I saw the *SS Great Britain* and noticed that when viewed side-on, the ship's wheel had order 10 rotational symmetry and 10 lines of symmetry (Figure 5.1). I thought that it might be interesting to ask whether it is possible to have a shape with 10 lines of symmetry that does *not* have order 10 rotational symmetry? (The learners knew that the opposite was possible.) What possible orders of rotational symmetry might there be? What would happen with numbers other than 10?

Task Openness

What could you do to make yourself more open to mathematical possibilities that might arise in everyday life?

How could you avoid losing these when they do appear?

While cultivating a state of mind that notices opportunities for mathematical ideas, you also need to be careful that work doesn't end up dominating your time off, so that you can't go on holiday without constantly photographing 'mathematical' objects! A sensible balance is needed. Saving ideas on a computer can be efficient and environmentally friendly. You can keep all the word-processing files you are ever likely to create in your career on one memory stick! Make sure that you begin with a sensible folder structure. I sort resources and ideas by topic rather than by age or stage, as I frequently find that the same thing will work well with all sorts of different ages. Material doesn't have to be a

Figure 5.1 A ship's wheel

polished and perfected worksheet: if you have an idea, type it into a file and save it – it takes only a few seconds, and you can always come back and develop it when you have more time or are looking for something on that topic. The main thing is not to lose your ideas – it is worth keeping everything, even things which didn't seem to work very well. Sometimes you will think back to something you did and have an idea about what could turn it into something more successful. And, of course, do back everything up regularly!

5.2 Creating a lesson

> From the very beginning of his education, the child should experience the joy of discovery.
>
> Alfred North Whitehead

Although a good mathematics lesson depends on having a good idea, the lesson is more than just an idea, and we will look more in chapter 6 at the process of transforming an idea into a lesson.

5.2.1 Making choices

> Try not just going with the first thing that comes to mind. Wait until you have more than one idea and then choose the best. It stops you from being an automaton!
>
> Mathematics teacher

This may sound like doubling (or more) the amount of work that you have to do, and may not always be feasible – sometimes you will be glad if just *one* idea occurs to you! But when you are in less of a hurry, the act of weighing up options can be valuable. Forcing yourself to consider at least two alternatives before settling on a plan of action can lead you into doing things that you might never have done otherwise. Avoiding the 'easy' option that first presents itself can be a good discipline, but it is important to be realistic. Mathematics teachers may begin their career idealistically but gradually get ground down by reality, becoming a little more cynical as time goes on. Sometimes that can happen if new teachers try to do too much too quickly at the start. The average full-time mathematics teacher may teach six or more lessons a day, five days a week. Probably nobody can present this many astoundingly interesting lessons every week. If you see experienced colleagues who seem to be able to do so, then it is almost certainly because they are not starting from zero with every lesson. They will be using ideas that have worked for them before and adapting them to their current class and/or making use of published materials. An experienced teacher may be able to do this sort of preparation very quickly, perhaps without writing anything down – maybe in the time it takes to wash up their coffee mug in the staffroom! Don't be discouraged if it takes you much longer, especially in the first few years or if you are changing your teaching style.

Task Realism

What approaches to lesson planning have you seen among colleagues or tried yourself?
What expectations are there in your school?
What do you think is realistic for you?

If you want to develop your teaching, perhaps moving away from an over-reliance on textbooks, you will probably not be able to transform all of your lessons overnight into amazing learning experiences. But maybe you could concentrate your energies on one particular class or aim to have one 'super' lesson each week. Every time you develop something good, you will find that you are in a better position to do so next time – and the lesson you have created may also serve you well again on another occasion. Sometimes you might construct a task-sheet; on other occasions it might work better just to pose a problem orally or put something provocative on the board. These choices might depend on how you prefer to work and what seems to work best for the particular classes that you teach. (See pages 73–76 for more discussion of the use of resources.)

Ainley *et al.* (2006) highlight what they call a *planning paradox*: if the teacher plans the lesson too precisely, there is no room for manoeuvre, and learners have less opportunity to show what they can do; but if there are just some open-ended starting points, then anything may happen and it may be hard to assess what learners have learned. Most mathematics teachers probably aim for something somewhere between these extremes. When you have some experience, one practical approach is to aim to plan *series* of lessons in more detail than individual lessons. If you can devise (or find) a really good open-ended task, then this might occupy learners for three or four lessons, and the preparation that you do lasts longer. Also, an open task may be more suitable for a wider range of learners, so you may not need to plan lots of different things for different learners. Learners will naturally *self-differentiate* by the way in which they choose to approach the task, and you will assist this process during the lesson. With exploratory work, planning for differentiation may consist mainly of thinking about the different learners within the class and anticipating the sorts of things that each might achieve with the task and how you could help. This way, you don't have to produce multiple versions of a worksheet or worry about managing different learners using different textbooks with different page numbers. By not revealing to learners in advance what you are anticipating that they might achieve, you will be leaving open the opportunity to be surprised, but you will also have strategies available for encouraging learners to choose appropriate aspects of problems to work on (see chapter 7).

5.2.2 Surprise

> If you do not expect the unexpected you will not find it, for it is not to be reached by search or trail.
>
> Heraclitus

Human beings have an ambivalent relationship with surprise: many people enjoy the thrill of a shock in the theatre, and the technical crew go to great lengths to create dramatic effects; but then a sign is put up in the foyer warning that there will be gunshots, say, during the performance. Do we want to be surprised or don't we? Surprise can be a powerful enabler in the mathematics classroom. As Mason and Johnston-Wilder (2004: 311) put it, 'It is the unexpected which strikes the learners' attention, and activates the sense-making apparatus'. Movshovitz-Hadar (1988) suggests that:

> all school theorems, except possibly a very small number of them, possess a built-in surprise, and that by exploiting this surprise potential their learning can become an exciting experience of intellectual enterprise to the students. ... Every single theorem can be turned into a surprise by considering the unexpected matter which that theorem claims to be true.
>
> (p. 34)

This provocative claim is worth trying to apply. Locating the potential surprise in what you want to teach and then constructing a task that exposes learners to it can be interesting. For Bruner (1986: 46), 'surprise is an extraordinarily useful phenomenon to students of mind, for it allows us to probe what people take for granted. It provides a window on presupposition: surprise is a response to violated presupposition'. Sometimes tasks offer a short, sharp shock, such as this one.

Task Six zeroes

If there are six zeroes in a million, how many zeroes will there be in *half* a million? Or in two million? Why?

There are the same number of zeroes in 'a million and one' as there are in 'half a million', and learners may be initially surprised by this sort of thing. (There are possible links here to indices and logarithms.) Learners might be asked to try to find a number with six zeroes, half of which *does* have three zeroes. You will be able to think of other tasks which offer a challenge to inappropriate *linear thinking*.

Other tasks might support a longer period of mathematical work. For instance, learners could use calculators (or a spreadsheet) or just pen and paper to begin this next task and then try to make sense of the patterns obtained.

Task Squaring

Work out:

$15^2, 25^2, 35^2, 45^2, 55^2, 65^2, 75^2, 85^2, 95^2$
$51^2, 52^2, 53^2, 54^2, 55^2, 56^2, 57^2, 58^2, 59^2$

What patterns can you find in the answers? Can you explain them?
Do they continue beyond these values?

When learners are confronted by something mysterious, puzzling, ambiguous or counterintuitive, energy is often created, which can be harnessed in pursuing the problem to some kind of a resolution (Foster, 2011a). Something that began for me as a real-life mathematics problem developed into the following task, although I changed the numbers to make it more interesting.

Task Doughnuts

A nice mathematics teacher wants to buy doughnuts for all 27 learners in the class.
Identical doughnuts can be bought in two different quantities:

Number of doughnuts in bag	Price per bag
4	£2.50
10	£6.00

What is the cheapest way to get at least 27 doughnuts?

Table 5.1 Doughnut calculations

Number of bags of 4	Number of bags of 10	Total cost (£)	Number of leftover doughnuts
2	2	17.00	1
7	0	17.50	1
0	3	18.00	3
5	1	18.50	3
3	2	19.50	5
1	3	20.50	7
6	1	21.00	7
4	2	22.00	9

Learners might discover that buying seven bags of four (with one doughnut left over – the nice teacher can have one too!) is cheaper than buying three bags of 10 (with three doughnuts left over). It is impossible to buy exactly 27 doughnuts anyway, since both 4 and 10 are even numbers, so at least one doughnut must be left over. But a better solution is possible, consisting of two bags of 4 and two bags of 10, making a saving of 50 pence (see Table 5.1). As with most 'real-life problems' (see chapter 4), learners might be encouraged to question the terms of the question – maybe not everyone will want a doughnut, or someone will be away, or maybe eating doughnuts is not particularly healthy anyway! Learners might suggest that since the teacher is buying in bulk they could try to negotiate a better price with the shopkeeper, or that buying smaller bags could enable them to get a bigger variety of flavours. These sorts of comments could be welcomed as part of dealing with the 'real' world. Learners could try changing the numbers in the problem to make the optimal answer even more surprising and difficult to find. Other extensions could relate to finding out what possible numbers of doughnuts can be bought if only bags of 4 and 10 are available (could you buy exactly 198 doughnuts, for instance?). With different numbers of doughnuts in the bags (e.g., bags of 5 and bags of 6), or with more than two different bag sizes, the problem could occupy learners in productive mathematical thought for quite some time. Could it ever be cheaper to have a doughnut left over than to buy exactly the right number?

5.3 Learners' perspectives

> Maths teachers are just on some other planet – well, I wish they were!
>
> Mathematics learner

Task Perspective

If you have the opportunity to talk to some pupils, ask them what they enjoy or don't enjoy about mathematics lessons. (Perhaps you could hunt down some pupils in a corridor or form room during lunch time?)

You might want to discourage them from naming particular teachers and ask them to describe things that happen rather than the people involved.
Do they say anything that surprises you?
Do they describe specific lessons or more general teaching attitudes or approaches?

Teachers sometimes think that there is no point asking learners what they think, because they will prioritize 'fun' at the expense of 'learning' and favour teachers who set little homework or give out sweets, regardless of whether they learn much mathematics. Maybe you object to the *consumer culture* which overvalues students' views. Interestingly, giving this sort of power to the learner is not a modern idea. Mlodinow (2001) describes the medieval university system:

> Typically, a university had no buildings at all. Students lived in cooperative housing. Professors lectured in rented rooms, rooming houses, churches, even brothels. The classrooms, like the dwellings, were poorly lit and heated. Some universities employed a system that sounds, well, medieval: professors were paid directly by the students. At Bologna, students hired and fired professors, fined them for unexcused absence or tardiness, or for not answering difficult questions. If the lecture was not interesting, going too slow, too fast, or simply not loud enough, they would jeer or throw things. In Leipzig, the university eventually found it necessary to promulgate a rule against throwing stones at professors.
>
> (pp. 64–65)

Nowadays, it is normal for learners to have some input into appointments of teaching staff and for school councils to have responsibility for aspects of how the school site is run. If our lessons are intending to cater for our learners' needs, then although learners may not always know what those needs may be, their viewpoints must be important in informing what we do.

Task Practice

Which of these things have you done before?
Which have you done recently?
Do you regard them as part of your practice? Why/why not?

- a mathematics lesson in the hall, drama studio or equivalent; i.e., without tables and chairs or writing anything down;
- a mathematics lesson on the school field/playground;

- leaving the school site for a mathematics lesson;
- a learner taking charge for a lesson;
- an 'unplanned' mathematics lesson, where all the questions and ideas come from the learners (e.g., a 'question-box' approach).

Learners normally appreciate it when imaginative mathematics lessons contain variety, flexibility and spontaneity. Sometimes you may be able to capitalize on some numerical feature of the day's date or a topical event or occasion; sometimes you will gauge the mood and be able to enjoy going with the grain of the learners' interests, rather than against it, such as doing some mathematics connected with snowflakes when it begins to snow and all the learners are excited about it (Foster, 2009).

Task Summary task

Here is a list of some 'external' things that could happen during a mathematics lesson and which might be potentially 'disruptive' to the lesson. (You could add others.) Instead of trying to ignore them ('the elephant in the room'), can you think of ways of turning them to mathematical advantage, exploiting them for a spontaneous mathematical task?

- Someone starts cutting the grass or blowing leaves about outside the classroom window.
- It starts snowing and learners get excited looking out of the window.
- Somebody sneezes very loudly and everybody laughs.
- In a noisy classroom, there is a sudden moment of silence where virtually everyone stops talking at once, and several learners notice.
- The deputy head arrives asking for four volunteers to do a job.
- A wasp flies in through an open window and terrifies some learners before flying away again.
- A message arrives that school will be closed one day next week because of a teachers' strike.
- Someone leaning back on their chair slips and falls on the floor.
- There is a power cut and the lights and data projector suddenly go off.
- The flat roof above the classroom is leaking and water is dripping into a bucket in the corner.
- The teacher has had a haircut and as the lesson starts a learner says, 'Sir, have you had your hair cut?'
- Several members of the class are away on a school trip.
- A learner is wearing a big badge declaring that it is their birthday.

Comments on mathematical tasks

Task: Squaring

For the number '$a5$' (i.e., 'a-ty-five' [sounds like 'eighty-five'], $10a + 5$), the last two digits are always 25 and the 'hundreds' is $a(a + 1)$. This follows from the fact that $(10a + 5)^2 = 100a(a+1) + 25$. For the number '$5a$' (i.e., 'fifty-$a$', $50 + a$), the last two digits are a^2 and the 'hundreds' is $25 + a$. In algebra, $(50 + a)^2 = 100(25 + a) + a^2$, and both results can be effective 'tricks' for mental squaring.

Task: Doughnuts

For example, if the costs are £1 and £2 for bags of 4 and 10, respectively, then seven small bags (28 doughnuts) are more expensive than three large bags (30 doughnuts). This could be related to work on inequalities.

Further reading

Mason, J. and Johnston-Wilder, S.J. (2006) *Designing and Using Mathematical Tasks*, St Albans: Tarquin Publications.

Watson, A. and Mason, J. (2005) *Mathematics as a Constructive Activity: learners generating examples*, Mahwah: Erlbaum.

Useful resources

Banwell, C.S., Saunders, K.D. and Tahta, D.S. (1986) *Starting Points for Teaching Mathematics in Middle and Secondary Schools*, Norfolk: Tarquin Publications.

Love, E. and McIntosh, A. (1980) *Points of Departure: book 1*, Derby: Association of Teachers of Mathematics.

Hardy, T. and Haworth, A. (1982) *Points of Departure: book 2*, Derby: Association of Teachers of Mathematics.

Association of Teachers of Mathematics (1989) *Points of Departure: book 3*, Derby: Association of Teachers of Mathematics.

Association of Teachers of Mathematics (1989) *Points of Departure: book 4*, Derby: Association of Teachers of Mathematics.

Ball, D. and Ball, B. (2011) *Rich Task Maths*, volumes 1 and 2, Derby: Association of Teachers of Mathematics.

Bills, C. (2000) *Eight Days a Week: puzzles, problems and questions to activate the mind*, Derby: Association of Teachers of Mathematics.

Bloomfield, A. and Vertes, B. (2005) *People Maths: hidden depths*, Derby: Association of Teachers of Mathematics.

Foster, C. (2009) *Mathematics for Every Occasion*, Derby: Association of Teachers of Mathematics.

Martin, C. (2011) *Big Ideas: a holistic scheme for pupils aged 11–12*, Derby: Association of Teachers of Mathematics.

Ollerton, M. (2002) *Learning and Teaching Mathematics Without a Textbook*, Derby: Association of Teachers of Mathematics.

Ollerton, M. (2005) *100 Ideas for Teaching Mathematics*, London: Continuum.

Useful websites

www.risps.co.uk
http://nrich.maths.org/

Chapter 6

Tasks, timings and resources

Many will fail in schools because they are forced to do work they hate and are deprived of work they might love.

Nel Noddings (2003: 81)

The quickest, easiest and dullest approach to planning a mathematics lesson is to find some exercises in a textbook or on an internet worksheet. Colleagues from other subject areas may believe that setting some mathematics work is so straightforward that when they are running a detention they may go straight to the child's mathematics teacher for 'something to keep them busy for half an hour'. A diet of routine textbook exercises which are sufficiently unproblematic for a learner to work through unaided, without much thought, is unlikely to lead to significant mathematical learning, although practice for fluency may have its place as part of a more interesting programme of study (see chapter 4). Sometimes dull exercises are dressed up to appear more significant than they are. For example, a mathematics teacher wanting a seasonal activity for the end of term photocopied some fractions questions onto red paper and titled it 'Christmas Fractions', but this doesn't make the experience of doing them any more worthwhile mathematically and is unlikely to fool the learners. Textbooks which are dominated by routine, repetitive questions are ultimately unstimulating for learners (and their teachers). Ollerton (2002) describes how he found alternatives to textbooks:

By the time I had become a head of mathematics I was using textbooks sparingly and at times despairingly! ... A three week period of not using a textbook soon became half a term period, when by Christmas I had not needed to use one I realised I had gained so many different strategies that I did not need to use one again.

(p. iv)

In this chapter, we will consider some alternative approaches to traditional exercises.

Task Good, poor, superb

What, in your opinion, makes a *good* mathematics lesson?
What, in your opinion, makes a *poor* mathematics lesson?
What, in your opinion, makes a *superb* mathematics lesson?

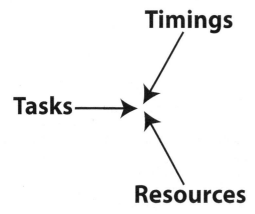

Figure 6.1 Tasks, timings and resources

Every mathematics teacher will answer these questions in different ways, and few will match published inspection criteria. In this chapter, we will consider mathematics lessons as being composed of three elements: tasks, timings and resources (Figure 6.1). Most issues concerning mathematics lessons can be related to one or more of these aspects of the classroom.

6.1 Tasks

> Study hard what interests you the most in the most undisciplined, irreverent and original manner possible.
>
> Richard Feynman

It is obvious that learners develop mathematically by working on mathematics for themselves. They need time and space to construct their understanding. Teachers cannot give concepts to learners ready-made – people don't learn well from being told (see chapter 4). The teacher's role is to provide tasks which will lead learners into thinking deeply about mathematics and making connections. Ollerton and Watson (2001: 57) suggest that 'a good starting task should intrigue and motivate students and lead them to a rich network of mathematical concepts and techniques'. Designing and using tasks employing *rich starting points* is the subject of this section.

6.1.1 Preconceptions

> My old teacher said that 1 was a prime number.
>
> Learner

Learners may arrive in your class from primary school, or from being taught by another mathematics teacher, with a quite different perspective. Many learners seem to arrive at secondary school believing such things as:

- *maths is about being quick with numbers,*
- *there is always one right answer* and
- *it's the teacher's job to say what's correct.*

They have probably not been told these things explicitly, just as no one may have actually told them that 1 is a prime number, but somehow they have acquired these beliefs. If you are seeking to challenge notions such as these, then learners may experience a degree of *culture shock* as they make the transition into the 'big' school or into your class. Learners who have always been successful, as defined by finishing their work quickly and accurately, may find deeper mathematical tasks deeply unpleasant and threatening. They may initially say that they used to enjoy mathematics and don't any more, but what they enjoyed was perhaps the feeling that they were better than their peers, which in a more inclusive classroom is not being fed. They may claim to have 'done' topics before when the teacher seeks to build on procedural competence in order to develop underpinning understanding. It may be helpful for secondary mathematics teachers to visit primary feeder schools from time to time to keep up-to-date with what a primary mathematics lesson feels like.

One approach to challenging learners' preconceptions about mathematics lessons is to use tasks that don't have one right answer, where a range of responses is acceptable, and where it is up to learners to construct a valid justification for the things that they offer.

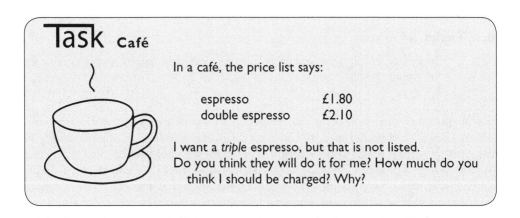

Task Café

In a café, the price list says:

espresso £1.80
double espresso £2.10

I want a *triple* espresso, but that is not listed.
Do you think they will do it for me? How much do you think I should be charged? Why?

Perhaps I will just be told to get lost – learners might advise that it wouldn't be very healthy anyway! – but there are many other possible responses. Learners might add the two prices (espresso + double espresso = triple espresso), or they might reason that since there was an extra 30 pence for the second shot, so another 30 pence must be added for a third shot, giving £2.40. Or that since there was an extra 30 pence for the second shot there should be an extra *60* pence for the third one. Other answers are possible and very likely. Tasks such as this can encourage the acceptance of different ways of thinking, justification and perhaps generalization for an '*n*-tuple' espresso.

6.1.2 Open-endedness

> Success is not a place at which one arrives but rather the spirit with which one undertakes and continues the journey.
>
> Alex Noble

Banwell *et al.* (1986) advise that:

> In selecting, or recognizing, starting points that will be fruitful, the teacher may wish to seek a balance between those that are genuinely open for himself as well as his students, and those that he knows through experience or insight are very likely to lead to structures already known to him if not his students. In the latter case, it may be difficult for him to restrain his influence on the choices that have to be made.
>
> (p. 66)

It is intended that at least some of the mathematical tasks offered in this book will be unfamiliar to the reader, enabling you to come to them freshly, as a learner might. It can breathe new life into a topic if the teacher addresses it by using a task that they are not personally over-familiar with. Open-ended tasks can be approached in a variety of ways. For example, learners could begin the following task with plastic shapes or by making sketches or by using computer software (see section 6.3). There are many possible answers, but as answers are accumulated and examined some patterns will emerge.

Task   Meeting shapes

A square (4-gon), a regular hexagon (6-gon) and a regular dodecagon (12-gon) are placed together at a point.

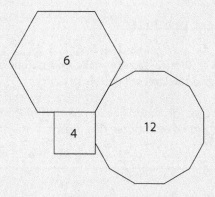

How can you be sure that they fit together *exactly*?
What other regular polygons will fit together *exactly* at a point?

There are many possible criteria that might be laid down for 'good' mathematical tasks, and three suggestions are given below. A good task:

- *doesn't require too much explanation from the teacher.*
  It is quick to work out what it is all about – there aren't too many technical terms or definitions before you can get going. For Ollerton (2009: 14), 'it is worth contemplating how to get a class started on a task as quickly as possible, thus negating the possibility of turning the front of the classroom into a stage'. Such tasks may be described as *low entry* – you don't need to know much mathematics to be able to do something to get into the problem. If you ask the learners, 'Does the task make sense?', everybody says yes, even though no one knows yet how to solve it or very much about it.
- *seems challenging and (potentially) 'deep'.*
  It is apparent to learners that the problem is not trivial. Some serious thinking will be required. This shows that the teacher respects the learners' mathematical abilities and believes that they can all work with complexity. There is no suggestion at the start that some people won't be able to do it, but the 'do it' is perhaps helpfully vague – everyone will achieve something; no one will achieve everything that could be achieved. This is sometimes referred to as *high ceiling*.
- *has the potential to be* engaging *for the learners.*
  It is very hard to say what makes this happen. Problems don't necessarily need to be relevant to everyday life (see chapter 4)—learners can enjoy pure mathematics problems and puzzles for the sake of the challenge of using their powers to think about them. If learners say, 'When will we ever need this?' or question why you are asking them to do it, then they are probably not very interested in the task.

Sometimes relatively small tweaks can significantly alter how a task is experienced. This is a skill in preparing a lesson but also something that the teacher will employ in the classroom as learners work on a task (Prestage and Perks, 2001).

Task **Biggest product**

1 2 3 4 5 6 7 8 9

Use the digits 1 to 9 once each to make two numbers which, when multiplied together, give the largest possible product.

Would you use this task (or a modification of it) with learners? Why/why not? If you would, what would you hope that learners might gain from working on it?

This task has two interrelated elements: *procedural* and *conceptual* (Silver, 1986), as outlined in Figure 6.2. Many tasks commonly found in textbooks and on worksheets are largely or entirely procedural, whereas a task such as this aims to offer plenty of opportunity for practising procedural skills while something a bit more interesting is going on. A teacher might use this task in different ways. If the teacher's intention were primarily

procedural	*conceptual*
the mechanics of written methods of multiplication (i.e., practising gelosia or long multiplication, etc. by hand)	understanding place value and the impact of a particular digit occupying different positions in the numbers

Figure 6.2 Procedural and conceptual elements in the 'Biggest product' task

procedural (to practise multiplying numbers), then they would probably not want learners to use calculators, other than perhaps for checking their answers. The task would be generating lots of practice products for them to do, in which (unlike random questions from a textbook) there is some incentive within the task for learners to get them right, because they are comparing the answers that they get (perhaps with each other) to try to find the biggest. Any incorrect answers (especially if they are large) are likely to be challenged vigorously!

On the other hand, if the teacher's intention were mainly to focus on the *conceptual* aspects of this problem, then they might *encourage* calculator use in order to allow learners to attend to the answers that they are obtaining and their significance, without the 'distraction' of 'doing the sums'. Both approaches could be valid on different occasions or for different learners. It would be dangerous to characterize procedural goals as more suitable for 'lower attainers' and conceptual ones for 'higher attainers'. All learners can solve problems strategically and all are entitled to opportunities in mathematics lessons to do so (see chapter 7). Tahta (1981) contrasts the *outer task*, which is what the learner is being explicitly asked to do, with the *inner task*, which is what the teacher really hopes that they will encounter while doing it. Figure 6.3 suggests that a small number of outer tasks

Figure 6.3 Inner and outer tasks

might contain many more potential inner tasks. Here, superficially, learners are practising multiplying numbers together, but at a deeper level they may be thinking strategically about where to place the digits in order to maximize their answers, thus developing a deeper sense of place value.

Having settled on a suitable task, the teacher might consider the following questions:

- *How could I adapt this for a learner who is finding it hard to start?*
  Perhaps they could use just the digits 1, 2, 3 and 4 to begin with. In that case, they must do either a 2-digit by 2-digit or a 1-digit by 3-digit multiplication, so there is still something significant to think about beyond the calculations. This strategy of simplifying a problem is one that learners might in time employ for themselves.
- *How could I adapt this for a learner who says that they have 'finished' or 'done it before'?*
  There is no need to be fazed by such comments; indeed, the teacher might welcome the experience that the learner brings. They could begin by asking the learner to explain what they know – either to the teacher, if they have time, or if they are needed elsewhere in the classroom the learner could write it down or tell another learner about it. Another option would be to recruit the 'know-it-all' as a 'helper' and encourage them to circulate around the room, listening rather than telling. Some learners might love this; others not. Alternatively, developing an extension, or asking the learner to do so, would be appropriate.

To extend the task (see chapter 12), you could remove digits, but you can't add any more unless you go to a base other than 10 (e.g., hexadecimal), which doesn't seem to offer anything substantially new. An obvious modification would be to ask for the *smallest* possible product, which might be a good test of their understanding of what they have done. Do they start all over again or do they modify their previous work? Another extension would be to ask for *three* numbers to be multiplied, rather than two – or perhaps any number of numbers. That would seem to make things quite a bit more difficult. Addition and subtraction might be interesting, instead of multiplication. There are also related problems such as using the digits 1 to 9, once each, to make *two* multiplications which have the same answer. If all else fails, you could ask 'What other puzzles like this could you make from the digits 1 to 9?' Mathematics teachers who are accustomed to giving learners pages of short simple questions sometimes worry about working with just one task over an extended period of time – what if learners 'finish' (see chapter 12). So it is helpful before the lesson to reassure yourself of the depth and breadth of the task, so that you can feel confident that the learners are not going to run out of interesting things to tackle.

If you wanted a starter, you could rehearse possible methods of multiplication by asking learners how they would work out 15×823 or 192×643, say, without a calculator. The answers are quite neat, and learners who are competent at this could try to construct other products with 'interesting' answers, like these. Before you make or find a worksheet of repetitive exercises, it can be worth trying to think whether learners could generate the same opportunities for practice themselves by giving them a richer starting point.

6.1.3 Tweaking tasks

Change in all things is sweet.

Aristotle

Another good way to develop an interesting task is to start with a less interesting one and give it a twist (e.g., Figure 6.4). Even relatively small changes can have a big effect on how the task is received and what learners gain from working on it (Prestage and Perks, 2001). In the hands of a skilful teacher, even apparently boring tasks can be made into worthwhile lessons; one should never judge a teacher by their resources – it all depends on how they are using them (see chapter 15).

Task Twisting

Find a 'mindless', repetitive, routine exercise in a textbook. (Sadly, this shouldn't be difficult!)

Can you give it a 'twist' to turn it into something more interesting and purposeful?

6.2. Timings

> The only reason for time is so that everything doesn't happen at once.
>
> Albert Einstein

A key concern of beginning mathematics teachers is time management (Adams and Krockover, 1997). This includes the teacher's personal organization and use of time as well as the handling of lesson time. For many mathematics teachers, it is essential to have a clock on the wall at the back of the classroom, so that they can keep an unobtrusive eye on the time without it being too distracting for the learners. In comedy, *timing is everything*, and in a mathematics lesson timing can also make a big difference to how well a task goes. Different learners will operate in different ways and at different speeds, so it can often be difficult to gauge what to do (see chapter 12). Sometimes the energy level in the room will suddenly seem to change – there will be a lull in the conversation level, or somebody will make a particularly pertinent discovery. There may be no 'right time' to move on, but just as toddler tantrums can sometimes be prevented by giving a warning that 'we are leaving in 5 minutes', so with older learners (and adults) it can be helpful to suggest roughly how long they have to spend on something before you will be urging them onto something else. In classrooms where learners take greater responsibility for their learning, sometimes these choices can be made by the learners themselves, either individually or as a group.

Task Clock

On an ordinary analogue clock, what is the angle between the hands at 10:10?

What about at 1:50?

Could be boring/routine	Could be more fun/stimulating
Find all the factors of 24.	The number 24 has 8 factors. What are they? Find another number with 8 factors. Try to find numbers with 1, 2, 3, 4, 5, 6 and 7 factors.
Work out the area of this triangle.	Draw some more triangles with the same area as this one. How do you know that they all have the same area?
Solve this equation. $$3x - 2 = x + 10$$	Put numbers in these boxes so that when you solve the equation you get an integer answer. $$\square x - \square = x + \square$$
Rotate this shape through 90° clockwise about the origin.	Rotate the point (2, 3) through 90° clockwise about the origin. What are the coordinates of the image? Rotate the point (2, 3) through 90° clockwise about some other point. What are the coordinates of the image this time? Find out how the image coordinates depend on the coordinates of the centre of rotation. What happens if you start with a different point? What happens if you try 90° *anticlockwise* instead?
Work out the mean, median and mode of these numbers. 2, 2, 4, 5, 7, 10	Find six numbers with a mean of 5. Work out the mode and the median of your six numbers. Find some more sets of six numbers with a mean of 5. • Can you make the mode bigger than 5? • Can you make the median smaller than 5? What if you have fewer than six numbers?
Work out $$\frac{2}{3} \times \frac{3}{5}.$$	Find pairs of fractions that multiply to make $\frac{2}{5}$. Find *three* fractions that multiply together to make $\frac{2}{5}$. Can you find 10 fractions that multiply together to make $\frac{2}{5}$?

Figure 6.4 Procedural versus richer tasks

Teachers are often under a great deal of pressure to 'cover' topics within tightly speci-fied amounts of time (see chapter 15). This can lead to a superficial treatment, with the teacher claiming to have 'done' things that the learners later say they do not remember. When learners appear 'stuck' with a particular topic, it may sometimes be worth spend-ing more time than you had planned, perhaps coming at it from another direction or giving an extra lesson for ideas to 'bed in'. On other occasions, you might reassure learn-ers that you will be revisiting a particular topic but choose to take a break from it – perhaps for your sake as well as theirs, if the lessons have been fraught! For me, this reflects my own approach to being stuck on a mathematical problem: sometimes I want to stay up late and see it through; other times, I want to shove it in a drawer and come back to it.

Encouraging learners to value mathematics lesson time, so that they arrive promptly with all their necessary equipment, is important. Questions such as 'If everybody came 10 minutes late for every mathematics lesson all year, how many people-minutes would we lose?' can be effective in attuning learners to the value of time!

6.3 Resources

> What did you do in maths today?
> Nothing – we spent all lesson copying off the interactive whiteboard.
>
> Conversation at home

No technology is ever a guarantee that high-quality learning will take place. *Electronic whiteboards*, for instance, may or may not be used in ways that can reasonably be termed *'interactive'* (Tanner *et al.*, 2005). It would be naïve to suppose that the more jazzy the technology, the better the learning. When I do mathematics at home, I am used to having ready access to paper, computer software and so on, but this availability and flex-ibility is hard to achieve for learners in the classroom, although hopefully this will improve in the future. Computers are still normally in short supply in schools, so mathematics teachers usually have to book ahead; and then, once they do get computer access, they feel that they need to make the most of it, so there is pressure to use the machines for the whole lesson rather than just when they might choose to. Increasingly, teachers have access to one machine with a data projector (with or without an electronic whiteboard) in their normal teaching room, but from the learner's point of view, watching someone else use a computer is not the same as using one yourself.

It goes without saying that, to get the most out of any technology, it is essential that teachers spend time familiarizing themselves with it first (Oldknow *et al.*, 2010). It is not sufficient that you do the *task* yourself – you need to know things like how to recover after clicking in the wrong place. In graph-drawing software, for instance, learners fre-quently zoom in or out repeatedly until they completely lose the image that they are trying to see. If the teacher can show them in an instant how to 'reset scales', it empow-ers them at a stroke. Reliability of technology is an ongoing problem in many schools, where having a standby alternative in case computers misbehave is sadly essential. Educational software is sometimes designed with very specific uses in mind, so that teachers can end up locked in to somebody else's choices; where possible, more flexible software is preferable (see below). Different schools will have access to different pieces of software, and increasingly it is becoming possible to use free versions of many programs, so there is less and less excuse for any school not having these wonderful resources. It makes sense to learn to use whatever your school has, but also to hassle whoever is responsible to get the latest versions of the best things.

6.3.1 Logo

(*MSWLogo™* is available free from www.softronix.com/logo.html.)

This was once very popular and currently seems to be making a welcome comeback. It is a programming language in which commands cause a *turtle* to move across the screen leaving a trace where it has been (learners sometimes refer to this track as 'turtle poo'!). There are many ways to use the program, and learners can profitably spend a great deal of time with it. (I have known learners install it on their home computers so that they can continue playing with it in their own time.) Papert (1993) advocated *constructionism*, where learners make things (e.g., drawings on a computer) as a way of learning mathematics. When using *Logo*, learners needn't ask you, 'Is this right?'; they can try it and see for themselves.

Task *Logo*

Use *Logo* software to...

- Draw a picture; e.g., a road with a dashed white line down the middle; a house; a row of houses (use a procedure and a repeat loop); a skyscraper with windows all the way up.
- Draw regular polygons.
- Draw star shapes.
- Draw a spiral.
- Make animations.
- Reproduce (or produce a variation on) a drawing that someone else has made (e.g., the rings of polygons below).

 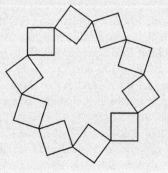

6.3.2 Graph-drawing software

Software such as *Autograph* can now do a great deal more than simply draw a graph, having superb 3D capabilities and the ability to transform shapes, represent vectors and carry out statistical procedures (see www.autograph-math.com). There are many excellent resources that detail how graph-drawing software can be used in the classroom (see the list at the end of the chapter). To take a simple example, learners can explore how the graph $y = mx + c$ changes as m and c are varied or look for pairs of perpendicular graphs and examine the relationship between their gradients.

Task Graph-drawing

- Draw a snowman using ellipses.
- Make some regular polygons from straight-line graphs.

6.3.3 Dynamic geometry

Many schools have *Cabri Géomètre II+*, *Geometer's Sketchpad* or *Cinderella*, but *GeoGebra* is now increasingly widely available (and free, from www.geogebra.org), so every child should now be able to access dynamic geometry in their mathematics lessons. Frequently, it is merely used by the teacher to *verify* the (approximate) truth of a theorem in a few special cases. However, it can be an extremely powerful tool for visualizing the meaning of a geometrical statement. Pre-prepared files, in which learners have limited control, can be easier to use, but learners can also start with a blank sheet and learn to use the various functions themselves. A common use for dynamic geometry is for getting a sense of properties and relationships and forming conjectures prior to a proof.

Task Dynamic geometry

- Look at the angles and angle sum for a polygon as you drag some of the vertices around.
- Look at the lengths of the sides in a triangle as it changes from acute-angled through right-angled to obtuse-angled.
- Explore angles in shapes inscribed in a circle, prior to learning circle theorems.
- Investigate what happens to the area of a triangle as you drag its vertices around. What is the locus of one vertex that preserves area?

6.3.4 Internet

It is impossible to summarize here the wealth of mathematical materials available (mostly for free) on the internet. Learners can access information about mathematical ideas (often presented in animated and/or interactive ways) and statistical data (e.g., www.censusatschool.org.uk). There is a huge number of applets (e.g., www.fi.uu.nl/wisweb/en/ and www.waldomaths.com) relevant to a wide range of topics. In particular, www.wolframalpha.com attempts to bring together a huge amount of relevant knowledge. Supremely useful for high-quality rich mathematical tasks is http://nrich.maths.org/, and for information about the history of mathematics, www.gap-system.org/~history/.

There is also a lot of software specific to mathematics education. Some of this could be characterized as 'textbook-with-bells-and-whistles', but there are also some great resources; in particular, *Grid Algebra*, which offers a powerfully intuitive approach to algebra. There is also a lot of potential in more mundane software, such as spreadsheets and word-processors. Unlike in the 'real world', where software is supposed to make our lives easier (even though it doesn't always), in the classroom it often makes sense to do the opposite and go *against* the grain of a particular program and try to do something that doesn't come naturally. Some elements of the task below may constitute 'real-life' challenges for a mathematics teacher preparing a task sheet!

Task Drawing

Try using the drawing tools in a word-processing package to:

- draw an equilateral triangle
- produce a rectangle inscribed in a circle
- make a tessellation of equilateral triangles
- make a series of concentric circles
- make a 12-pointed star
- make a tessellation of irregular polygons

Try to avoid making any judgements 'by eye' – by setting 'snap to object' it should be possible to construct a definite location for every point.

Besides computers, you will need to think about when and how to give learners access to calculators (graphical and not), mini-whiteboards, practical equipment (*manipulatives*) such as linking cubes, Cuisenaire® rods, 2D and 3D shapes (obviously the 2D shapes are really 3D but just thin!), dice, cards, geoboards, mathematical activity tiles (MATs), trundle wheels and clinometers, mathematical games, scissors, glue and squared, isometric, dotty, graph and tracing papers (see chapter 7).

Task Summary task

What mathematical resources do you have access to in your school? How often are they used?

Are there any additional resources you would like to obtain?

Which classes would you use them with and what would you do with them?

Comments on mathematical tasks

Task: Meeting shapes

Learners may be familiar with *regular tessellations* but not with the situation where *different* shapes meet at a point (but do not tessellate the entire plane). There are many possibilities, such as a regular 3-gon, 10-gon and 15-gon. A total of r regular polygons, the ith one having n_i sides ($n_i > 2$), will fit together exactly at a point if and only if $\sum_{i=1}^{r} \frac{1}{n_i} = \frac{r}{2} - 1$. For more information, see Mason and Murphy (1999).

Task: Biggest product

The biggest product is 87 531 × 9642 = 843 973 902. There are 11 solutions, such as 23 × 158 = 46 × 79, to the two equal products problem (Dudeney, 1970; www.puzzles. com/puzzleplayground/NineDigits/NineDigitsPrintPlay.pdf).

Task: Clock

Did you notice that the angles are not exactly 120°? When using this task in a lesson, it can be interesting to ask learners whether they think that each angle is more or less than 120° before trying to work it out exactly. The angle in each case is 115°. Can you generalize to *any* time?

Task: Logo

Drawing pictures involves learners in estimating distances and angles. When they try to draw an equilateral triangle, for instance, they will often enter something like `repeat 3 [fd 100 lt 60]`, which will produce half a regular hexagon. This can be a good way into working on interior and exterior angles. Drawing a 7-pointed star, for instance, can be an interesting challenge. Learners will need to think carefully, and perhaps make a sketch, to get the correct angles. They might draw either a star 7-gon or a concave 14-gon (left and right, respectively, in Figure 6.5). By putting repeats within repeats, some beautiful drawings can be made (e.g. Figure 6.6).

Figure 6.5 A star 7-gon and a concave 14-gon

Figure 6.6 `repeat 36 [repeat 9 [fd 100 rt 40] rt 20]`

One way to do animations is:

- Draw a shape many times on top of itself using the repeat command – this is just to 'waste' time.
- Go into 'tippex' mode (`pe` = penerase).
- Draw the shape once more, to delete it.
- Move the turtle a little.
- Put the 'tippex' away (`px` = pen normal).
- Repeat these instructions.

This can be a lot of fun and requires some serious thought to make it work. There is less flickering if you hide the turtle (`ht`) before your start.

Further reading

Mason, J. and Johnston-Wilder, S.J. (2006) *Designing and Using Mathematical Tasks*, St Albans: Tarquin Publications.

Prestage, S. and Perks, P. (2001) *Adapting and Extending Secondary Mathematics Activities: new tasks for old*, London: David Fulton Publishers.

Oldknow, A., Taylor, R. and Tetlow, L. (2010) *Teaching Mathematics Using ICT*, London: Continuum International Publishing Group.

Useful resources

www.chartwellyorke.com

Grid Algebra, Derby: Association of Teachers of Mathematics (software)

There is a useful series called *Getting Started with Interactive Geometry Software*, published by the Association of Teachers of Mathematics, covering *Geometer's Sketchpad*, *Cabri Géomètre II+* and *GeoGebra*.

Chapter 7

Equality and difference

Everyone is kneaded out of the same dough, but not baked in the same oven.

Yiddish proverb

One reason why some people become mathematics teachers is to advance social justice (Povey, 2002). However, attempts to promote equality in schools can often be simplistic and miss the complexity of reality on the ground. It may even be that schools are institutionally inequitable; part of the problem rather than part of the solution. As Dweck (2010) comments:

> Much talk about equity in education is about bricks and mortar—about having equal facilities and equal resources. Those factors, although extremely important, are relatively easy to quantify. What may be harder to capture are the beliefs that administrators, teachers, and students hold—beliefs that can have a striking impact on students' achievement.
>
> (p. 26)

Equity is a particularly sensitive issue for mathematics teachers, since failing to obtain a necessary mathematics qualification can shut the door for many young people to opportunities in later life (see chapter 15). Yet the situation is complicated. What if education necessarily increases the range of variation among learners? As Feynman (1992: 281) puts it, 'In education, you increase differences. If someone's good at something, you try to develop his ability, which results in differences, or inequalities. So if education increases inequality, is this ethical?'

7.1 Dealing with difference

Once the game is over, the king and the pawn go back in the same box.

Italian proverb

Our perspective on difference may be informed by our experiences as members of different majority or minority groups. A mathematics teacher who has lived in a foreign country or among an unfamiliar community for a period of time may have some insight into what it is like to belong to a minority, but a short-lived experience can be quite different from living permanently as a minority person, and an adult's perspective may be quite different from a child's. In any class of more than one learner, diversity will be expressed in many dimensions, such as age (perhaps), gender, ethnicity, disability, social, economic and cultural background, mood, interests and preferred ways of learning. It may seem like an impossible task for any human teacher to cater for all of these differences, yet each learner is entitled to access the mathematics curriculum (Davis, 2001). Heterogeneity is healthy in biological systems, and diversity also brings life and interest to the classroom. However, sensitive teachers can nevertheless have a tendency to put learners in boxes and to pander excessively and unhelpfully to difference.

7.1.1 Ability and intelligence

> I'm in two minds about the left-brain–right-brain theory.
>
> Anon.

Much of the unequal treatment of learners of mathematics in schools stems from popular views about *ability* and *intelligence*. Moon and Bourne (2002: 28) 'question the claim that overall ability either exists or is measurable. ... Talking of a child as able/less able therefore in a broad general sense seems inevitably inaccurate'. Dweck (2000: 2) criticizes an *entity theory* of intelligence, which sees it as a 'fixed trait' which learners 'have a certain amount of ... and that's that'. Students fixated on how intelligent they think they are (or are not) may put a premium on looking smart. Dweck (2000: 3) explains that 'The entity theory, then, is a system that requires a diet of easy successes. Challenges are a threat to self-esteem'. By contrast, an *incremental theory* stresses the malleable nature of intelligence and focuses on how it can be developed: 'everyone, with effort and guidance, can increase their intellectual abilities'. The idea that qualities such as intelligence reside in fixed locations of the brain is ridiculed by Hofstadter (2000):

> In the human brain, there is gullibility. How gullible are you? Is your gullibility located in some "gullibility center" in your brain? Could a neurosurgeon reach in and perform some delicate operation to lower your gullibility, otherwise leaving you alone? If you believe this, you are pretty gullible, and should perhaps consider such an operation.
>
> (p. 309)

Gardner (2006) has helpfully pluralized the concept of intelligence, believing that people contain varied combinations of different intelligences. His theory of *multiple intelligences* began with seven and has since increased to eight (and possibly nine):

- linguistic intelligence
- logical-mathematical intelligence
- spatial intelligence
- bodily-kinesthetic intelligence
- musical intelligence
- interpersonal intelligence
- intrapersonal intelligence
- naturalist intelligence

He deliberately chose to call these talents or capabilities *intelligences* so as to elevate them to the status of what is often referred to as 'intelligence'. He believes that everyone has all of these intelligences, but different amounts of each, and that everyone can develop them further (Armstrong, 2009). Others have suggested numerous additional intelligences that might be added to the list.

A rather rough-and-ready cerebral categorization of learners results from the notion of *brain lateralization*. According to this, the dominant left cerebral hemisphere is the logical, verbal half while the right cerebral hemisphere is the more imaginative, spatial and emotional side. Scientifically, this is at best over-simplified and at worst dangerously misleading (Hines, 1987). Modern brain-scanning techniques reveal that both sides of the brain are involved in most processes. As a metaphor for different kinds of thinking, provided that it is not taken too literally, the left–right description may be helpful and can encourage teachers to strive for a balance of activities in their mathematics lessons. But when learners are labelled as 'left-brainers' or 'right-brainers' according to the perceived dominance of one side, and treated differently as a result, this '*neurobabble*' (Claxton, 2005: 29) can limit the learning opportunities that they are given. Such designations can sometimes be presented as hard-wired fact and it can be hard for learners to object to their classification or do anything about it. In recent years, *Brain Gym*® (www.braingym.org.uk) became popular and was purchased by thousands of UK schools. It is a commercial programme consisting of exercises, which learners may enjoy, but there is a lack of evidence that it improves learning (Hyatt, 2007), and some of its claims have been ridiculed as 'pseudoscience' (Goldacre, 2006).

Task Difference

They showed me a picture of three oranges and a pear. They asked me, 'Which one is different and does not belong?' They taught me different was wrong.

Ani DiFranco

If $a = 10$ and

- the difference between a and b is 1, and
- the difference between b and c is 2, and
- the difference between c and d is 3,

what are the possible differences between a and d?
By choosing *different* values for the *differences*, can you produce *more* possible answers?
Can you produce *fewer* possible answers?

7.1.2 Gender

The belief that mathematics is predominantly a male domain creates problems for many female learners (Leder and Forgasz, 2003). Stereotypical gender roles may be reinforced by school mathematics departments dominated (numerically, managerially or both) by men. Books, examination papers and classroom examples from 'real life' may contribute to this (Hanna, 2003). As a consequence of these factors, along with societal/parental pressures, girls are under-represented in post-compulsory mathematics, may receive less attention in the classroom and frequently underachieve relative to boys. The traditional stereotype that men like to solve problems whereas women like to communicate could suggest a helpful balance to common classroom practice. Instead of being answer-focused, learners might be encouraged to engage for a while in *problem-gazing*: wallowing in the mathematics, discussing features of the problem and exploring connections between the elements, rather than rushing to a resolution. Masculine military metaphors involving 'tackling' and 'nailing' problems could be balanced by more relational language. A feminist perspective on the learning of mathematics could bring insights from different ways of thinking (Gilligan, 1982). Sensitive accounts of the history of mathematics reveal the role of women and minority groups, confirming the potential part that learners might play in the story of mathematics (du Sautoy, 2008).

7.1.3 Learning styles

The idea that different learners may have different preferred *learning styles* has been widely promoted in schools, with categories such as *visual, auditory* and *kinesthetic* (Fleming and Baume, 2006). Sometimes the impression is given that some learners cannot operate in all of these, which is clearly unwise. For example, constructing triangles with compasses is going to be a kinesthetic activity whoever is doing it, although learners with *dyspraxia*, for instance, may need more support than others. The popular *meshing hypothesis*, that learners learn better when the teaching style is tailored to their preferred learning style, has not been confirmed (Pashler *et al.*, 2008). Indeed, there is a danger of stereotyping learners with labels; in the most extreme cases, giving learners badges declaring 'I am a visual learner'.

When a teacher identifies a learner preference, there is a tension between wanting to capitalize on it and wanting to build up other *less*-developed styles of working. Always catering to what is already well formed is likely to diminish learners' versatility and trap them into a restricted range of ways of working. For example, if a learner always converts fractions into decimals, because 'I don't do fractions', then if this is just accepted by the teacher as a neutral preference then the learner may become entrenched in their aversion to fractions. Similarly, learners who refuse to draw diagrams because they do not see themselves as 'visual' may be the ones who would most benefit from them. However, awareness of learning styles is helpful when it encourages teachers to seek variety in their teaching and avoid an over-emphasis on auditory work. Clausen-May (2005) describes learners with *learning differences* as those:

> who favour a visual and kinaesthetic, rather than an auditory, thinking style, and for whom the conventional print-based curriculum may not be appropriate. Their learning differences may, on occasion, lead to learning *difficulties*, but such difficulties are an outcome of inappropriate teaching. They are not, in themselves, a cause of failure.
>
> (p. 84)

7.1.4 Accepting heterogeneity

To make progress with algebra, it is necessary to recognize that two or more expressions can be different in kind but equal in value; for example, $5 + 5 + 5 = 3 + 3 + 3 + 3 +$

$3 = 3 \times 5 = 5 \times 3$ or $x + x + x = 3x$. Notice that in the case with x we don't know the value of either side, since it depends on what value x takes, but we do know, nevertheless, that they will be equal to each other, whatever the value of x. We can say for definite that two things are equal without knowing the value of either. Parallels might be drawn here between being unable to ascribe a precise value to any human being, yet asserting, nonetheless, that people are equally precious, though different.

Task Equality

Can any of these expressions be equal to each other?
If they can, say when (for which values of x); if they can't, say why not.

$$3x^2 - x \qquad 4x + 2 \qquad 2x \qquad 2$$

In the nineteenth century, mathematicians became forced to accept plurality within their discipline. Geometry, which was solely Euclidean, became *geometries*, embracing elliptical and hyperbolic perspectives flowing out of different assumptions (Mlodinow, 2001). Algebra became algebras, infinity became infinities (Hofstadter, 2000: 19). Accepting difference should be natural for the modern mathematics teacher.

7.2 Setting and all-attainment teaching

> We don't have to make human beings smart. They are born smart. All we have to do is stop doing the things that made them stupid.
>
> John Holt (1990: 161)

Most teachers like to think that they are not prejudiced, yet it is very easy to make assumptions based on little information. When I walked past the head teacher's office one day and saw a particular learner sitting on his own at a small desk outside, I naturally assumed that he must be in trouble and, knowing him, I was unsurprised. But later I discovered that in fact he was being bullied and had been extracted for his own safety. It is easy to jump to conclusions in the classroom too, and, for instance, simply assume that you mis-heard a learner who you believe to be 'good' when they make a mathematical mistake.

Setting learners into different classes according to teachers' perceptions of *'ability'* is particularly common in subjects such as mathematics, science and modern foreign languages, which are popularly perceived as *hierarchical* (Ruthven, 1987). *Streaming* involves using a notion of 'overall ability' to place learners into different teaching groups across a number of different subjects—effectively separate schools within the same site. Working-class learners are typically over-represented in the lower sets, given less experienced and less qualified teachers and a diet of less interesting and less demanding mathematics (Boaler, 2010). The UK has a shameful history of allocating learners to grammar schools or secondary modern schools on the basis of their performance in the '11 plus' examination at the end of primary school (Hodgen, 2007). Nowadays, children as young as

6 or 7 are sometimes setted for mathematics. Affluent parents fear that their children will be 'held back' in mixed classes, yet Watson (2006) warns of the:

> inescapable fact that the system of grouping which we use in school replicates society as a whole, so that learners from already disadvantaged groups are most likely to find themselves gathered together in the lowest sets for mathematics, hence with the least possibility of being empowered and enfranchised through mathematics.
>
> (p. 14)

Ollerton and Watson (2001: 94) comment that 'In discussions with teachers about their plans for teaching lower sets the focus is often found to be on settling, calming, keeping busy, giving simple tasks or practical tasks, and relating mathematics to the outside world'. Dweck (2000) complains that:

> what we do with students who learn more slowly than others at a given point in time is to relegate them, secretly, to a lower level of intelligence, assign them easier things to learn, and try to make them feel smart learning the easier things—to protect their self-esteem. In this way, we doom them to fall further and further behind.
>
> (p. 129)

Instead, she advises (2000: 129) that 'we give students an honest choice. If they want to get ahead they have to put in what it takes. But we also have to be prepared to help them learn what it takes'.

Setting by marks in mathematics tests frequently unintentionally segregates learners by race, class or gender. Such actions become self-reinforcing and teachers' assumptions about the learners in particular sets become self-fulfilling prophecies (see chapter 14). When lots of effort has been put into testing and sorting the learners, teachers are likely to believe that the benefit to be gained from this is more homogeneous classes, who will be easier to teach together. Yet if a teacher believes that the learners in their set are 'approximately the same', they may be inclined to *teach to the middle*, thereby missing the majority—a compromise that meets nobody's needs very well.

Task Setting

Are learners setted according to attainment in your school?
If so, in which subjects does this happen and at what ages?
What do you think are the main reasons for this?

The practice of 'ability'-grouping remains controversial (Hallam, 2002; Abraham, 2008), yet evidence shows that setting disadvantages learners at every level. Boaler *et al.* (2000) found that:

> Ability-grouping was associated with curriculum polarisation. This was enacted through restriction of opportunity to learn for students in lower sets, and students in

top sets being required to learn at a pace which was, for many students, incompatible with understanding. ... Teachers employed a more restricted range of teaching approaches with 'homogeneous' groups than with mixed-ability groups which impacted upon the students' experiences in profound and largely negative ways. Almost all of the students interviewed from 'setted groups' were unhappy with their placement.

(p. 631)

Jo Boaler, professor of mathematics education at Stanford University, California, worked in the UK for many years, and her short article in *The Independent* newspaper (2005) is easy to read and highly suitable for referring interested parents to:

One of the enduring problems of English schools is their practice of setting by ability, which means that many thousands of students languish in low sets on diets of low-level, uninteresting work. Most of these are capable of achieving infinitely more, but their experience of being told that they are incapable turns them against learning and against school. ... England is more committed to setting than most countries, and this practice continues despite numerous reports pointing to its ineffectiveness. ... Some people believe the practice is right because it keeps the high achievers away from low achievers. The irony is that high achievers do not do any better in high sets than in mixed-ability groups, and for some students, being in a high set is a source of considerable anxiety. Comparisons of test performance in different countries always show that countries that set students the least and latest have the highest performance.

7.3 Differentiation

He calmly rode on, leaving it to his horse's discretion to go which way it pleased, firmly believing that in this consisted the very essence of adventures.

Miguel de Cervantes Saavedra, *Don Quixote*

Differentiation—learners doing different tasks (or different variations on the same task)—is an attempt to give each learner the maximum opportunity to learn. Such a practice can be defended as promoting justice. According to Lucas (1980):

Justice is not equality, because equality is concerned only with results, and not how they are arrived at, and equality is concerned only that people should be treated the same, whereas justice is concerned to consider each individual case on its own merits, treating, if necessary different people differently.

(p. 4)

However, the idea that *there is nothing so unequal as the equal treatment of unequals* would seem to open the way to differentiation as 'setting by the back door' within an otherwise mixed class. *Differentiation by task* involves giving different learners different mathematical tasks that are supposedly tailored to their prior attainment. However, 'appropriate for their level' can easily become patronizing and a route to low-level undemanding work that is mathematically unprofitable (see chapter 4).

There are genuine difficulties with all-attainment teaching (Ollerton and Watson, 2003). Ollerton (1995: 35) describes taking groups of children walking and the difficulty of 'keeping them together', with those at the front getting more and more frustrated by constantly being asked to wait for the ones at the back, who seemed to be going ever more slowly. He uses this analogy to explain teachers' perceptions of an 'ever-widening gap' of 'ability' as students progress (or not) through their schooling. However, he comments:

> In my mathematics classrooms I do not worry about the "gap" because I do not expect to keep my class together, nor do I expect all the pupils to reach the same destination. Indeed, to set out to achieve either of these outcomes is to deny the differences which exist ... the issue is not therefore how I operate with a large gap, but how I operate with any gap whatsoever.
>
> (p. 35)

He then describes using open-ended rich tasks which allow all learners to access a wide range of relevant mathematical ideas. From a similar standpoint, Watson (1995) asks rhetorically:

> How should I differentiate between children? Can I choose to offer to one what I do not offer to another? Can I choose to give one a wide vision to explore and another a sequence of small steps to follow? ... There is an obsession running through much current thinking in education about making simplistic judgements about the complexities of the intellect, or other developing human aspects, and using these inducements to treat people differently.
>
> (p. 42)

She concludes by contrasting the self-fulfilling nature of differentiation by task with the more complex and 'un-neat' nature of what she calls *differentiation-through-interaction*.

One of the features of a good mathematical task is that it cannot be ascribed a single 'level'. It depends how it is used – the *response* to the task is what matters. *Differentiation by outcome* allows different learners to make whatever they can out of a given task, but this works only if the task is sufficiently open. Ollerton and Watson (2001) argue that their approach:

> of using common starting points with the whole mixed-ability class, allows all students to work on a topic, though this may be understood by students in different ways at different times. It is supported by discussion, group work, and the overt use of the teacher's special knowledge and mathematical expertise.
>
> (p. 2)

Ollerton and Watson (2001: 2–3) show how 'the whole class approach allows for mixed-ability teaching in ways which value the contribution and ways of learning of all students, not just the brightest nor just the "average" student in the group'. Such attitudes and ways of working allow learners to develop their mathematics without imposing an unnecessary glass ceiling on what they might achieve.

7.4 Special educational needs

> All the people like us are We, And everyone else is They.
>
> Rudyard Kipling, *We and They*

Everyone has their own particular educational needs, but the term *special educational needs* (SEN) is generally applied to learners with particular sorts of differences (Ernest, 2011a). Learners of mathematics may have *physical disabilities* of various kinds, *speech and language disorders* (difficulties in communication), *autistic spectrum disorder* (ASD) or *Asperger's syndrome* (difficulties with social interaction). They might have problems concentrating (*attention deficit disorder*, ADD), perhaps also exhibiting hyperactivity or impulsiveness (*attention deficit hyperactivity disorder,* ADHD), being generally fidgety and finding it hard to sit still on a chair (Chinn, 2010). Active mathematical tasks can provide opportunities to harness surplus energy, and such learners can sometimes be asked to hand out practical equipment or take responsibility for organizing something. Being tolerant of some movement, where this does not hamper anybody's learning, can also be sensible.

More common than these are the *specific learning difficulties* (SpLDs), which refer to particular problems with learning that are not the result of a wider condition. The most common SpLD is *dyslexia*, a term which covers a broad range of difficulties with fluency and accuracy in reading. Mathematics teachers may notice dyslexic learners experiencing confusion with reversals (e.g., letters such as *b* and *d* in algebra or < and > signs) and with left–right symmetry in geometry; they are also likely to find wordy problems particularly hard to disentangle. *Dyspraxia* refers to difficulty in planning and coordinating movements, which may impair learners' writing or lead to clumsiness when using mathematical equipment (e.g., clicking cubes together). *Dyscalculia* covers particular difficulties with learning mathematics, particularly number (Bird, 2007; Chinn, 2004). Other learners will have emotional and behavioural difficulties or may have a different first language from English, often termed *English as an Additional Language* (EAL). Various kinds of extra support, such as a specialist teaching assistant or an interpreter, will need to be made available if all learners are to be successfully accommodated in the mathematics classroom.

Whether *acquired* (e.g., through injury) or *developmental*, learning difficulties often come together (*co-morbidity*); for instance, learners may have both dyslexia and dyscalculia or both dyspraxia and Asperger's syndrome. The exact appearance of any of these difficulties will vary from learner to learner, and perhaps from day to day, and may be categorized as mild, mid-range or severe. For some, describing these differences as 'difficulties' is unhelpful. A learner may have a physical impairment, but whether it is a disability for them depends on how the classroom is structured (Clausen-May, 2005). A *deficit model* problematizes difference as an inadequacy, inability, deficiency or weakness. Noddings (2003: 152) comments that such perspectives are 'properly frowned on today. Educators should not assume that students whose native language is not English are therefore suffering a cultural deficiency'.

Learners with particular difficulties may be accompanied by other adults in a supportive role, and working constructively with, for example, teaching assistants (TAs) is important. A quick briefing can be helpful, so that if, for example, your task involves learners in working out a method to solve a problem, the TA doesn't inadvertently impose one. Helpful adults can sometimes help learners too much, and excessive *path-smoothing* of tasks can remove too much of the challenge. Mason's (2000: 101) dictum that we should 'only do for people what they cannot yet do for themselves' is always worth bearing in mind. Although such actions as 'structuring' a solution by 'breaking down' a problem into short steps can make life easier and less stressful in the classroom, they can lead to *learned helplessness* (see chapter 13). Watson (2006) comments:

> [I]t is said that learners who cannot concentrate for long periods need frequent changes of task; they grow bored if you do not change the topic every lesson; they need activity which uses their energy because many are so-called "kinesthetic" learners; they need the quick success which comes from getting things right easily; and so on. The irony of these arguments is that if you follow these guidelines low attainment is the inevitable *result* ...
>
> (p. 103)

Boorman (1997) describes how he chose:

> a new picture of my role as a teacher. My job was to find a suitable field for [the learners] to explore and to sit up on the hillside above and roll down rocks for the kids to jump or climb or scramble over.
>
> (p. 40)

He believed that he did not have to make things easy but instead supported learners as they worked on things that were hard.

Task SEN

He's not very academic.   *She's an underachiever.*   *He's a slow learner.*
She has poor short-term memory.   *He's lazy.*   *She's a late developer.*

Would you appreciate comments such as these from a colleague describing learners in a class that you are about to take over?
How might they be helpful/unhelpful?

The language which teachers use about learners can easily become self-fulfilling. In particular, although 'they can't ...' *may* be accurate for today, it must never be allowed to imply '... and they never will'. Indeed, the fact that a learner, for example, *did not* correctly say the multiples of 3 today does not mean that they *cannot*. On another occasion, in a different context, they might. It is important to be open to being surprised by learners and not constrained in your expectations by previous poor performance. It is important not to let a label dominate your view of a particular learner. Reeves *et al.* (2001) found that teachers underestimated learners who had previously been identified as having 'special educational needs'. People with dyslexia may have certain similarities, but the differences that make each person individual are far more important.

Sometimes teachers are cynical about designations of SEN and suspect that parents who can afford to pay an educational psychologist to assess their child are more likely to obtain a recommendation that their child should have extra support in school and extra time in examinations, even when the child might appear to be in less difficulty than another less advantaged child. However, it is up to each teacher to do the best for every one of the learners that they teach. Many of the strategies that have been developed to support learners with special educational needs can be seen as 'corrections' for uninspiring and dry teaching. The appeals to make lessons engaging and to use practical equipment are relevant to *all* learners. All learners will have difficulties with mathematics, only some of which have well-known names. As time goes on, more of those difficulties will be studied and labelled, but in the meantime it is important to focus on helping all learners develop in their mathematics. Clausen-May (2005) acknowledges the popular wisdom that '*If it's good for special, then it's good for mainstream*'; however, she cautions that:

> even more significant here is the inverse: *If it's bad for mainstream, then it's bad for special.* Teaching that relies on the pupils' acquisition of meaningless algorithms will serve the highest achievers poorly—but for those in the 'bottom set' it can be a disaster.
>
> (p. 84)

It may be useful to bear in mind in general that:

- words present a barrier to many people,
- not everyone finds a diagram or a graph easy to take in,
- fiddly tasks such as using compasses to draw a circle, or measuring something accurately with a ruler, will be extremely frustrating for some learners,
- sitting still for long periods of time may absorb a great deal of energy and create boredom and fatigue,
- listening to the teacher talking for long periods is likely to be dull at best and infuriating at worst, and
- some people remember things much more easily than others and different things help different people.

Although kinesthetic experience can be helpful, physical games and manipulatives (see chapter 6), such as cubes or Cuisenaire® rods, are not a panacea (Uttal *et al.*, 1997). As Ball (1992: 47) memorably puts it, 'Although kinesthetic experience can enhance perception and thinking, understanding does not travel through the fingertips and up the arm'. She explains that:

> One of the reasons that we as adults may overstate the power of concrete representations to deliver accurate mathematical messages is that we are "seeing" concepts that we already understand. ... But for children who do not have the same mathematical understandings that we have, other things can reasonably be "seen".
>
> (p. 17)

How best to cater for learners with a variety of needs is an important matter for mathematics departments to discuss among themselves as well as with the school *special educational needs coordinator* (SENCO), who may have useful expertise and knowledge of individual learners.

7.5 Gifted and talented learners

> If you don't make mistakes, you're not working on hard enough problems.
>
> Frank Wilczek

Murphy and Dweck (2010) found that prevalent assumptions about intelligence being a fixed asset had a considerable effect on how people thought about themselves and behaved. According to Dweck (2000), the term 'gifted':

> implies that some entity, a large amount of intelligence, has been magically bestowed upon students, making them special. Thus, when students are so labeled, some may become overconcerned with justifying that label, and less concerned with seeking challenges that enhance their skills. ... They may also begin to react more poorly to setbacks, worrying that mistakes, confusions, or failures mean that they don't deserve the coveted label.
>
> (p. 122)

In recent years, there has been increasing concern that schools do not provide well for the highest-achieving learners. Rather than picking out particular learners and labelling them as 'gifted' or 'talented', many mathematics teachers prefer to regard all of their learners as 'gifted and talented' in all sorts of ways and to seek to have high expectations of them all. Borovik and Gardiner (2007: 4) list some 'traits of mathematically able children' such as the '[a]bility to make and use generalisations, often quite quickly', the '[a]bility to concentrate on mathematics for long periods without apparent signs of tiredness', the 'instinctive tendency to approach a problem in different ways' and find alternative solutions and a 'striving to find the most economical ways to solve problems, for clarity and simplicity in a solution'. Most learners will show some or all of these tendencies at various times, if given the opportunity.

Task Best foot forward

Design an experiment to test the hypothesis that 'high-achieving people' are more likely to enter a room on their right foot, even if they are left-handed/ footed.

Tasks such as this one engage learners in issues of fairness. It has been claimed that if you watch film of world leaders entering a room, most of them put their right foot through the door first. Learners might consider the social and educational background of politicians and how they have obtained their power.

Some schools advocate *acceleration* for the highest attainers, such as early-entry GCSE or beginning sixth-form studies before age 16. Others argue that this is damaging socially if the learner is isolated and expected to learn independently of the rest of the class, and also detrimental mathematically if depth of understanding is sacrificed in order to acquire qualifications at the fastest possible rate. Borovik and Gardiner (2007: 8) warn that 'more of the same' is not acceleration, and caution that acceleration 'fails to ensure that earlier techniques become sufficiently robust, or that these techniques are linked together to provide a sufficiently strong foundation for subsequent work'.

Enrichment is an alternative approach, in which learners' needs are catered for within the normal class for their age. If rich *high-ceiling* tasks are offered (see chapter 6), then it is possible for a more advanced learner to develop their mathematics alongside their peers. Online communities such as www.nrich.maths.org can provide contacts with like-minded learners at other schools (Piggott, 2004), and the UK Mathematics Trust (www.mathcomp.leeds.ac.uk) runs individual and team challenges which can be highly stimulating for keen mathematicians. When enrichment is on the agenda, it can benefit everyone, not just an elite few, if it leads to more interesting and richer mathematical tasks being offered to all. By planning for gifted students within the normal lesson, greater opportunities may consequently be given to *all* learners to develop their mathematics.

Task Summary task

How important do you think the differences are between the learners that you teach?

In what ways do you seek to cater for these differences?

Comments on mathematical tasks

Task: Difference

Visualization on a number line can be helpful. Setting a equal to zero, rather than 10, would afford the possibility of learners working with negative numbers. Given that $a = 0$, $|a - b| = 1$, $|b - c| = 2$ and $|c - d| = 3$, d can take the values 4, 6, 8, 10, 12, 14 and 16 (7 possible values), so $|a - d| = 0$, 2, 4 or 6 (4 possible values). Learners might notice that b and c must have the opposite parity (odd or even) from a and d. Clearly, if you set $|a - b| = |b - c| = |c - d| = 0$, then $d = a$ and thus $|a - d| = 0$ would be the only solution. For the related problem involving sums rather than differences, see Stanley *et al.* (1991). You might like to think about what would happen with *complex numbers*.

Task: Equality

Six equations can be formed:

$$3x^2 - x = 4x + 2 \Rightarrow x = 2 \text{ or } -\frac{1}{3} \quad 4x + 2 = 2x \Rightarrow x = -1 \quad 2x = 2 \Rightarrow x = 1$$

$$3x^2 - x = 2x \Rightarrow x = 0 \text{ or } 1 \quad 4x + 2 = 2 \Rightarrow x = 0 \quad 3x^2 - x = 2 \Rightarrow x = 1 \text{ or } -\frac{2}{3}$$

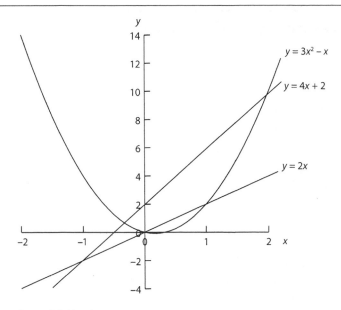

Figure 7.1 Equality

When $x = 1$, three of the expressions are equal; when $x = 0$, two of them are equal to zero and the other two are equal to 2. This can be visualized graphically (Figure 7.1). Can you construct four expressions such that all six possible equations have *integer* solutions?

Further reading

Boaler, J. (1997) *Experiencing School Mathematics: teaching styles, sex and setting*, Buckingham: Open University Press.

Boaler, J. (2010) *The Elephant in the Classroom: helping children learn and love maths*, London: Souvenir Press Ltd.

Clausen-May, T. (2005) *Teaching Maths to Pupils with Different Learning Styles*, London: Paul Chapman.

Ernest, P. (2011a) *Mathematics and Special Educational Needs*, Saarbrucken, Germany: Lambert Academic Publishing.

Ollerton, M. (2003b) *Everyone is Special*, Derby: Association of Teachers of Mathematics.

Ollerton, M. and Watson, A. (2003) 'I teach them but they don't learn', *Equals*, 9(1), 17–18.

Watson, A. (2006) *Raising Achievement in Secondary Mathematics*, Maidenhead: Open University Press.

Chapter 8

Starters, fillers and finishers

The best starters tend to take the whole lesson.

Mathematics teacher

In this chapter, we consider in more detail some elements that could make up a lesson: the bricks and mortar out of which a mathematics lesson might be built. How you select the pieces and put them together will depend on you and your class. Despite some confident assertions to the contrary, there is no magic formula for the perfect mathematics lesson, and anything will become a straitjacket if imposed relentlessly. Sometimes teachers try to cram too many good things into one lesson—particularly if it is going to be 'observed'. It is probably more practicable to aim to include a wide variety of experiences over a more lengthy period of time, say half a term. It is interesting that many teachers return from professional development events complaining about the way in which sessions were run, and such experiences can provide much food for thought regarding the learners' experiences in their classrooms.

8.1 Variety

Nothing is pleasant that is not spiced with variety.

Francis Bacon

The most traditional mathematics lesson tends to follow the *exposition–practice* model, which might be parodied as the teacher talking and writing on the board for as long as they can get away with it, and when the learners become too fidgety they give them some exercises to do (see chapter 4). However, seeing the lesson as comprising subsections (*multi-episodic lessons*), which may take various forms (e.g., plenary, individual work, pair-work, people maths, ICT-based tasks, etc.), can bring some welcome variety. On the other hand, if learners are given sufficiently stimulating tasks they may happily work away, perhaps in groups, for several lessons on productive mathematics with minimal teacher input 'from the front' (Martin, 2011).

Parallels are sometimes drawn from the ways in which television programmes (or advertisements) seek to keep our interest, with constant lively changes of pace, attempting to jerk the viewer back to attention. Even if the teacher might prefer a 'straight' approach without the 'bells-and-whistles', it is important to recognize that many learners may benefit from a different strategy. A traditional system may have worked for many mathematics teachers—perhaps we would not have become teachers if we had not, at least to some extent, survived under it—but we may unintentionally exclude large numbers of learners unless we offer mathematics lessons that they can access. On the other hand, education is not simply entertainment, and gimmicks may simply become annoying. The three tasks below might stimulate some different ways of working in the classroom.

Task Mosaic

Look at this pattern. How would you describe it? Say what you see.
Can you make something like it?

A task such as this provides learners with an opportunity to use mathematical language to describe the intricacies that they notice. They might spend some time creating or recreating a similar design as a response to this stimulus. Some learners will be challenged by the idea that mathematics can be a creative endeavour.

Task Largest/smallest

What is the *largest* number you can write down in words without using any letter more than once?

What is the *smallest* number you can write down in words without using any letter more than once?

What other questions like this can you ask?

In this task, we probably don't really care what the answer is; the value in the task rests on the process of thinking through and examining closely the makeup of the words we use for our number system (see the comments at the end of the chapter).

Task My PIN

I can't remember my four-digit PIN for the cash machine. But, strangely, I can remember four things about it:

- All the digits are different.
- The first two digits are a two-digit multiple of 23.
- The last two digits are a two-digit multiple of 24.
- The middle two digits form a prime.

If I get it wrong three times in a row, the machine will keep my card.

Is it possible to avoid losing my card?

Can you make up other puzzles like this one?

In this task, learners are invited to construct something similar to the problem given, using whatever properties of number they wish. There is much potential for creativity and examining all possible cases.

Varied tasks can result from responding to learners' particular interests. On one occasion a learner who was particularly interested in Sudoku planned and taught a lesson to the rest of the class. Similarly, learners who have had a talent for origami have led the class through the construction of various different animals.

8.2 Structure

> I usually do my starter at the end of the lesson.
>
> Mathematics teacher

Like human beings, mathematics lessons come in all shapes and sizes—there is no perfect model (Wilson *et al.*, 2001). It may be possible to say that every lesson can be thought of as having, in a trivial sense, a 'beginning, middle and end', which you might call 'starter, main phase and plenary'. However, 'plenary' doesn't mean 'ending'—it means something the class does all together – and it is not obvious that you will always necessarily want to have that sort of a finish to your lesson. Nor will you necessarily always want to begin with a separate 'starter'; sometimes you might just start with the main event.

Some mathematics lessons feel a little over-engineered. The teacher offers a series of tasks, each lasting no longer than a few minutes, and each dependent on the previous one and building to some conclusion, but there is little space for learners to make a significant contribution to the direction. My wife once attended a wedding on a hot day where the spectacular multi-tiered cake that had been created began to collapse under its own weight. The guests saw it beginning to move and several of them rushed forwards to try to save parts of it, getting covered in gooey icing in the process. Sometimes lessons are over-intricately structured and seem unable to support their own weight. A more desirable approach might be to try to find a starting point rich enough that it seems to generate its own energy – the teacher sets it off at the start, but it seems to continue to some extent under its own momentum without the teacher constantly pushing. Of course, this may be easier said than done!

Task Structure

Do your mathematics lessons (or those that you have observed) follow any kind of regular structure?
Does your school encourage any particular model?
What purposes might there be in a 'starter' or 'finisher' that is to some extent separate from the rest of the lesson?

Whatever structure you opt for in a particular lesson, it can be very useful to have shorter tasks, either to provide variety and a change of pace/mood, or as 'fillers' for spare moments. When making a cake, the icing and the filling give a change of flavour and texture, but are normally not the main body of the cake. *Fillers* (which need not necessarily happen at the start) can serve one or more of the following purposes:

- reviewing some mathematics from another time,
- introducing some ideas that might be needed for a later task,
- calming and settling a lively class,
- occupying learners who have arrived at the lesson before everyone else, and
- offering a pace and mood which contrast with the rest of the lesson.

Task Serial sevens

Can you count backwards from 100? Of course you can!
What about in *sevens*?

$$100, 93, 86, 79, ...$$

What questions might emerge from this activity?

Here learners might continue past zero and into negative numbers. Possible questions might include:

- Will we get to zero *exactly*? If not, how close will we get?
- How many numbers will we have said by then?
- What if we started at 1000 instead of 100?
- What if we went down in *sixes* instead?
- If we start at 100, will we get to −100 if we keep going long enough?

So a task such as this could either be used as a filler or as something that might occupy learners on sequences for a whole lesson or more. It is often the case that a good filler can be developed into something substantially more.

If the teacher consistently uses a starter as an overture to the main theme of the lesson, this can result in learners assuming that there will always be a ready-made connection. I once heard the exchange below, following a starter on the multiples of 5:

Teacher: How big are the angles in an equilateral triangle?
Learner: 60 degrees
Teacher: Why?
Learner: Because 60 is a multiple of 5?

Encouraging learners to draw on mathematics that they have learned at other times is obviously important, but not if this is limited to the last thing mentioned. It might be suspected that *if the only tool you have is a hammer, then every problem is seen as a nail*, so it is important that connections are not too obviously set up. Learners benefit from a varied approach in which different elements in a lesson sometimes connect naturally and sometimes don't. Sometimes a filler might involve learners practising skills that they are going to need later—simultaneously allowing the teacher to assess who can do what and judge what support might be needed. On the other hand, fillers can support classroom management, with goals such as 'warming up' and 'calming down'. These are matters that each teacher must decide for themselves, sometimes 'in the moment'.

Task Late

What do you do when learners arrive over an extended period of time, in twos and threes? (Perhaps they have come from different parts of the school or were changing from PE?)

What do you do when learners arrive 'hyped up', highly excitable from whatever has just happened?

What do you do when learners arrive exhausted and sleepy? (Perhaps it is the lesson after lunch and it is a hot summer afternoon.)

Some starters can be displayed on the board (or given out on paper) at the beginning of a lesson and learners can start straightaway, as soon as they arrive. (It can feel unnecessary to *wait* for a starter, like in a restaurant!) This can be advantageous if there is a long delay between the first and last people arriving. Here is one possibility.

Task Boxes

Can you put the numbers 1, 2, 3, 4, 5 and 6, once each, into these boxes to make the statements true?

$$\Box + \Box = \Box$$

$$\Box \times \Box = \Box$$

Can you put the numbers 1, 2, 3, 4, 5, 6, 7, 8 and 9, once each, into these boxes to make the statements true?

$$\Box + \Box = \Box$$

$$\Box - \Box = \Box$$

$$\Box \times \Box = \Box$$

Can you put the numbers 1, 2, 3, 4, 5, 6, 7, 8, 9, 10, 11 and 12, once each, into these boxes to make the statements true?

$$\Box + \Box = \Box$$

$$\Box - \Box = \Box$$

$$\Box \times \Box = \Box$$

$$\frac{\Box}{\Box} = \Box$$

If you *can*, see whether you can do it in *more than one way*.
If you *can't*, find a list of positive integers (all different) that *will* work.
You could try to do it keeping the integers as small as possible.

Fillers don't have to be numerical, although many good ones are. Mental visualization is an important skill to develop, so fillers with a geometric element can also be useful.

Task How many?

How many triangles are there in this drawing?
There are more than 3.

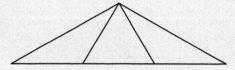

Make up another drawing that contains more triangles than it might at first appear.
Make sure you know *for sure* how many triangles are in it!
Try it on someone else.

Some learners may think there are 4, when they see the 'big' triangle containing the three small ones, but you can also count each triangle together with its neighbour, giving 6 altogether. Learners could explore other drawings in the same family, such as the one shown in Figure 8.1, and find out how the number of triangles increases. The task below also calls on mental visualization.

Task Net

Do you think this will fold up to make a cube?

1	2		
	3	4	
		5	6

If you *don't*, try to explain why not.
If you *do*, which numbers will be next to each of the other numbers?

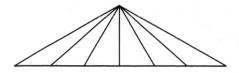

Figure 8.1 How many triangles are there now?

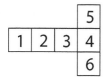

Figure 8.2 Which numbers will be next to each other when this is folded into a cube?

You could make this task easier by using an easier net of a cube, such as the one shown in Figure 8.2. Learners might have views about which numbers' neighbours are easiest to imagine.

Having ideas such as these up your sleeves (or in your planner/bag)—just in case—can help you to be prepared for the unexpected. You may even find that they come in handy outside of mathematics lessons, when there is a problem with set work when you are covering somebody else's lesson, or another teacher is called away suddenly and you are looking after their class, or you have a spare slot with your tutor group (although they may not appreciate always doing mathematics in these situations!). Knowing that you always have faithful standbys waiting in the wings, ready to go at a moment's notice, can give you confidence, especially if you are trying other tasks that you are unsure will work.

> # Task Ending
>
> Have you ever misjudged the timing of the end of a lesson and finished 10 minutes early by mistake? What could you do with the spare 10 minutes?
> Suppose that learners have already packed away all their things and you don't want them to get everything out again. Could you manage 10 minutes without any materials?

Many schools have a strict policy of not allowing learners out of lessons early. Fillers, including 'oral and mental' ones, that you might be able to do without any equipment, are very handy. Frequently, games that you might use in situations such as this become class favourites, so you can use the same idea again and again—learners might request it when there appears to be a bit of slack time. On other occasions, fillers might require pencil and paper, mini-whiteboards, cubes or other mathematical equipment.

8.3 Games

> We don't stop playing games because we grow old; it's the other way round.
>
> Anon.

Many people have commented that human beings naturally play games, and there are many reasons why games could have an important role to play in mathematics lessons

(Ernest, 1986). One day some learners told me that they had been playing '21 Dares' during a wet break time. Their 'dare' had been to 'lick the floor', which I couldn't allow, but the principle of the game seemed highly mathematical.

Task Twenty-one dares

We're going to count up in integers from 1. You have to carry on from the last person, and you can say either one number or two numbers or three numbers. Whoever has to say '21' loses.

For example, suppose that Ana, Ben and Cayla were playing:

Ana:	1, 2
Ben:	3, 4, 5
Cayla:	6
Ana:	7, 8, 9
Ben:	10
Cayla:	11, 12
Ana:	13
Ben:	14, 15, 16
Cayla:	17, 18, 19
Ana:	20
Ben:	21 (loses)

What questions might emerge from this activity?

One way to use games in mathematics lessons is to play a game such as this and then to seek to analyse it mathematically. Possible questions might include:

- What is the best strategy to win (or avoid losing)?
- How many players makes this a good game?
- How might you modify the game?

There is relatively little at stake for learners when playing 'silly' games such as this, where those 'in the know', who can beat anyone else, clearly know something that is useful only in this one limited context. It can be more difficult where games are used with an obvious intention that learners should rehearse or memorize some particular mathematical skill or knowledge. In the game *fizz-buzz*, for instance, learners take it in turns to say the next natural number, but instead say 'fizz' when they hit a multiple of 2, 'buzz' on a multiple of 3, 'fizz buzz' on a multiple of 6, etc. (Stephenson, 1998). This can be a nice way to experience prime factorization (e.g., 'fizz fizz buzz' for $12 = 2^2 \times 3$), yet if everyone laughs when a learner gets one wrong this can be embarrassing and might be reason enough to prevent a teacher from using it.

Task 1089

Write down a 3-digit number.

Now reverse the number (writing the digits in the opposite order).

Subtract the smaller number from the larger one and write down the answer.

Reverse this number and add it on.

What happens with different starting numbers?

What happens if you start with a *four-digit* number instead?

If you start with a palindromic number, such as 636, you will get zero; otherwise, with one caveat, you should get 1089 (Acheson, 2010). One way to see why this happens is to start with the number '*abc*', where $a > c$ (Brown and Coles, 2008: 92)—see the example in Figure 8.3.

Games can be an excellent way to familiarize learners with 'important' numbers such as triangle numbers, squares, cubes, primes and powers of 2. In a conference workshop that I attended on the '1089' task, another delegate pointed out that she had immediately been struck that 1089 was 33 squared. This reminded me of Sacks (2007) quoting the mathematician Wim Klein describing his love for numbers:

> Numbers are friends for me, more or less. It doesn't mean the same for you, does it—3844? For you it's just a three and an eight and a four and a four. But I say, 'Hi! 62 squared'.

> (p. 219)

$$
\begin{array}{ccc}
{}^{5}\cancel{6} & {}^{12}\cancel{3} & {}^{1}\cancel{2} \\
-\quad 2 & 3 & 6 \\
\hline
3 & 9 & 6 \\
\hline
+\quad 6 & 9 & 3 \\
\hline
1\,0 & 8 & 9 \\
\hline
{}_{1} & &
\end{array}
\qquad
\begin{array}{ccc}
{}^{a-1}\cancel{a} & {}^{b+9}\cancel{b} & {}^{c+10}\cancel{c} \\
-\quad c & b & a \\
\hline
a-1-c & 9 & c+10-a \\
\hline
+\quad c+10-a & 9 & a-1-c \\
\hline
1\,0 & 8 & 9 \\
\hline
& {}_{1} &
\end{array}
$$

Figure 8.3 Getting 1089

The classic anecdote in this area comes from when Hardy was visiting his friend Ramanujan in hospital (Newman, 1960):

> I had ridden in taxi-cab No. 1729, and remarked that the number seemed to me rather a dull one, and that I hoped it was not an unfavourable omen. 'No', he

replied, 'it is a very interesting number; it is the smallest number expressible as a sum of two cubes in two different ways'.

(p. 375)

Number games can assist learners in recognizing 'special' numbers as 'friends'. Mathematical games are frequently associated with *numeracy*, which is generally considered very important despite uncertainty over exactly what it is (Gardiner, 2004)! They are also a good way to develop learners' confidence and ability to interact in a relaxed way with others. The internet can be a great source of interactive games (such as various versions of *Countdown*).

There are many excellent books of games and ready-made games to purchase. There are also many that are almost certainly not worth the money and unlikely to be played more than once, so it is well worth reading reviews before you buy (e.g., at www.atm. org.uk/reviews/). Very often, the process of *making* the game seems to involve more mathematical thinking than *playing* it, so it can be more fun to ask learners to invent their own games—perhaps on a specified mathematical topic. Often learners interpret 'game' as 'board game' and spend lots of time creating little cards containing questions that they might find in any textbook, and the process may be of questionable value. Instead, if they are set on making a board game, it may be worth encouraging them to incorporate the mathematics into the board itself, not just the questions. For example, in a board game on transformations, the counters could move around by translating or reflecting or rotating, according to whatever comes up on a spinner or by a throw of some dice.

> # Task Summary task
>
> What sorts of structure do your lessons tend to follow? How happy are you with that?
> What short mathematical tasks (fillers) do you have at the ready?
> How often do you use them?

Comments on mathematical tasks

Task: Largest/smallest

Usually learners end up with 'five thousand' for the largest and 'minus forty' for the smallest. (Those who think that 'forty' contains a letter U may be confused by this!) Sometimes learners check 'special' numbers such as 'googol' or 'infinity' or utilize other languages: a Year 7 learner once offered me 'tin lakh', which is 300 000.

Task: My PIN

Using the first three conditions, the possible numbers are:

| 6924 | 2348 | 6948 | 9248 | 4672 | 6972 | 2396 |

Two of these (4672 and 6972) have a middle two digits that are prime, so it must be one of these. So, if we are smart, we are bound to get it by at most the second try.

Task: Boxes

One solution for the first one is $1 + 4 = 5$ and $2 \times 3 = 6$, but since addition and multiplication are commutative, these can be turned around. For the second one, $1 + 7 = 8$, $9 - 5 = 4$ and $2 \times 3 = 6$ but, as well as the commutativity, the addition and the subtraction are also interchangeable. For the third one, a bit of logical reasoning is required to see why it is impossible. The multiplication and division must (between them) use the relations $2 \times 5 = 10$ and $3 \times 4 = 12$, and frustratingly this doesn't allow the addition and subtraction to be made with what remains. Swapping 11 for 13, though, allows $6 + 7 = 13$ and $9 - 8 = 1$, and is one way of completing it.

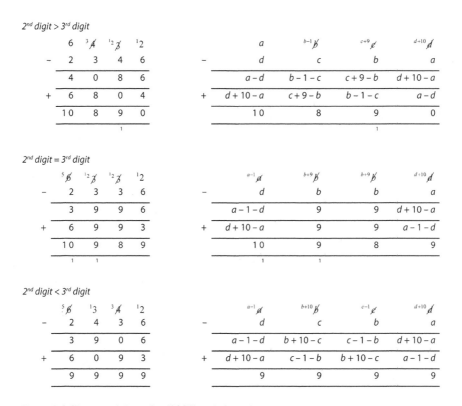

Figure 8.4 The possibilities for '1089' with four digits

Task: 1089

If the first and third digits differ by only 1, then 99 is obtained in the first stage, and unless a 'leading zero' is included, then 198 will be the final answer. With a four-digit starting number, there are three possible answers (other than zero), depending on the relative sizes of the second and third digits of the number, as shown in Figure 8.4.

Further reading

Foster, C. (2008) *Variety in Mathematics Lessons*, Derby: Association of Teachers of Mathematics.

Useful resources

Fourbidden, Derby: Association of Teachers of Mathematics (game).
Hatch, G. (2004) *What Kind of Game is Algebra?*, Derby: Association of Teachers of Mathematics.
Hatch, G. (2005) *Geometry Games*, Derby: Association of Teachers of Mathematics.

Part 2

Teaching mathematics

Make a habit of two things – to help, or at least to do no harm.

Hippocrates, *Epidemics*, Book I, Section XI

In the first part of this book, we have focused on *preparation*. We now turn to what goes on in the classroom when the learners are with you. Clearly, the two aspects are closely interrelated: what you plan affects what happens in the classroom; what you experience in the classroom informs your future planning. In some respects, the preparation is under the teacher's control: provided you have the time, and subject to certain constraints (see chapter 15), you can plan whatever you like. But reality hits when you walk into the classroom and try to make it work with unpredictable young people. Classrooms are full of uncertainties and a perfectly good plan may fall flat because of circumstances outside your control – other things that have been going on that day, fallout from a previous lesson or a playground dispute, or even something as mundane as wet and windy weather!

However, there is much that the teacher can do 'in flight' to maximize the possibilities for success in a mathematics lesson. In this part, we will think about the 'softer' skills that are useful for dealing with learners in lessons, whether *en masse*, in groups or as individuals. In the quote at the top of this page, Hippocrates suggests that hard-working sincere doctors might unintentionally do more harm than good to their patients. It is a sobering thought that the same could be true of conscientious mathematics teachers. When teachers complain that learners become less resourceful and less confident as they 'progress' through school, the thoughtful teacher will pause to consider what else is being learned besides the mathematics and how the mathematics teacher's behaviour in the classroom might be responsible.

Chapter 9

A mathematical classroom community

A leader is best when people barely know that he exists. ... Of a good leader, who talks little, when his work is done, his aims fulfilled, they will all say, "We did this ourselves".

Lǎozǐ (*Tao Te Ching*, chapter 11)

This chapter examines the *ethos* of the mathematics classroom and considers how a mathematics teacher can establish a supportive atmosphere of productive mathematical thinking, especially when beginning with a new class. A class of learners that look after one another mathematically is much less tiring and stressful to teach; when everything is functioning well, there may be times when you can 'stand back' and enjoy the spectacle of learners learning mathematics together without an excessive need for your constant input. If you are away from school, whoever looked after your class will say how 'great' they were and how they sorted themselves out with very little fuss.

9.1 First impressions

You never get a second chance to make a first impression.

Anon.

A lot goes on in the first few moments with a new class. Willis and Todorov (2006) suggest that a few tenths of a second may be all that it takes before people form judgements that are subsequently hard to change. Certainly, by the end of the first lesson, learners will have formed plenty of opinions about the teacher, the others in the class and even about mathematics itself. What a teacher chooses to say or not say, do or not do, and how they react to situations that develop in the first few lessons, will be taken as indicators of the kind of teacher that they are and what their attitude is to mathematics. On this basis, learners will form expectations of what is likely to happen in subsequent lessons (Patrick et al., 2003). As mathematics teachers, we inevitably, in many small ways, implicitly broadcast our view, not only of mathematics, but of what it means to learn.

9.1.1 The mathematics classroom

Can we sit anywhere?

Learner

It is not only the teacher who will be assessed in those first few moments – the classroom is likely to come under equal scrutiny, perhaps even before the teacher has had a chance to say anything. There is a saying that 'walls have ears', but they talk as well, and what we choose to have on display on the walls in our classrooms says something about what we consider to be important:

- ready-made mathematical posters or learners' own work?
- only the 'best' work or a variety of different things?
- 'finished' items or work in progress?
- passive things to read or provocative images and text that might become interactive?
- stale faded items from years ago or recent business?
- memory aids for examination questions or open-ended thought-provoking problems and puzzles?
- items from a multitude of cultures or predominantly Western-influenced?

Task   Classroom audit

What is on the walls of your classroom? Why?
What immediate impression do you think your classroom creates? (Perhaps you could ask somebody who is not familiar with it.)
How are the tables laid out? Why?
Are there better or worse places to sit? Why? What could you do about that?

It may be that you do not have the luxury of your own specialist mathematics teaching room. Perhaps you teach some of your classes in several different rooms. Nevertheless, it is important to make the best of your situation, report damaged items so that they can be replaced, get graffiti removed and develop a good relationship with the person who cleans the classroom. Classroom climate includes such mundane issues as having an adequate temperature, an absence of clutter and freedom from extraneous noise from neighbouring rooms or outside (Inan, 2009; Clayton and Forton, 2001). It can be worth trying out some of the 'cheaper' seats in your classroom and seeing how well you can view the board when it is sunny or whether you can hear what someone is saying across the room. Sometimes small changes to the environment can alter learners' behaviour significantly (Guardino and Fullerton, 2010). Perhaps there are computers or other items of technology in your classroom, and this may attract learners' attention when they first arrive. For some time, I have had the first few hundred digits of π winding around the walls of my classroom, and it has never ceased to be a talking point. Sometimes at break time learners bring in their friends from other classes to show it to them, and children I don't know occasionally pop in to ask me about it. (A convenient printout if you want to do the same is available at www.cleavebooks.co.uk/trol/trolgf.pdf.)

9.1.2 The first lesson

Is she strict?

Learners talking about their new teachers

Meeting a new class for the first time can be nerve-wracking, even for an experienced mathematics teacher. Learning learners' names as quickly as possible will help to build relationships, and showing interest in learners beyond their learning of mathematics is also important. If you are wanting to change some of the ways in which you work and start the year differently from how you have managed it previously, then this can be doubly hard. Sometimes things are difficult at first simply because you – and perhaps the learners – are doing them for the first time. It can take everyone a little while to adapt to new routines, so it is wise not to assume too quickly that something new that you try 'doesn't work', but to give it a chance.

Task Getting to know you

 As learners enter the classroom, the teacher shakes hands with each one, which some of them find surprising or funny.

When the learners are seated, the teacher asks:

- If you all shook hands with each other, how many handshakes would there be?
- If each of you introduced each person to every other person, how many introductions would there be?

What impressions might an initial task such as this convey?

In a lesson such as this, it is possible to start with a group of just three or four learners, who could stand up and do the handshaking, while someone else counts the number of shakes. When learners have investigated the number for the whole class (or the whole school, or ...), then *more than two* people could shake hands at a time, and this could build into a bigger investigation. The task attempts to value those present by engaging with a relevant theme and some demanding mathematical ideas.

The application of Lave and Wenger's (1991) concept of a *community of practice* to mathematics education has led to the recognition of the importance of the entire classroom situation, and not merely the teacher's 'performance' at the front. From this perspective, learning is *social* rather than individual, as a group of people come together to do and learn mathematics (Winbourne and Watson, 1998). What happens has more to do with behaviour that fits within the group than with absorbing facts and procedures in isolation. Many mathematics teachers see creating a vibrant, mutually supportive mathematical classroom community as one of their highest priorities (Goos, 2004). David and Watson (2008) explain:

> Theories of situated cognition focus our attention on the social structures and activities in the learning environment, and suggest that learning is a movement from novice, peripheral, participation towards mature participation in the practices of communities. Learning, in these models, is the process of participating in an

increasingly expert manner, and knowledge is a property of people and their interactions and activities in situations.

(p. 31)

Task 1 to 50

Take the integers from 1 to 50 and come up with something interesting to say about each one.

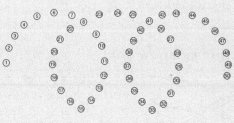

This task could work well in groups, where everyone can have something different to contribute. The results can read rather like acrostic poems, giving possible cross-curricular links with English. If some of the statements are wrong (or could be nuanced), that can lead to useful discussion. (A fascinating book extending this idea is Wells [1997].) Two samples of learners' work are shown in Figure 9.1.

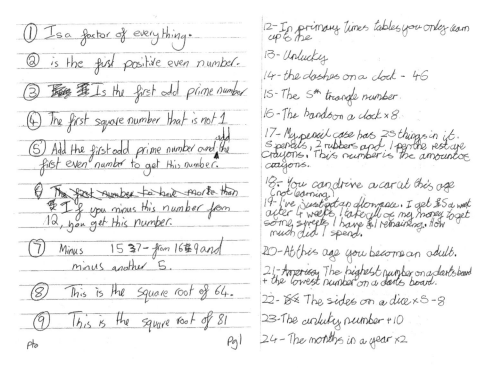

Figure 9.1 Facts about some numbers

> # Task Peripheral vision
>
> Human beings have a horizontal field of vision of about 190° without turning
>   their heads. For goats, it is said to be about 330° and for deer about 350°.
> Make an accurate diagram using as many of these animals as you can, but placing
>   them so that *no animal can see any other animal*.
>
> How many can you accommodate in your drawing?
> When do you need to include objects as cover? Why?

Everyone knows that teachers develop eyes in the back of their head, or *'withitness'*
(Kounin, 1970), sometimes even using reflections to see what is happening in the room,
thereby astonishing learners with their 'sixth sense'. A teacher's interest and involvement
in what is going on everywhere in the classroom is vital.

> # Task Acting
>
> I would ... urge every teacher to become an actor. His classroom technique
> must be enlivened by every device used in theater. He can be and should be
> dramatic where appropriate. He must not only have facts, but fire. He can
> utilize even eccentricities of behavior to stir up human interest. He should
> not be afraid of humor and should use it freely. Even an irrelevant joke or
> story perks up a class enormously.
>
> Morris Kline (1956: 171)
>
> Do you agree with the sentiments expressed in this quote?
> Do you feel that you can be yourself in the classroom or do you intend/pretend
>   to be 'someone else'?
> If your best friend came to watch you teach, would they see the same 'you' that
>   they know or another *persona* altogether?

The *performance* element of teaching clearly attracts some people to the profession, but
genuineness, being someone whom learners can get to know as a real human being, is even
more important (Rogers, 2002).

9.2 Classroom talk

> It is the mark of an educated mind to be able to entertain a thought without accepting it.
> Aristotle

It is well established that teacher talk dominates in most mathematics classrooms (Corey,
1940; Mercer, 1995) and that learners frequently struggle even to ask questions, let alone
participate more fully in meaningful discourse (Dillon, 1988). In the next chapter, we

will look at some ways in which teachers can manage the tension between listening and intervening (Goos, 2004), but here we will restrict ourselves to ways of encouraging learners to engage in mathematical talk.

Task Contributing

Teacher: What could you do to improve in maths?
Learner: Not talk?

What do you think prevents learners from making greater (in quality as well as quantity) oral contributions to mathematics lessons?
What might help them to do so?

Even very young children learn to put up their hand to speak, with or without accompanying sound effects to attract the teacher's attention! However, some classrooms operate a *no-hands-up-for-answering* policy, in which learners are invited by the teacher to speak, sometimes by a random system such as pulling lolly sticks (each with a student's name written on it) out of a cup (Black *et al.*, 2003). This aims to involve all learners and to prevent anyone from opting out. They could still raise their hand if they want to make a comment or *ask* something. On the other hand, some mathematics teachers avoid directing questions at learners who have not indicated that they wish to answer (*cold calling*). Noddings (2003) explains how she told students that she was:

> to an important degree, at their mercy because I will not call on anyone who has not volunteered. Perhaps, as a result, some relax, daydream, and miss important opportunities to learn, but at least they need not be afraid. I do not want learning to be associated with pain and fear.
>
> (p. 246)

Classrooms that fall into an adversarial 'quiz show' mentality, in which someone is 'put on the spot' and 'wins' if they can answer and 'loses' if they can't, can lead to tactical behaviours, such as learners attempting to communicate answers to one another by whispering, writing notes or using non-verbal cues. When you observe such actions in your classroom, this could indicate that there is an opportunity to work on modifying the classroom climate.

Mason (2009) promotes a *conjecturing atmosphere*, in which everything that is said in the mathematics classroom is treated as a conjecture rather than a fact. If I disagree with you, then I may 'invite you to modify your conjecture'. This shifts the emphasis from 'right answers' towards more varied contributions to a discussion:

> Establishing a conjecturing atmosphere or ethos takes time. Attention needs to be drawn to the status of assertions and assumptions as conjectures needing confirmation and justification. Those who are uncertain need to be encouraged to try to articulate their conjectures and be overtly respected for modifying their conjecture as a result; those who are confident or certain need to be encouraged to ask helpful questions of

others, to try to find counter-examples to other people's conjectures, and to probe themselves and others for justifications and reasoning. Most importantly, conjecturing is most effective as a collaborative rather than a competitive interaction with others. Everybody learns when someone modifies a conjecture or proposes a counter-example.

(p. 32)

Whether learners are naturally tentative (Rowland, 1995) or overconfident, this approach encourages them to use words like 'suppose' rather than 'assume' and to question the implications 'if' something is taken to be the case – without claiming that it *is*. Rowland (2000: 141) has coined the term *zone of conjectural neutrality* to describe 'the space between what we believe and what we are willing to assert'. By encouraging learners to contribute *thinking-in-progress*, rather than the 'finished article', mathematics teachers can create a safer space for discussion.

Part of the teacher's role is to avoid *evaluation* of what is said, so as to prevent *premature closure*. The teacher does not act as *arbiter of truth* but as an *organizer of debate*, deliberately prolonging, even intensifying, disagreement at times. As Simon and Blume (1996) comment:

It is the teacher's job to promote the establishment of a classroom mathematics community in which mathematical validation and understanding are seen as appropriate and important foci and to endeavor to make mathematical ideas problematic in ways that students are likely to see a need for deductive proof and "proofs that explain".

(p. 9)

Colleagues in other subject areas may have valuable experience to share with mathematics teachers, such as this advice from Dean and Joldoshalieva (2007):

Establishing an open discussion climate is a prerequisite for conducting effective discussions as students must feel free and secure to share their views and argue with each other. The teacher's role is to act as a moderator to ensure that diverse and competing perspectives are fairly heard, to ask questions and challenge ideas, eg, by playing devil's advocate.

(p. 178)

The manner of public discourse in the classroom (*whole-class discussions*) is also likely to influence to some extent the sorts of peer discussions that take place during group work.

Task Highlights

Imagine teaching a mathematics lesson when everything is going 'really well'.
In your thoughts, what are the most important elements?
What would you want someone to notice if they walked in on the lesson?

Some teachers imagine themselves giving a word-perfect explanation at the board, with the whole class listening in rapt attention. The opportunity to have a captive audience is attractive to many teachers, who long to hold people spellbound with a visual aid or anecdote that cements a particular point. Other teachers are happier when learners are working independently and they are less visible, 'floating' around, exercising control in more subtle ways. For some, the pinnacle would be a learner (or several) standing at the front talking about mathematics to their peers, so that the teacher was merely a (proud) bystander.

Most teachers would agree that it is much easier to teach a class that you know than one that you don't. The process of getting to know a class is dynamic – they will change you and you will change them. Classes frequently develop different characters and, although their mood may seem to depend on such things as whether it is a morning or an afternoon, there will be some consistency and predictability about how learners behave as a group. Ultimately, a safe classroom is one where learners will not suffer deliberate embarrassment or be laughed at by anyone. What they have to say will be listened to and respected, so learners will give one another time to speak and be listening, not just thinking about what they are going to say when it is their turn. When a learner 'dries up' while speaking to the class, the class will wait and let them get back on track – such silences can be productive, as someone 'thinks out loud', but can also be punishing if prolonged, and judgment is obviously needed.

9.3 Power and control

> She's scary!
>
> Learner talking about her mathematics teacher

Smiling

> Don't smile till Christmas – and don't smile too much even then!
>
> Advice from a mathematics teacher

Why do you think teachers give advice like this?
What might the negative consequences be?
Do you aspire to be a 'strict and scary' mathematics teacher? Why/why not?

Much has been written about power relationships in the classroom (Richmond and McCroskey, 1992) and learners' attempts to subvert the prevailing order (Candela, 1998). In the mathematics classroom, power can be intimately related to notions of mathematical proof (Simon and Blume, 1996) since, unlike in some other subjects, mathematical results are not true because the teacher says so, but because learners *reason* so for themselves. However, this is not always how the subject is experienced, and it is easy for a confident mathematics teacher to use mathematics as a weapon to intimidate and embarrass less competent learners. But for adolescents, whose emotions are in flux, the certainty of mathematical reasoning – when it comes internally, rather than from an external authority source – can be extremely powerful.

9.3.1 Rules and routines

> Report all accidents to your teacher – however small.
>
> Sign seen in a school laboratory (apparently even small teachers like to be kept informed!)

Whether or not mathematics teachers feel disposed to smile in the classroom (and different sorts of smiles might be perceived as 'weak' or 'confident'), the atmosphere that the teacher seeks to create will be influenced by the power that they choose to wield and the ways in which they do so. Teachers sometimes demonstrate a power to calm when they enter an excitable classroom on a windy day and, by moving slowly and talking quietly, enable learners to *entrain* (catch their mood), rather than the other way round (not that this always works!).

Seating plans are a common way in which teachers seek to take control of their classroom – perhaps by dictating 'boy/girl' arrangements or splitting up beautiful friendships. Table layouts in rows facing the board may communicate a different view of learning from those in which learners are to some degree facing each other, such as 'islands' or 'horseshoe' arrangements (see chapter 11). Space can limit what is possible, and in many classrooms the teacher has to trade off being able to move around the room against ensuring easy visibility of the board by everyone. Whether you choose seating arrangements to maximize opportunities for discussion or to prevent them will depend on your beliefs about classroom talk and your perceptions of your class. Sometimes teachers feel the need to dominate the classroom and claim it as their territory, either by body language or by rules such as learners lining up in the corridor until they arrive or standing up when the teacher comes in. Once in the classroom, learners may not be permitted to help themselves to resources (as may have been normal practice at primary school), but have to put up their hands even to ask for a piece of paper. This contrasts sharply with the situation where learners who arrive early are expected to enter and begin working on some mathematics unsupervised.

Task Beginnings

When you meet a new class, are there certain things that you particularly want to do or say?

Are there particular rules or expectations that you try to lay down?

Are there particular mathematical tasks that you feel are especially appropriate? Why do you use these?

Some classrooms contain posters of 'classroom rules', which may be imposed from on high but are sometimes 'negotiated' with learners at the start of the year. However, it is

Mathematicians...

...ask questions

...make conjectures

...explain their reasoning

Figure 9.2 Mathematical behaviours

understood that in such negotiations there is an enormous imbalance of power (rather like a powerful Western state 'negotiating' with a tiny developing country). Generally, the teacher enforces these rules however they see fit, and may or may not follow them themselves. Does the teacher shout, interrupt people and flout school uniform rules, rather like the actors on stage in a theatre who are allowed to smoke despite the 'no smoking' signs that the audience must obey? On the other hand, some classrooms have posters such as the one shown in Figure 9.2, listing some characteristic behaviours of 'mathematicians'. Of course, mathematicians come in many shapes and sizes, and these characteristics are not set in stone, yet a practice such as this gives the teacher an opportunity to draw learners' attention to when they are doing one or more of these things. As learners become adept at behaving in these ways, the poster could be changed to include other elements that the teacher wishes to encourage. It is well to resist the temptation to abuse this process by asserting things like 'Mathematicians always tidy away their equipment' or 'Mathematicians hand their work in on time'! It is probably even incorrect to say things like 'Mathematicians always show their method clearly'.

Task Twenty-four

On centimetre-squared paper, draw a triangle with area 24 cm².
Now draw some more triangles with area 24 cm², but make them as different from each other as you can.
Draw a quadrilateral with area 24 cm².
Try to draw examples of different kinds of quadrilaterals, each with area 24 cm².
Draw a pentagon with area 24 cm².
And so on...

With a task such as this one, it is natural to invite learners to come to the board to share some of their shapes, perhaps leading to the additional constraint that every new shape must fit into the space left on the board by all the shapes drawn so far! Getting learners up to the front of the classroom early on may communicate the view that that area is *our* space rather than the teacher's personal domain. Language can be important, and replacing the phrase '*my* desk' with '*the* desk' and 'Can you tell *me*...' with 'Can you tell *us*...', and so on, although subtle, can contribute, if repeated again and again over a period of time, to a more positive climate. I was reminded of the complex power structures in place in my own classroom when I once asked a Year 7 learner to tell us the area of a shape that we had been working with. He said, 'Fourteen'. I wanted him to include the units so I continued to look at him and raised my eyebrows. He looked a little uncomfortable, so I asked, 'Fourteen *what*?' He looked even more uncomfortable and said, 'Fourteen, *sir*'! A related incident concerning units, where notions of power would also seem to be important, is reported by Houssart (2009). A primary learner wrote '250' on the board as his answer to a money problem:

> He did not write in the units and the teacher reminded him by saying "Were they elephants?" Damian smiled and wrote p after the number on the board. The teacher smiled as well and said "Good, now we all know what they are". As Damian went back to his place on the mat, he added in a whisper "Potatoes".

(p. 69)

9.3.2 Rewards

> I feel that the greatest reward for doing is the opportunity to do more.

Jonas Salk

Task Rewards

Do you give merits, housepoints, sweets or other rewards in your school? When? Why?
What are the advantages of doing this?
What are the dangers?

Different schools and departments have differing policies with regard to this sort of thing: some learners will get very excited about accumulating them, whereas others will remain aloof. However, *extrinsic rewards* can militate against learning for its own sake, on its own terms (Middleton and Spanias, 1999), whereas *intrinsic motivation* tends to lead to increased 'time on task', greater persistence in the face of failure, greater creativity and more risk taking (Lepper, 1988):

> The presence of salient extrinsic incentives or constraints, or the desire to demonstrate one's superior mastery of the activity, is likely to focus students' attention and

efforts more exclusively on those aspects or parameters of task performance that have potential instrumental value, that are likely to lead to the attainment of external goals.

(p. 298)

As Ariely (2010: 36) explains, 'when the incentive level is very high, it can command too much attention and thereby distract the person's mind with thoughts about the reward. This can create stress and ultimately reduce the level of performance'. Rewards can also alter the manner in which a task is approached (Lepper, 1988: 295): 'When an activity is considered an end, decisions are more likely to be based on a "least-effort" or "minimax" principle in which the student seeks to maximize extrinsic rewards with a minimum investment of thought and effort'.

If you are working in an environment in which rewards have become very desirable, it may be more realistic to seek to wean learners off them gradually rather than to declare boldly from day one that you don't 'do' them. A more positive approach is to seek to offer tasks which give learners opportunities to derive enjoyment from exercising their own natural powers to think mathematically. When learners are so engrossed in their mathematics that they have forgotten all about the stickers and prizes, and begin to see them as props that they no longer need, they are beginning to derive satisfaction from mathematics as an end in itself.

Task $111\ 111\ 111\ 111^2$

Put away your calculator.

Can you work out $111\ 111\ 111\ 111^2$ exactly?

Can you work out $111\ 111\ 111\ 111^2 - 111\ 111\ 111\ 110^2$ exactly?

How can you be sure that your answers are correct?

What other difficult-looking calculations can you do without a calculator?

Can you do some more accurately than your calculator can?

Learners may gain a sense of power from tasks such as this, where they sit in judgment on their calculators, which normally go unchallenged, and realize that their brains can achieve greater accuracy.

9.3.3 Targets

> If you aim at nothing, you are bound to hit it.
>
> Anon.

Targets, aims and objectives are currently ubiquitous in education, but it may be that some things are best obtained by *not* aiming for them directly. For example, happiness often comes as a by-product of aiming for something else; aiming to be happy as a goal in itself can be counterproductive, as many celebrity lifestyles sadly illustrate. Some of the most important things we might wish for in education cannot effectively be prescribed and aimed for directly. For instance, as Noddings (2003: 183) remarks, 'We can't establish self-esteem as a learning objective and teach directly for it'. Some people find that having personal targets enables them to achieve what they wish to achieve; others find them unnecessary and constraining. Targets that an individual freely constructs for themselves (like new year's resolutions) may be helpful; ones imposed by others are much less likely to be.

Noyes (2007: 125) comments that 'Writing the Learning Objective on a little white-board, normally about 1 metre to the side of the larger whiteboard, is de rigueur – like a talisman that somehow ensures quality learning'. The teacher then becomes obsessed with demonstrating that this has been achieved by the end of the lesson, searching for simplistic markers of superficial progress. However, as Mason and Johnston-Wilder (2006: 31) explain, 'Although it is often advocated that learners be told what the purposes and goals of a lesson are, some of the teachers' purposes cannot be made explicit, at least to begin with, without being self-defeating'. Announcing publicly that today we are going to discover Pythagoras's theorem is likely to prompt the question, 'What is Pythagoras's theorem?', which is exactly what you are *not* planning to tell them. It can be hard to articulate where you are going until you get there.

 **Task** **Fraction lives**

The *half-life* of a radioactive substance is the time taken for its radioactivity to decrease to a half of what it was.
What do you think that *third-life* would be?
Which is more radioactive: something with a *half-life* of 2 days or a *third-life* of 3 days? Why?
Can you extend this idea?

Poorly conceived targets tend to be too simplistic; once people know that they will be judged by a certain target, the temptation arises to seek to achieve it by means that the target-setter did not anticipate (e.g., copying other learners' work, achieving correct answers without understanding, or rushing to a conclusion and missing important elements along the way). *Goodhart's Law* says that once a measure becomes a target it ceases to be a measure (Elton, 2004). This becomes an aspect of the so-called *didactic contract*: that the teacher does the teaching and the learner does the learning. This can lead learners to believe that if they merely complete the tasks that they are set, then learning will arise automatically. Watson and Mason (2007) explain:

> There is always a didactic contract between teacher and learners, giving rise to an inevitable tension: the more clearly the teacher ... indicates the behaviour sought, the easier it is for learners to display that behaviour without generating it from themselves, that is, without learning.

(p. 210)

Sometimes aiming to solve a mathematical problem may be too big and learners need to break it down and begin, say, by aiming to explain to someone else the difficulty that they are having. Teachers can help by suggesting such steps, but must be careful not to do so in ways that generate dependency. In a healthy classroom, learners become increasingly able to do such things for themselves and less reliant on the teacher to break things down for them (see chapter 13).

9.3.4 Being real

> Reality is merely an illusion, although a very persistent one.
>
> Albert Einstein

A teacher who is comfortable with learners exercising some measure of control in the classroom will want to exploit their interests and take opportunities that arise, such as special occasions or references to what is happening in the wider world (see chapter 6). They will avoid simple closed tasks that restrict the opportunity for learners to develop their own ideas, and will embrace complexity and variety. They will probably have more flexible ideas about what constitutes 'off task' behaviour, and be keen to exploit the mathematical possibilities of situations that arise spontaneously. They might invite a learner to teach a lesson, encourage peer marking of mathematics and perhaps ask learners to vote for what to work on or how to achieve a specified purpose.

Task   Date

Find something interesting about the numbers in today's date.

When will what you have found happen again? Why?

Learners may appreciate some measure of consistency and structure that they can depend on in their mathematics lessons (see chapter 8), but they will also enjoy the occasional surprise, such as a mathematical trick or a task that incorporates their names or something about them, or a mathematical situation which leads to an unexpected outcome. Teaching is a caring profession, and pastoral issues can arise at any time. Being the sort of teacher who keeps an eye out for problems and ultimately is always a human being will help to engender caring in learners and support the kind of classroom climate that you are striving for.

Task   Summary task

If you have time, read McCallum et al. (2000) – learners' views on what makes for good learning. Do you agree?

What elements of what happens in the mathematics classroom are most important to you?

What particular features would you seek to incorporate into your first few lessons with a new class? Try to prioritize.

Comments on mathematical tasks

Task: Getting to know you

The handshakes task is well known and leads to triangle numbers, so for n learners there will be $^nC_2$ shakes. If each of the n learners has to introduce every other pair of learners, then each learner must introduce $^{n-1}C_2$ pairs, meaning that there will be $n\,^{n-1}C_2 = \frac{1}{2}n(n-1)(n-2)$ introductions altogether.

Task: Peripheral vision

Learners could explore this using dynamic geometry software or pencil, protractor and paper. Two deer, for instance, could be invisible to one another in an arrangement such as the one shown in Figure 9.3. Could you have a human being in between who couldn't see either deer and who couldn't *be seen* by either of them? (The beginning of the short Laurel and Hardy film *Berth Marks* (1929) offers an amusing illustration of two people moving around but – just – unable to see each other.)

Task: *111 111 111 111²*

Although learners are asked to 'put away' their calculators, ordinary calculators almost certainly wouldn't display enough digits to be very helpful, although more sophisticated machines, such as *Wolfram | Alpha* (www.wolframalpha.com) would. The answer is 12 345 679 012 320 987 654 321. It is possible to think of 111 111 111 111² as 111 111 111 111 × (1 + 10 + 100 + 1000 + 10 000 + 100 000 + 1 000 000 + 10 000 000 + 100 000 000 + 1 000 000 000 + 10 000 000 000 + 100 000 000 000), leading perhaps to a vertical addition as shown in Figure 9.4, which is nothing like as formidable as it looks! It is

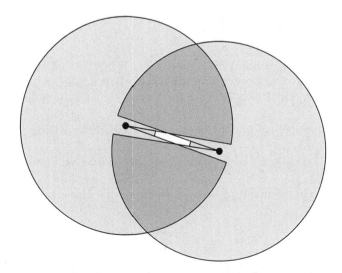

Figure 9.3 Two deer, shown by dots, located back to back, in each other's blind spots

```
                                               1 1 1 1 1 1 1 1 1 1 1 1
                                             1 1 1 1 1 1 1 1 1 1 1 1 0
                                           1 1 1 1 1 1 1 1 1 1 1 1 0 0
                                         1 1 1 1 1 1 1 1 1 1 1 1 0 0 0
                                       1 1 1 1 1 1 1 1 1 1 1 1 0 0 0 0
                                     1 1 1 1 1 1 1 1 1 1 1 1 0 0 0 0 0
                                   1 1 1 1 1 1 1 1 1 1 1 1 0 0 0 0 0 0
                                 1 1 1 1 1 1 1 1 1 1 1 1 0 0 0 0 0 0 0
                               1 1 1 1 1 1 1 1 1 1 1 1 0 0 0 0 0 0 0 0
                             1 1 1 1 1 1 1 1 1 1 1 1 0 0 0 0 0 0 0 0 0
                           1 1 1 1 1 1 1 1 1 1 1 1 0 0 0 0 0 0 0 0 0 0
                       +  1 1 1 1 1 1 1 1 1 1 1 1 0 0 0 0 0 0 0 0 0 0 0
                       ─────────────────────────────────────────────────
                         1 2 3 4 5 6 7 9 0 1 2 3 2 0 9 8 7 6 5 4 3 2 1
                                   1   1   1   1   1   1
```

Figure 9.4 Working out 111 111 111 111²

intriguing that 123 456 789² contains no 3's or 6's, that 123 456 789³ contains no 2, that 123 456 789⁴ has no 6 and that 123 456 789⁵ has no 5. If someone asked you why this was, what might you say?

The second one is a difference of two squares, so 111 111 111 111² − 111 111 111 110² = (111 111 111 111 − 111 111 111 110) × (111 111 111 111 + 111 111 111 110) = 222 222 222 221. Learners might experiment with shorter examples, such as 111² − 110², where they can calculate more easily, to get a sense of what is going on, and see, for instance, that the answer isn't just 1.

Task: Fraction lives

With a *half-life*, it doesn't matter whether we say 'reduce *to* half its value' or 'reduce *by* half its value', as the result is the same, but with third and other lives it does, so there are at least two possible interpretations of *third-life*. Taking $t_{\frac{1}{3}}$ as the time for the radioactivity to reduce *to* one-third of its original amount, at time t the radioactivity will be $\left(\dfrac{1}{3}\right)^{\frac{t}{t_{\frac{1}{3}}}}$ as much. Since $\left(\dfrac{1}{3}\right)^{\frac{1}{3}} < \left(\dfrac{1}{2}\right)^{\frac{1}{2}}$, a material with a *third-life* of 3 days is *more* radioactive than one with a *half-life* of 2 days. Continuing the pattern, a *quarter-life* of 4 days is *equivalent* to a *half-life* of 2 days.

Further reading

McCallum, B., Hargreaves, E. and Gipps, C. (2000) 'Learning: the pupil's voice', *Cambridge Journal of Education*, 30(2), 275–89.

Goos, M., Galbraith, P. and Renshaw, P. (1999) 'Establishing a community of practice in a secondary mathematics classroom', in L. Burton (ed.) *Learning Mathematics: from hierarchies to networks*, London: Falmer Press, pp. 36–61.

Ollerton, M. (2004) *Creating Positive Classrooms*, London: Continuum.

Wells, D. (1997) *The Penguin Dictionary of Curious and Interesting Numbers*, London: Penguin.

Chapter 10

Listening and intervening

He talks too much!

Learner describing their mathematics teacher

The traditional perception of the teacher – particularly the mathematics teacher – seems to be as the 'fount of all knowledge', standing at the front of the classroom, broadcasting to all (Mercer, 1995). Many mathematics teachers learned mathematics that way, and were successful; they may indeed have fond memories of university lecturers who held the audience spellbound with their presentations. Computer software and video clips can bring 'bells and whistles' to this sort of approach, yet the *transmission* model of teaching has severe limitations (see chapter 4). Only by taking the time to *listen* to learners can we really begin to understand their mathematical thinking and so help them more effectively.

10.1 Listening

We have two ears and one mouth so that we can listen twice as much as we speak.

Epictetus

Despite perhaps using this appeal to anatomy to encourage *learners* to listen to the *teacher*, mathematics teachers do not always recognize *their* need to listen to the learners (*we* have two ears as well!). Numerically, it might seem that with a class of 30, say, the teacher needs to listen a great deal more than *twice* as much as they speak, so we perhaps need to envisage ourselves with many more than two ears!

Task Attention

Are you listening to me?

Mathematics teacher

Do you wish that your learners listened to you more carefully?
Do you get frustrated by 'short attention spans'?
What do you do about this?

Everyone knows that a teacher's voice is easily tuned out. If the teacher spends a lot of time talking to the class, learners may become *desensitized* to the sound, so that it begins to function like background music. Most people can become *habituated* to even quite a loud ticking of a clock, for instance, so that after a while they are no longer really aware that it is even there. This works even when the sound is not a constant monotonous one. If you have not been to a railway station for some time, your attention will very likely be caught when you hear over the speakers: 'This is a security announcement ...'. Your ears will prick up and you will probably stop talking. However, if you are a frequent rail traveller, then you will know that it is likely to continue '... Will all passengers please make sure that they keep all of their belongings with them at all times ...' It is just a repeat of an instruction that you have heard many times before, and consequently seasoned travellers tend to ignore announcements completely and continue talking over *any* message – even a potentially serious one, rather like in the story of the boy who cried wolf. In such cases, less is more. Likewise, somebody must have thought that it was wasteful having the emergency signs over motorways switched off for most of the time, so they are now used for general advice messages, such as 'don't drink and drive', 'check your fuel level' or 'take regular breaks'. Yet, when they are used in this way, people end up ignoring them and not bothering to read them even when it could be a matter of life and death. Likewise, if the mathematics teacher chatters away at the front of the classroom more or less constantly (sometimes even when learners are supposed to be thinking about a task), then when they *do* have something important to say they may find that no one is paying much attention.

For some mathematics teachers, listening is the learner's job; the teacher's job is to impart information (see chapter 4). There is a tendency to think that teachers earn their money by 'performing' at the front of the room. Unless we are telling the learners something, then we assume that they won't know it, so we begin to see ourselves as indispensable sources of information, constantly broadcasting our messages and getting frustrated if we feel that people are not listening to us. We would talk faster if we thought they could handle it; we end up seeing moments when the teacher is *not* talking as a waste of precious classroom time. Yet many learners (those with dyslexia, for example) can find it very difficult to work on a task while instructions are being given simultaneously. More learning may take place if the teacher *stops* talking. This is not to say that silence is always golden, but that questioning and explaining are helpful only when we have gained some prior understanding of the learners by listening to what they are saying.

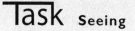

Seeing

Say what you see.
What mathematical questions might you ask?

A task such as this can be useful for encouraging learners to listen to one another's ideas, use mathematical language and find the mathematics in something for themselves. It can be very interesting for the teacher to see what emerges. Some learners might find a sense of wonder in the gradually increasing number of sides; they might or might not be moved to count them, or the vertices. Noting that the number of sides increases by 1 each time, learners might be able to 'see' how many sides the outermost polygon has without counting them all. Learners might explore how the picture could be extended/ continued or how they might reproduce it (or make a similar one), with or without computer software. There are no right or wrong answers – the purpose is to understand better the way the learners are thinking and to help them, through their articulations, to notice new connections. If they are not used to a task like this, one way to get them talking about it might be to ask them to describe it sufficiently clearly for someone else to make a copy without seeing it. One way to adapt this would be to seat learners in pairs, back-to-back, and have one draw a simple shape and describe it to the other, who has to make a copy without looking. (In the easier version, the 'copier' can ask questions; in the harder version, they are not allowed to.)

In such situations, it is not that the teacher is just passively listening in and offering nothing; the teacher is seeking to engage in *transformative listening* and to encourage this in the learners. According to Brown and Coles (2008):

> Evidence of transformative listening and mindfulness in a classroom includes a willingness to alter ideas in a discussion, to engage in dialogue, to entertain other points of view, and hold them as valid, independent of whether they are accepted or not.
>
> (p. 97)

It is much harder to listen than is commonly thought. Many people think that they are good listeners but, as counsellors know, *really* listening to someone is hard work and is a skill that takes time and effort to develop. Very often, people think that they are listening, but really are mainly *evaluating* what is being said, thinking of objections or formulating what they are going to say next. One sign of this is when one person finishes speaking and another immediately starts, with no pause in between. In many conversations there appears to be a fear of silence, so that any gap must be filled in order to avoid embarrassment. Becoming comfortable to be in the presence of someone who is thinking can be hard; becoming comfortable to *be* thinking in the presence of others can be even harder.

Every teacher knows that learners will sometimes ask a question that has just been answered by the teacher or someone else, but teachers are not always much better at paying attention to the learners. Sometimes mathematics teachers question the purpose of listening to a learner who *doesn't* know something when the teacher *does* and could just tell them. Wouldn't it be easier for everyone just to say that they are wrong and tell them? Yet people don't learn well from being told and can, understandably, be resistant to changing their thinking if they do not see the need for it. Taking learners' *preconceptions* (including *misconceptions*) seriously and seeking to understand them is important in helping learners to move on from them. Attempting to sweep them under the carpet by saying 'Don't think about it like that; think about it like this' may not really address the problem.

> ## Task Attentiveness
>
> What things make it hard to listen well to what learners say in mathematics lessons?
> What could help?

An experienced mathematics teacher can easily develop unspoken assumptions such as 'I know what your problem is – I've seen it a thousand times – and I know how to fix it. Now listen to me ...' For instance, when you see a learner adding fractions by adding the numerators and adding the denominators, your heart may sink – 'Oh no, another one'. But learners are individuals, not clones. Although difficulties may have similarities, they may not be identical, and learners will benefit from expressing what they *do* understand. There is a view that 'wrong' ideas are not worth thinking about – may even do the learner some harm if aired – yet it is hard to help someone develop their thinking without attempting to understand where they are now.

Time pressure can be a big problem. In a busy classroom, it can be hard for a mathematics teacher to find the time to attend properly to each individual; indeed, good classroom management may entail fixing one eye firmly on them while the other roves around the room, monitoring what is going on elsewhere! It is also very hard to listen truly to what a learner says if you have something very specific in your mind that you *want* to hear them say. Holt (1990: 27) describes a teacher who 'was so busy thinking about what she wanted [a learner] to say, she was so obsessed with that *right answer* hidden in her mind, that she could not think about what he was really saying and thinking'. The importance of suspending judgment and letting people finish what they are saying is nicely illustrated by this sort of silly children's tale:

A: Last week I went on an aeroplane ride.
B: Oh that's good.
A: It wasn't – I fell out!
B: Oh that's bad.
A: But I had a parachute on.
B: Oh that's good.
A: But it didn't open!
B: Oh that's bad.
A: But as I was falling I saw a nice soft haystack.
B: Oh that's good.
A: But it had a pitchfork sticking out of it.
B: Oh that's bad.
A: But I missed the pitchfork.
B: Oh that's good.
A: But I missed the haystack as well.
B: Oh that's bad.

Premature evaluation makes person B look silly – they don't have all the facts, yet they keep attempting to conclude. Instead of seeking closure, they would be better off waiting and seeing. Rogers (2002: 18) comments that 'Our first reaction to most of the statements which we hear from other people is an immediate evaluation, or judgment, rather than an understanding of it'. Changing such 'habits of a lifetime' can be hard.

Task Disagreeing

Find someone you strongly disagree with about something. (This could be a political canvasser or a member of a religious organization at your door, a friend or member of your family. It may be best not to try it with your line manager!) Get them to tell you their views about something and why they hold them, and as they do so, attempt just to listen. Don't interrupt or make your own points. From time to time, you might ask questions of clarification, but not 'pointed' questions that introduce things they haven't mentioned or attempt to expose problems with their views. You are not trying to 'make them think': make it your whole aim to understand their point of view well enough to explain it to someone else (in the first person) as if you were them.

The aim is not that you will change your mind about the issue – the purpose is to put your own feelings to one side and focus completely on how this person sees something.

For some people, such a task is almost physically painful; they just cannot bear keeping silent when things are said that they disagree with. If they really aren't allowed to say anything, then their objections will trickle out in facial expressions and gestures! In the mathematics classroom, a teacher may struggle to watch a learner making mathematical mistakes or saying things that are false, and be desperate to 'put them right', but the intervention may be much more powerful if it comes *after* the learner has expressed what they want to say (see section 3.2). In fact, the learner may discover their ideas changing as they begin to articulate them; an aspect of *emotional intelligence* that mathematics lessons may enable learners to develop (Claxton, 2005). Little changes to your practice can sometimes have massively disproportionate effects: a little more attention to holding back and just respectfully listening can completely transform a teacher's relationship with learners.

10.2 Questions and responses

> Any questions? No? Good.
>
> Mathematics teacher

For some mathematics teachers, a question from a learner is a little bit of an insult – it implies that they didn't think that you explained everything well enough. It might be more comfortable to assume that they weren't listening properly or are too impatient: 'Put your hands down – I haven't finished explaining yet!' The importance of high-quality discussion in the mathematics classroom is widely acknowledged (Walshaw and Anthony, 2008), but many teachers assume that it is mainly their job to ask the questions and mainly the learners' job to answer them – if they can.

> # Task Limerick
>
> What number words can go in the gaps to make this limerick correct?
>
> A dozen, a gross, and a score
> Plus three times the square root of four
> Divided by seven
> Plus _____ times eleven
> Is _____ squared and not a bit more.
>
> Adapted from Leigh Mercer (Brooke, 1980)
>
> What possibilities are there?
> Can the same word go in *both* gaps?
> What happens if you blank out other words instead?
> Can you make up your own number limerick/poem?

Much has been written about the process of questioning in the mathematics classroom (Mason, 2002); mathematics teachers frequently mention it as something that they want to improve. A starting point is to be aware of the spectrum from *closed* questions, such as 'What is the answer to 4 + 6?', to more open prompts, such as 'Say two numbers that add up to 10'. (Learners used to working in this sort of way may reply to a prompt such as '4 + 6 = □' with an 'answer' such as '12 − 7 + 5', rather than the expected '10'.) However, the distinction is by no means straightforward and, as Watson and Mason (1998: 5) put it, 'most "closed" questions can be opened up, and many apparently "open" questions are nevertheless constrained'. As Watson (2002: 34) remarks, 'The almost Orwellian mantra "open–good; closed–bad" is clearly misleading'. However, the practice of asking a more demanding question combined with extending the *wait time* (Black *et al.*, 2003), or asking learners to discuss in pairs before saying anything publicly, can be very helpful in obtaining more extended and thoughtful responses.

Ainley (1988) has categorized classroom questions as:

- *pseudo-questions*: where the teacher seeks compliance; for example, 'We factorize here, don't we?';
- *testing questions*: where the learner knows that the teacher knows the answer; for example, 'What does equilateral mean?'
- *directing questions*: where the teacher attempts to point the learner to something; for example, 'What do you notice about the tens column?' and
- *genuine questions*: where the teacher does not know the answer; for example, 'How would you work that out?' or 'What did you find out?'

It seems that teachers over-use the first two kinds, especially *rhetorical questions* that seek to manage learners' attention and behaviour rather than develop their mathematical thinking. One way to increase the number of *genuine questions* you ask is to inquire honestly about a *learner's thinking*, such as asking a learner who says, 'I'm confused' to 'Tell me about your confusion'. Putting the ball back into the learner's court in this way gives the teacher more opportunity to listen and avoids an unhelpful tendency to try to *'move them on'*. Questions are genuine only when they are sincere; in other words, when you don't know the answer, you want to know it and you think that the person you are asking might be able to tell you. It is socially awkward to be constantly asking questions to which you think you know the one right answer, particularly if you don't think that the learner that you are asking is going to give it. Learners frequently perceive questions as *traps* and as *requests for display rather than information*. Genuine questions release this tension and enable you to keep your thinking fresh, because you are truly curious about how this particular learner is thinking.

The most common kind of classroom discourse follows the triadic structure: *initiation – response – feedback* (Sinclair and Coulthard, 1975). The teacher asks a question, a learner answers it and the teacher evaluates their response or develops it in some way. This can easily descend into *leading questions*. Holt (1990: 199) cautions us not to think that 'guiding children to answers by carefully chosen leading questions is in any important respect different from just telling them the answers in the first place'. In its most extreme form, increasingly tightly focused *funnelling questions* (Bauersfeld, 1995) push a learner nearer and nearer to a pre-determined end point, and might be regarded as the teacher being manipulated by the learner into doing their work for them! Breaking out of this sort of cycle, so that learners make a more significant contribution and a learner comment is followed by *another* learner comment, can afford the teacher much greater opportunities for listening and entering into the learner's world.

Different categories of question can de extended to produce varied rich tasks (Bills *et al.*, 2004). However, asking a 'good' question is really just the start; the crucial thing is how it is followed up. If your question creates a stir, learners may start arguing about it and you have succeeded in setting the cat among the pigeons, but this is the beginning, not the end. In some ways, a starting question is a bit like a serve in tennis or an opening move in chess: it is important to think about it in advance, but your subsequent moves can only be planned to a very limited extent if you are really to be sensitive to the circumstances (Figure 10.1). *Closed* questions are like 'aces' in tennis; if you can reliably deliver 'aces', you control the game – your opponent is little more than a spectator. We might admire a tennis player who can serve a long sequence of aces, but it makes for dull tennis. This is what happens in classrooms where the teacher has tightly defined expectations about what is going to happen. The learner either plays ball or doesn't. If a learner says something unexpected and the teacher is wrong-footed, everyone wakes up at the surprise – like when an opponent manages to return an 'unreturnable' shot.

Facilitating a sequence of volleys is fun, but it can be difficult to plan for the 'what-nexts'. Being at home in the topic is obviously important, having an awareness of possible productive avenues to explore – but more important still is an attitude of not being too fixed in what you want or expect. It is embarrassing to watch a teacher attempting, by increasingly pointed questioning, to elicit a particular response that is obvious to the observer but not to the learners. When that is happening, you might just as well say whatever you want to say and then move on. Watson (2002) lists the following 'dynamics of questioning':

- varying wait-time, before and after answers;
- using open questions;
- not commenting on answers but asking for more;

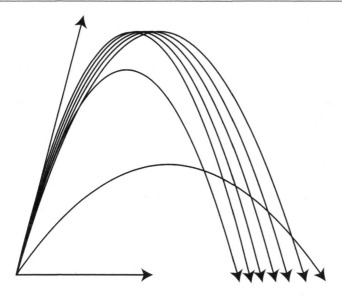

Figure 10.1 The same question may lead anywhere

- bringing in other people;
- collecting a range of responses on the board;
- seeking agreement, alternatives or dissent;
- using, or not using, 'hands-up';
- using names to get particular people to answer;
- remaining silent until something else is said.

It can be worth referring to this list from time to time to see whether there are potential strategies that you are exploiting only rarely.

Some of the most productive and useful prompts in the classroom are not clever questions and don't look very impressive when written down on paper: an inquiring look, a smile, a nod, a pause. Comments like 'Er – what do you mean?', 'I don't get it' or simply 'Why?' can be surprisingly effective, and longer, more impressive-sounding questions can be self-defeating. Just think of any self-important TV interviewer, wanting to make their name by asking clever questions to the politician on their programme: the more complicated the interviewer's question, the less time the interviewee spends 'on the spot'.

10.3 Intervening and explaining

> She's a really good teacher: she explains things really well.
>
> Learner

So far this chapter may have given the impression that teacher talk is unimportant, but that was not the intention; it *is* important (Khisty and Chval, 2002). The aim was to counterbalance the common perception that the chief role of the teacher is to *explain*.

Sometimes mathematics teachers seem to have an almost magical belief in the power of their words. Holt (1967) describes this as an 'astonishing delusion':

> We think that we can take a picture, a structure, a working model of something, constructed in our minds out of long experience and familiarity, and by turning that model into a string of words, transplant it whole into the mind of someone else. ... Most of the time, explaining does not increase understanding, and may even lessen it.
>
> (p. 178)

It is often said that *the person who benefits most from an explanation is usually the explainer*. By putting learners in the position of explaining mathematical ideas, they have the opportunity to clarify their thinking. But there are times when the teacher needs to explain a task or intervene in some way to help the learner, and it is to this side that we now turn.

Task Rectangle

How do you work out the area of a rectangle?

Learner

How would you respond to this? Try to be specific – what would you say and do?
Suppose that you have plenty of time and just this one learner to work with.
Suppose that you have just met them and don't know anything about them.
(Perhaps they have turned up at a 'maths clinic' at lunchtime.)

The danger of doing a little presentation on 'the area of a rectangle' is that you don't know what is blocking this for them. If they are at secondary school, then they have probably been told much the same thing before, and they don't seem to know it now, so repeating what hasn't worked previously is unlikely to be more than superficially successful. Clearly you need to probe a little. You might ask the learner to draw you a rectangle (do they know the word?) on blank or squared paper. They might draw a square, which you could work with, since a square is a special case of a rectangle. By operating with the specific rectangle obtained here, you might hope to generalize later. Every child has some sense of 'area', but it can be hard for anybody to put into words. By seeking to build at each stage on the understanding that the learner expresses, the teacher avoids lecturing *at* them and instead engages in a conversation *with* them.

Once learners have been given a task, and they understand what has been asked, the teacher may see their job as mainly to ask questions rather than to *tell*. Hewitt's (2001) distinction between the *arbitrary* and the *necessary* suggests *telling* things which are arbitrary (e.g., what we mean by the word 'rectangle') but actively *avoiding* telling things which are necessary (e.g., what the factors of 12 are); instead, supporting learners as they work them out. The teacher's behaviour can be likened to that of a moderator in a nuclear reactor: it is not the active ingredient, the fuel that drives the process; instead, the moderator slows down the neutrons so that they are absorbed better, allowing the chain reaction to take place. In a similar way, the teacher sometimes intervenes to slow down or help to make explicit a learner's thinking, or to point out something about what they have said, while avoiding firing energetic particles into the mixture. The teacher might reflect back to a learner what they have just said or encourage them to write it down or record their results in some way. They might ask them to have another look at what they have just done or compare it with what they had done earlier. Also, they encourage mathematical interactions *between* learners: 'Why don't you talk to Zaina about what she has done?', 'Can you explain that to Aga?' All of this attempts to channel energy into deeper mathematical thinking.

Counsellors warn of the danger of giving advice. Rogers (2007) describes the all-too-frequent result of giving advice within a counselling setting:

> The counselor who has made directive suggestions to clients (and what counselor has not?) will perceive the … grudging, incomplete type of action which follows a direct suggestion, in those cases where the suggestion is not disregarded entirely. In response to direct suggestion and advice the client delays taking action. He carries out part of the suggestion, but not the crucial portion. He carries it out in such a way as to defeat the counselor's purpose. He carries it out halfheartedly, and then reports its failure. All this contrasts very sharply with the type of action taken by the client who has been freed by the counseling situation to a point where he can attain insight and formulate actions in line with his newly chosen goals. Here is no halfheartedness, nor action taken only after prodding. The step is taken in clear-cut fashion. The client is pleased with the results.
>
> (pp. 215–6)

When learners seek help from the teacher, rather than giving advice and hints, it can be much more helpful to leave the learner with the problem partially unresolved, so that they make the 'key step' when you are not present. That way you break the association with you being with them when things are sorted out and you avoid creating a dependency relationship. If you leave them with some strategies to try, then when something 'clicks' you are over the other side of the room working with someone else, and they may call across that 'they' (rather than you) have cracked it. This would seem like a far more preferable dynamic.

An important aspect of intervention in mathematics lessons is frequently the attempt to shift learners from stating *conjectures*, and perhaps verifying them in a finite number of cases, to working towards *proof* (Stylianides and Stylianides, 2008). In daily life, over-generalizations are rightly seen as ignorant, small-minded and arrogant, betraying a limited viewpoint. When someone says 'Maths is boring', they are over-generalizing crassly. So thoughtful learners are often cautious about making bold, absolute claims, and one aim for mathematics teaching would be to help them to see when it is justified to make such mathematical statements and when it isn't. Moving from a *conjecturing climate* (see chapter 9) to a place of rigour is a vital step. There are at least two sides to proof in school mathematics: *demonstration* and *explanation*. As Cohen (2001) points out, philosophers such as Hegel and Schopenhauer have criticized mathematical proof for demonstrating:

> *that* something is true without displaying *why* it is true. The kind of proof Hegel disliked was one after the provision of which it could remain *mysterious*

that the theorem in question was true, even though it had certainly been *proved* to be true.

(p. 58)

Hanna (1990: 9) suggests that 'whenever possible we should present to students proofs that explain rather than ones that only prove'. A *proof by exhaustion* that checks all possible cases, such as the proof of the *four-colour theorem*, may convince us that it is true, but fails to give much insight into the reason why (Wilson, 2002). Tasks addressing proof sometimes focus excessively on convincing (e.g., to self, to friend, to enemy) rather than on explaining. A proof that emerges from focusing on why a specific example works (*proof by generic example*), such as many visual *proofs without words*, can lead to such insights (Walther, 1984).

Task Proof

Proof is an idol before whom the pure mathematician tortures himself.
Arthur Eddington

What can you do to help a learner to develop their conjectures into proofs? Suppose, for example, that a learner notices that square numbers seem to have an odd number of factors.

If a learner were to find the factors of a number systematically, they might write them down in pairs. For example, when finding the factors of 24, say, you might encourage the learner to write '1 and 24, 2 and 12, 3 and 8, 4 and 6'. Since every factor comes with 'a friend', there will be an even number, but with a square number one number comes 'with itself', which we count only once, so there will be a 'missing' factor; hence, an odd total. Informal non-algebraic proofs, such as this, can be a powerful way for learners to appreciate generality.

Once a proof has been understood, learners frequently say that it is obvious. In a sense, all mathematics results are 'trivial', because they follow logically and inevitably from some previous result. The physicist Richard Feynman (1992) describes sharing the lounge at tea-time with the mathematics department at Princeton University. One mathematician was convincing another of a theorem he describes as 'trivial' and, after working through several complex steps involving some strenuous thinking, the other eventually agrees, 'Yeah, yeah. It's trivial':

> We physicists were laughing ... we decided that "trivial" means "proved". So we joked with the mathematicians: "We have a new theorem – that mathematicians can prove only trivial theorems, because every theorem that's proved is trivial". ... I said there are never any surprises – that the mathematicians only prove things that are obvious.

(pp. 84–5)

There is a sense in which proving a new result can often be seen as 'merely' understanding more fully the implications of previous ones, and so can indeed appear 'easy once you see it', although that hardly rules out the possibility of surprise (Watson and Mason, 2007).

Dealing with learners' individual needs as you circulate around a classroom can be one of the most challenging aspects of the job. Listening carefully and provoking further thought by asking appropriate questions takes a lot of judgment. It can be helpful to think about stirring things up rather than resolving them; creating problems for the learners, rather than making things easy. As Grosholz (2007) shows expertly, in the historical development of a subject, *ambiguity* is an essential stage, because as the subject grows it is inevitable that we lack formality at our current level (Foster, 2011a). This is also true as an individual learns, and this is not a problem to try to avoid but a necessary feature of constructing knowledge from the bottom up (Simon, 1995).

Task Summary task

Which of the skills described in this chapter do you think you most want to develop?
What steps can you take to do that?

Comments on mathematical tasks

Task: Limerick

The original answers are 'five' and 'nine', but there are infinitely many possibilities, provided that you don't worry too much about the 'scanning'! The number in the second blank space can be the square of any number that is either 2 more or 2 less than a multiple of 11, and 'thirteen' works simultaneously in both slots. Learners might consider what makes for an easier or a harder puzzle; clearly, some words rhyme, which would help to identify them. Deleting just 'nine' makes quite an easy puzzle, as you can just follow through from the start. Deleting 'three' would entail more working backwards and engaging with priority of operations conventions. There are cross-curricular links with English and history in the definition of 'gross', etc.

Further reading

Brown, L. and Coles, A. (2008) *Hearing Silence: learning to teach mathematics*, London: Black Apollo Press.

Houssart, J. and Mason, J. (2009) *Listening Counts: listening to young learners of mathematics*, Stoke-on-Trent: Trentham Books Ltd.

Graham, A., Mason, J. and Houssart, J. (2009) *Listening Figures: listening to learners of mathematics at secondary school and above*, Stoke-on-Trent: Trentham Books Ltd.

Rogers, C.R. and Freiberg, H.J. (1994) *Freedom to Learn*, New Jersey: Prentice Hall Inc.

Useful resources

Watson, A. and Mason, J. (1998) *Questions and Prompts for Mathematical Thinking*, Derby: Association of Teachers of Mathematics.

Bills, C., Bills, L., Watson, A. and Mason, J. (2004) *Thinkers: a collection of activities to provoke mathematical thinking*, Derby: Association of Teachers of Mathematics.

Chapter 11

Groups and individuals

> If nature is really structured with a mathematical language and mathematics invented by man can manage to understand it, this demonstrates something extraordinary. The objective structure of the universe and the intellectual structure of the human being coincide.
>
> Pope Benedict XVI

If you walk the corridors of a school after the learners have gone home, and look for clues as to what happens during the day, the layout of the furniture in a mathematics classroom may say something about the kinds of lessons that typically take place there. In many schools, the default seating arrangement has tables in rows, as in a theatre, all facing the board, where the teacher perhaps acts as a 'sage on the stage' (King, 1993). Simply walking into a room set out like this sets up an expectation that a 'performance' is going to begin at the front (see chapter 9). It may be that the tables are separated from one another, so as to keep learners as far apart as possible, which could indicate a view of learner–learner interaction as problematic—dangerous, even, or certainly to be avoided if possible. Some mathematics teachers would love to create a *panoptic space*, in which they could see each learner and what they are doing but no learner could see any other learner, and some school computer rooms attempt to be an approximation to this. Some learners might regard this as akin to being in a prison.

11.1 Mathematical Groups

> I always use group work in my lessons, but sometimes I think the optimal group size is 1.
>
> Mathematics teacher

In many schools, group work seems to be less common in mathematics than it is in other subject areas. So learners may experience the transition from another subject lesson to their mathematics lesson as an isolating one, in which they lose a lot of communication with their peers. They may attempt to subvert the organization of the mathematics classroom and engage illegally in social 'chat', whether orally, by passing notes or by texting.

Task **Talking and learning**

They worked so hard today – you could have heard a pin drop!

Mathematics teacher

Teacher   'You're here to *work*, not to *talk*'.
Would you say this to learners? Why/why not?
What is your attitude to 'noise' within your classroom?
When do you encourage learner–learner discussion, and why?
Who does most of the talking in your classroom? Why?

For many learners, talking in mathematics lessons is equated with misbehaving. Noyes (2007: 70) describes a teacher who 'told a boy to stop talking during his mathematics work because "you can't talk and do mathematics at the same time"!' Here 'talking' is understood to mean social conversation unrelated to mathematics (social chat), but the fact is that many learners *do* seem to be able to chat in this sort of way and do mathematical work at the same time. This multitasking might indicate that the learner is operating on 'auto-pilot' and could handle a more demanding task. Learners are sometimes particularly 'chatty' when, say, drawing axes for a graph or performing routine numerical calculations. However, when the intention is for learners to develop their fluency at some mathematical skill, not thinking too much about what they are doing may be exactly what the teacher wants. In these situations, social talk as a parallel activity in tandem with the mathematics could even be helpful, so there would seem to be some room for a varied approach.

Many mathematics teachers fear that learners who are working on their mathematics, but thinking mainly about other things, may well be *working* but not necessarily *learning*. Mason (1999: vii) warns that 'doing is not construing'. It is possible for learners to be engaged 'on task' with *busywork* that is of little mathematical significance for them. Of course, this can be true whether or not the learner is talking. In a silent classroom in which there is apparently a good '*working atmosphere*' there may well be no worthwhile mathematical learning taking place (i.e., a poor *learning atmosphere*). The entire class (perhaps including the teacher) might be 'daydreaming', or they might be thinking about mathematics but the thinking might not be benefiting them very much. Many learners, if they are not very interested in the mathematics being offered, might have talking priorities as shown in Figure 11.1. The teacher might attempt to switch the first two by offering more interesting tasks, perhaps choosing things that are puzzling or controversial in some way. If learners' interest in the subject grows, then the first inequality sign might, at least some of the time, reverse. But it is inevitable (and perhaps not completely undesirable) that some social talk will take place during group work, and it would be too simplistic to categorize this as 'off-task'—and unfair to criticize the teacher for not always preventing it.

There are many reasons for promoting communicative group work in mathematics lessons (Sfard *et al.*, 1998). If the learning of mathematics is viewed as an initiation into a mathematical *community of practice* (Lave and Wenger, 1991), then it is essential that

talk socially $\gtrless$ talk mathematically > not talk

Figure 11.1 Possible talking priorities

learners acquire the language and processes of mathematical discourse (see chapter 9). However, to establish productive group work it is not enough just to put learners together and tell them to discuss mathematics. Askew (2008) recounts his struggles with establishing purposeful paired work with 8- to 9-year-olds:

> I put up a calculation and launched into a "think–share–pair" routine: work out the answer and share your method with the person sitting next to you. The children begrudgingly engaged in the "think" part, but when it came to them "sharing" thoughts and methods with a partner, the atmosphere turned sour. Children argued over who was going to explain first—neither wanted to be the listener. Methods and answers were "secrets" to be kept to oneself and not "given away" to anyone else. In some cases, one partner would start to explain, but the other would sullenly turn away. Very few children were interested in what their peers thought and arguments flared up around the room.
>
> (p. 69)

Askew (2008) describes how he recovered this situation by using *parallel calculation chains* (each child doing a different calculation and then explaining their answer and method to their partner), *solver and recorder* (with one piece of paper and one pen between the two children, they took it in turns to come up with a method, which the other learner wrote down) and *clue problems* (each child—possibly in larger groups—had a 'clue card' containing some relevant information, and they were not allowed to show anyone else their card). Giving group members different roles can be a helpful way to structure group work, but more important is developing the sense that the group is responsible for each member's mathematical learning. This is apparent when a learner arrives half way through a lesson, and those seated near the newcomer automatically take the role of helping that person fit into whatever is going on.

There are different ways in which learners can work cooperatively with one another. For instance, each one might be carrying out their own unrelated investigation, but they might from time to time look at each other's work and make comments or ask each other questions about it. This might be termed *assisted individual work*. On the other hand, groups of learners might work together corporately through discussion to produce a joint solution to the problem, each person contributing ideas and relating their contributions to those of others. This might be termed *collaborative group work*. Sometimes the former masquerades as the latter: the teacher thinks that group work is taking place because learners are talking about their work, but at the end each learner submits their own piece of mathematics independently of anyone else. Lotan (2003) argues that effective mathematical tasks for groups must be *group-worthy* and not just ordinary tasks given along with the direction to 'do it together'.

Learners who are not used to working collaboratively in mathematics may benefit from physical objects, such as cards to sort or fit together into a jigsaw (Swan, 2006). The materials can provide a useful focus for emotions, taking away potentially threatening eye contact and uniting group members around the pieces and where they should go. For a quieter group member, silently sliding a piece into place may be a low-risk first step to getting involved. Another way into group work is to begin with *pair-work* ('two heads are better than one'), asking learners to talk to their neighbours about some aspect of the mathematics, perhaps initially for just a minute or two, either with subsequent feeding back or not.

Task Pairs

Suppose that the whole class gets into pairs today.

Next lesson, the teacher says, 'Get into pairs, but no one is allowed to be with the same person they were with last time'.

The following lesson, the teacher says, 'Get into pairs, but no one is allowed to be with anyone that they have already been paired with'.

For how many lessons can this continue? Why?

A task such as this immediately gives members of a group different things that they could do. Groups could even act out the process (*role play*) in order both to get a sense of what is being asked and to begin to appreciate the structure of the problem. Mason and Johnston-Wilder (2006) describe the structure of *doing–talking—recording*, where I have used a longer dash before 'recording' as a reminder not to rush to that stage. The teacher may choose to prompt groups to move from doing to discussing what they have done, or leave that to happen spontaneously.

The difficulty of managing large groups of people is mathematically captured by Ulam (1991), who explains:

> [W]hen I became chairman of the mathematics department at the University of Colorado, I noticed that the difficulties of administering N people was not really proportional to N but to N^2. This became my first "administrative theorem". With sixty professors there are roughly eighteen hundred pairs of professors. Out of that many pairs it was not surprising that there were some whose members did not like one another.
>
> (p. 91)

This is a rather pessimistic perspective. It might be argued that the more people you have the more potential there might be for *positive* interactions, mutual support and other people resolving difficulties as well. To work effectively with groups, it is necessary to trust learners to some degree to manage their affairs. The term *teacher lust* (Boole, 1931; Tyminski, 2010) has been used to refer to a teacher's desire (extreme at times!) to *tell* things to learners rather than allow them to work them out for themselves. Resisting this temptation can be the hardest aspect of 'letting go'. There is an element of 'losing control' as groups begin talking—the noise level goes up and you cannot observe everything that is happening everywhere in the room. Real discussions may not get going unless the teacher is willing to 'back off' to some degree ('a watched pot never boils').

It is impossible to micromanage every detail of every group, and teachers will almost certainly need to tolerate some social talk. The teacher may find that as they approach a group, with the noble intention of 'listening in', all conversation stops and the learners look expectantly at the teacher. If the teacher persists in walking up to the groups without speaking, learners will eventually realize that they can just continue. Alternatively, if the teacher arrives interrupting at once with something such as 'OK, so how are you getting on then?', it is less likely that this will happen.

Although the teacher may be seeking to create space for learners to work things out for themselves, it could be that within the groups learners are doing to one another exactly what the teacher is *avoiding* doing—one learner may be 'explaining' everything to the rest. There is a danger that groups of learners compensate for one another, leading to regression rather than progression. Harré and van Langenhove (1998: 1) use the language of *positioning* to describe how 'if someone is positioned as incompetent in a certain field of endeavour they will not be accorded the right to contribute to discussions in that field'. Such identities can arise gradually, perhaps without learners realizing it, and may be more subtle attributions, such as 'the one who has ideas', 'the one who spots problems', 'the one who checks things on the calculator' or 'the one who draws the diagrams'.

If someone can do quick mental calculations, for instance, others may grow reliant on them and become correspondingly deskilled. Any such persistent *division of labour* can be problematic in education in a way in which it might not in the 'real world', where some specialization might be less dangerous. When individuals become locked in to stereotyped behaviours, the group is becoming constraining, and putting learners into different groupings might be advisable. Ollerton and Watson (2001) comment that:

> groups who commonly work together create patterns of working that may be supportive and agreement-based rather than stimulating and challenging. Hence a change of groups can lead to new ways of working together and new insights into ways of thinking about mathematics.
>
> (p. 31)

You only have to play a game of charades to appreciate the value of language in communicating your thinking. As Mercer (2000: 16) explains, 'Every time we talk with someone, we become involved in a collaborative endeavour in which meanings are negotiated and some common knowledge is mobilized'. Mercer (2000: 153) categorizes three kinds of group talk:

- *cumulative talk*: where ideas from different people pile up on top of one another, without much critical examination or sifting;
- *disputational talk*: where people focus on defending their position or attacking someone else's, generating more heat than light;
- *exploratory talk*: where 'partners engage critically but constructively with each other's ideas ... reasoning is visible in the talk'.

Clearly, *exploratory talk* is the most desirable for the mathematics classroom, since here 'a dialogue happens in which differences are treated explicitly, as matters for mutual exploration, reasoned evaluation and resolution' (Mercer, 2000: 102).

11.2 Individuals

> You're a unique individual—just like everybody else.
>
> Anon.

It is often said that in Western culture there is an over-emphasis on the individual, in contrast to the greater valuing of groups in other parts of the world. However, treating a class as a homogeneous unit may lead to simplistic attempts to *teach to the middle*, completely overlooking the individuality of each learner and their mathematical needs. When mathematics teachers describe what they enjoy about their jobs, they often refer to incidents involving individual learners. While I was writing this chapter, a learner came to see me at lunchtime, as recounted in the following task.

Task Three-eighths

A learner had written $\frac{3}{8} = 0.38$. I had assumed that he had rounded 0.375 to 2 decimal places, and had asked him whether he could give the decimal version more accurately, but this comment had mystified him. He told me that he had not rounded anything; he had placed the numerator of the fraction in the tenths column and the denominator in the hundredths column.

This led me to wonder whether there any other fractions for which this method will give approximately the correct answer. Are there any for which it will give *exactly* the correct answer?

How would you have pursued this with the learner?

Working intensively with an individual learner can be difficult within the confines of a normal lesson (see chapter 10), where the teacher's attention has to be divided among many. When something unexpected arises, it would often be lovely to sit down and think about it at length, but circumstances do not always permit that, and many ideas must be saved for later.

Task Multiplying

When asked to work out 52 × 43, a learner wrote

$$
\begin{array}{r}
52 \\
\times\,43 \\
\hline
206 \\
\end{array}
$$

What do you think the learner has done?
How would you try to help them?

They appear to have multiplied the units digits (2 × 3) and written the answer in the units column, then multiplied the tens digits (5 × 4) and written the answer in the tens column – a common error (Hart, 2005). When faced with this, I asked myself:

- Does this give the same result the other way round, with 43 as the multiplicand and 52 as the multiplier?
- What would the learner do if the units digits gave a product more than 9? Would they carry, or just 'throw away' the tens, or would the algorithm 'crash' completely?
- Does this process *ever* give the right answer, other than in the trivial case of two single-digit numbers?
- Where might this incorrect process have come from? Was this a one-off error or something that was to some extent ingrained?
- What can I do next?

First, I wanted to see whether the learner would use this method consistently, and whether by provoking some more of this I could help him to see that it was wrong. So I asked him to work out 50 × 10 and 50 × 2. I hoped that he might know (or be able to find by some other means) the answers to these, and therefore be able to compare the correct answers with the results (50 in both cases) provided by this method. (In situations such as 50 × 2, the answer 52 is also quite common, resulting from thinking that $n × 0 = n$, rather than zero, but did not appear on this occasion.) In fact, he repeated the same process both times and did appear to experience some *cognitive conflict*. Although he did not readily know the correct answers, he did have a belief that 'multiplying makes things bigger' that was challenged by getting the same number as he started with. We then did some more work on place value to try to help with resolving the difficulty.

When learners are engaged in individual *seatwork*, it can be helpful if they are encouraged to take the view that the purpose of what they are doing is to *learn* something rather than to *produce* something. When teachers say, 'You're here to work', the misconception is perpetuated that school is like a factory, and teachers are like task-masters, exacting as much 'output' from their charges as they can. However, of course, really we do not solve equations in order to find out what x is, but in order to learn about solving equations. No one cares what x is: when an answer is obtained, unless the question forms part of something bigger, it has no significance—the learner moves straight onto the next question. The point of solving a mathematical problem is to develop an understanding of the class of problems of which it is an example. You know when you have done enough of them, not because you reach the end of the exercise, but because you can describe 'that' sort of problem and how to solve it, and do so fluently and confidently. When it becomes normative for learners to be trusted to make such decisions, they tend to do so wisely. The learner who comments, 'I've just done the hardest question in the exercise and got it right; why do I need to do any more?' may have a point.

Mason and Johnston-Wilder (2006) describe a framework of *seeing–experiencing—mastering*, where again I have used a longer dash before 'mastering' to suggest that learners need several exposures to an idea before they can be expected to be comfortable with it. Mathematics teachers sometimes need to be patient with learners who wish to repeat work that seems to the teacher too easy for them. However, in order to learn, pupils eventually have to step outside their comfort zone and tackle things that are 'too hard', *beyond* their current level, things with which they will struggle. The idea that learners must be working 'at their own level' is patronizing and limiting: learning happens when you go *above* your level (see pages 44–46). Bruner (1999: 13) advocated a *spiral curriculum*, which 'as it develops should revisit ... basic ideas repeatedly, building upon them until the student has grasped the full formal apparatus that goes with them'.

The *Peter principle* (Peter and Hull, 1969) proposes that in the commercial world people are promoted to the level of their incompetence: someone who does something well is promoted repeatedly until they reach something which they *don't* do well, and then they stay doing that job for the rest of their career. So positions everywhere are occupied by people who cannot quite cope with them, and if they could just step back slightly then they would be happier and do their jobs much better. But education is completely different. You constantly need to be trying things that are beyond you, so as to develop and progress. If you *can* do something, then there may be little point in doing it; learners need to attempt what they *can't* yet do. It can be tempting for the teacher to offer work which is slightly too easy, so as to avoid the stress and confusion present in classrooms where learners are struggling with challenging ideas. Lessons in which learners are not challenged can sometimes look impressive, as learners get through a lot of 'stuff' and their work is neat and correct. Parents are happy and some learners will be delighted with their 'success', but they are missing the point of why they are there. If you take on a class that is used to working like this, and offer something challenging instead, without making it clear that that is what you are doing, then the classroom will become disorderly, hands will go up in the air, the room will get noisy, learners will 'make a mess' in their books, crossing things out and the atmosphere may get stressful. When learners who are not used to being 'stuck' suddenly are when *you* start teaching them, they (and perhaps you) may assume that you are doing something wrong. Persuading learners that 'being stuck is an honourable state' (Mason *et al.,* 2010: viii) can be a long struggle.

Sometimes learners will be 'stuck' and may demonstrate blocking behaviours such as apparent indifference or lack of motivation. Some may clam up completely. Chesterton (2006: 757–8) comments how his character 'Father Brown had a way with him in getting people to explain at considerable length why they refused to say a single word'. It is important to give learners time and space and to recognize that events beyond the classroom can drastically affect how someone approaches a mathematical task. Sometimes the difficulty of a task can seem overwhelming. It is helpful for learners to have strategies for simplifying problems, such as trying smaller or easier numbers, or removing constraints, and such things might profitably be talked about during plenaries. Hofstadter (2000: 657–8) describes two 'ways to throw information out', which he terms *focusing* (directing attention to part of the whole) and *filtering* (viewing the whole but in one particular way, to the exclusion of alternative perspectives). Molina and Mason (2009) describe *gazing* or *holding a whole* as taking in the entirety of a situation, and contrast this with *discerning details*. Developing the ability to switch comfortably between 'microscope' and 'telescope' greatly facilitates problem solving. It can be useful to everyone if the teacher draws attention to instances where a learner has made use of such approaches.

> ## Task Summary task
>
> What balance between individual work and group work would you like to achieve with your classes? Why?
> What might enable you to move in this direction?

Comments on mathematical tasks

Task: Pairs

This is equivalent to arranging same-sex speed-dating. One way to tackle this is visually, by laying out the n people as the vertices of a regular n-gon and then joining up possible pairings (the thick lines for the six people in Figure 11.2). Clearly, when n is odd not everyone can pair up. However, when n is even, each person can pair up with a maximum of $n - 1$ people, so $n - 1$ is an upper bound for the problem (5 ways for 6 people). Is this always possible?

Task: Three-eighths

The only one that works exactly is, $\dfrac{1}{6} = 0.1\dot{6}$, but you have to include a dot over the '6' to indicate 'recurring'. If you round to 2 decimal places, then you can have $\dfrac{8}{9} = 0.89$,

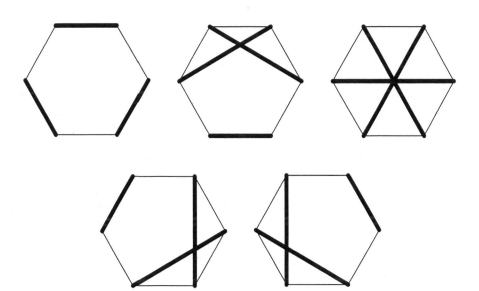

Figure 11.2 Possible pairings of six people

and, if you *truncate* rather than round, then $\frac{1}{6} = 0.16$ is also correct. You might also consider $\frac{9}{9} = $ '0.99' a possibility, since $0.\dot{9} = 1$.

You might like to prove algebraically (or by exhaustion) that the equation $\frac{a}{b} = \frac{a}{10} + \frac{b}{100}$ has no solutions for integers between 0 and 9. You might also like to explore the possibility of the denominator being a double-digit number, so could something like $\frac{2}{19}$ be equal to 0.219? You could also consider the situation in bases other than 10.

Further reading

Mercer, N. (2000) *Words and Minds: how we use language to think together*, Oxford: Routledge.

Swan, M. (2006) *Collaborative Learning in Mathematics: a challenge to our beliefs and practices*, London: National Institute for Advanced and Continuing Education (NIACE) for the National Research and Development Centre for Adult Literacy and Numeracy (NRDC).

Chapter 12

Extending and finishing

> You don't understand something until you understand it more than one way.
>
> Marvin Minsky

Starting off a task can be quite easy and can quickly lead to excitement and mathematical thinking. But as time goes on the teacher must decide how to develop it further and when to draw it to a close – or allow learners to make these choices. A task which on one occasion might be used for a 10-minute starter might in different circumstances occupy learners for a week or more.

12.1 Finishing

> Finished!
>
> Learner after spending 30 seconds on a problem that the teacher intended to occupy him for about half an hour

Learners sometimes arrive at secondary school, or from another teacher, with the notion that the best learner of mathematics is the one who finishes something first. They may be used to being praised for being quick—many mathematics classrooms, both primary and secondary, seem to operate in this way—and this may lead to an emphasis on quantity over quality and a sense of everything being rushed and dealt with superficially.

Task Speed

Who can be the first person to tell me...?
Who's finished?
Come on, hurry up ...
5 ... 4 ... 3 ... 2 ... 1 ... are you ready?

Mathematics teachers

In what ways do you encourage learners to be quick?
How do you deal with those who say they have 'finished'?
What do you do about those who take a long time?

A 'pacey' teaching style can look dynamic and impressive to an observer. The children may appear to be being kept 'on their toes' and the room seems to be filled with frantic energy. Fast-moving mathematical activities may help to develop learners' fluency with mathematical skills, and they will find it hard to work on demanding mathematical problems if they are worrying about how to do more 'basic' procedures, so there is much to be gained in developing sufficient confidence with routine work to be able to perform it quickly. Even those mathematics teachers who generally shun *behaviourist* approaches may nonetheless want learners to be conditioned to give the response '63' immediately when they hear 9×7. (On the other hand, it might demonstrate more mathematical sophistication if they worked out 9×7 by doing $10 \times 7 - 7$.) However, learning by heart does not necessarily follow from an excessive emphasis on practice. As Holt (1990) comments:

> When we give children long lists of arithmetic problems to do in school, hoping to create confidence, security, certainty, we usually do quite the opposite, create boredom, anxiety, less and less sharpness of attention, and so, more and more mistakes, and so in turn, more and more fear of making mistakes.
>
> (p. 75)

When it is appropriate, there may be nothing wrong with quick-fire question-and-answer sessions, but some mathematics classrooms seem to be characterized by short tasks and a constant frenzy to 'finish' things as quickly as possible. Learners are encouraged (bribed with rewards, perhaps) to answer quickly, both in oral and in written work, and praised when they are fast, especially if they are accurate as well. However, Dweck (2000: 121) suggests that if a learner has done something 'quickly, easily, and perfectly', instead of praising their intelligence, 'we should apologize to the student for wasting his or her time with something that was not challenging enough to learn anything from'.

Task Painting

A painting is never finished. It simply stops in interesting places.

Paul Gardener

Do you think that this could also apply to doing mathematics? Why/why not?

When mathematicians answer one question, they are likely to start asking other ones. Provided the task is rich enough, and learners are given enough time, follow-on questions will arise in their minds, particularly if 'good questions' are generally valued within the classroom. It is important to appreciate it when learners offer something related that you had not thought of, and to point out that such thoughts are highly mathematical. The best compliment for the learner might be to invite the whole class, or a group, to work on what is suggested. One way to encourage learners to give more considered answers is to ask more demanding questions, such as problems where a lot of work may be necessary before an 'answer' can be given.

> # Task Factors
>
> Which integer less than 100 has the most factors?
> Why?

Later in this chapter we will consider how a task can be modified (or extended) to make it more general, or just different, but a great antidote to the race to finish is to develop a prevailing culture in which learners are expected to *adjust* tasks that they find too easy or too hard. For example, in the task above, changing '100' to '10' might offer a more accessible way for a learner to begin, while changing '100' to '1000' would provide a significantly greater challenge! Learners might explore which numbers have an even or odd number of factors, or which numbers have exactly 4 factors, and so on. Another response to a learner having 'finished' is to ask them to find a different method of solution, or a way of checking their answer. Seeing something another way can be of great benefit and help to consolidate ideas. As E.M. Forster put it, 'Only what is seen sideways sinks deep' (Forster and Gardner, 1988).

> # Task Three equations
>
> Solve:
>
> $$x + y + z = 49$$
> $$x^2 + y^2 + z^2 = 949$$
> $$x^3 + y^3 + z^3 = 19\,999$$
>
> How did you tackle this?
> Could you have used a different method?

Tasks which extend across several lessons give learners the opportunity to take a break from a problem and return to it. This is what I do with mathematical problems that I find hard; I rarely solve them at one sitting. This can also create a sense of suspense – a cliffhanger that must be resolved in subsequent lessons, which might encourage learners to work on ideas between lessons, and avoids assuming that every lesson must end with a neat conclusion. On the other hand, all good things must come to an end, and there may be times when you do want to draw a line under something and reach some kind of closure. There are many ways to effect this in a mathematics lesson, all of which have pros and cons:

12.1.1 Plenary/presentations

Learners may get impatient listening for lengthy periods of time (which might be a good reason for seeking to develop this practice). They may need encouraging to treat with respect what other people say, even when they disagree. If you have a large class, it may not be possible in a reasonable amount of time for everyone to share what they have done. If someone has 'gone off on a tangent', it may be difficult for everyone else to follow all the details. If they have worked in groups, learners could mix up and talk in new groups about what they did in their group.

12.1.2 Writing up

Learners may dislike having to do a write-up (like writing up a science practical), especially if it is for homework. They may also spend a lot of time focusing on less-mathematical aspects, or describing the task at great length at the expense of saying *what they did*. But mathematical communication is an important element of learning mathematics, so it is worth trying to develop this. It might be possible to use mp3 recorders or video cameras to make a 'report' (e.g., a news bulletin) about what they found out.

12.1.3 Posters

This can be popular with older learners as well as younger ones. Each group can make a poster summarizing what they did—these can then be put on the wall and examined during the lesson or at other times. This can encourage learners to relate what they do in subsequent lessons to what they discovered before. Your school may have a policy about display work being 'correct', and you will have to decide what you are going to do about mathematical inaccuracies and spelling mistakes. If posters are produced on computers and emailed to you, you have the option of a little editing before printing them out, if that is felt to be necessary.

12.2 Pressure

> Be careful what you wish for, lest it come true.
>
> Anon.

One of the delicate judgements required of teachers is to decide when to push a learner and when to hold back from doing so. Many mathematics classrooms are characterized by high stress levels for all sorts of reasons and, as teachers are put under various pressures, such as to achieve examination results, this pressure can cascade down to the learners themselves (see chapter 15).

Task Pressure

What pressures do you think that learners experience in your classroom? (Perhaps you could ask them?)
Do you deliberately seek to *apply* pressure at times? When? How? Why?
Do you deliberately seek to *remove* pressure at times? When? How? Why?
Do you think that pressure is productive or counterproductive?

It is often said that a reasonable amount of pressure is beneficial: an actor who feels absolutely no stage-fright may not give quite such a good performance as one who does. Being too relaxed can lead to a slack and casual approach which doesn't do justice to the task being undertaken. Sportspeople need to psyche themselves up before a game in order to get the adrenaline flowing. To function at your best in an examination or pull off that 'all-singing-all-dancing' lesson, maybe a bit of tension is what you need? But there are problems with comparing performance-type situations with learning ones. The *Yerkes–Dodson law* (Ariely, 2010) describes the relationship between arousal and performance and is frequently taken to imply, in an educational setting, that there is an optimum amount of pressure that leads to enhanced learning—too little or too much and the experience will be less effective. But this seems to be true only for low-level tasks, such as memorizing lists of nonsense words, which are simple for psychologists to measure in their experiments. For more complex tasks, such as those that form the basis for worthwhile mathematical activity, pressure is unhelpful and the relationship is an inverse one. Skemp (1971) illustrates it by imagining someone being chased by a bull:

> The fiercer and closer the bull, the better [someone's] performance will be at running (a task of low complexity), jumping a ditch, or climbing a gate. But suppose that the bull breaks through the hedge, and the [person] seeks safety in his car: then in the slightly more complex task of finding the right key and unlocking the car, he might well fumble. If the key were not in its usual pocket, he might take longer to remember that he had hidden it where others of his party could also find it if they returned before him.
>
> (p. 126)

A little pressure may help a learner to speed up with something that doesn't require much thought, such as unpacking their bag at the start of the lesson, but is only going to hinder them in doing something complex, like solving a serious mathematical problem. Ariely (2010) concluded that in the world of business many bonuses are far too high to motivate people effectively:

> When the job at hand involved only clicking two keys on a keyboard, higher bonuses led to higher performance. However, once the task required even some rudimentary cognitive skills (in the form of simple math problems), the higher incentives led to a negative effect on performance.
>
> (p. 35)

Task Product

Without using a calculator or computer, can you work out 123 456 789 × 987 654 321?

If someone promised to give you £100 000 if you worked it out correctly in less than 5 minutes, do you think that that would help you to get it right? Or would it just make you panicky and jittery because so much was at stake?

Have you ever found yourself getting muddled when solving an unfamiliar problem on the board in front of a class, but once they have left the classroom you immediately see where you were going wrong? Ariely (2010: 44–5) found that participants solved about twice as many anagrams in private as they did when asked to work on a large blackboard in plain view of the other participants. An experienced mathematics teacher, with a class that they know and trust, may be almost as competent when working on the board as they are on paper, but in other situations the pressure will be a hindrance.

When learners are put under pressure, they look for short-term, face-saving coping strategies, seeking to remove the unpleasant stress as swiftly as possible. For instance, they may look for the first acceptable response, rather than the best one. In television political interviews, the quality of the interviewee's answers frequently degenerates as the interviewer turns the screw. And politicians spend a lot of time preparing for and enduring a grilling—the average person would probably be much worse. The same thing happens to the rest of us in job interviews or on dates, when people can make the most ridiculous statements, saying things that they would never say in a more relaxed setting. When someone feels threatened or embarrassed, nothing useful happens for them mentally. Panic sets in and a defensive (or offensive) approach is taken, which plays for safety and seeks escape, whereas what you want in an educational setting is a willingness to pause, take time to think, ponder difficulties and be open to taking risks, making mistakes and listening to others. Adrenaline does not lead to those sorts of behaviours—biology never intended it to—and although it may be a *performance*-enhancing substance, it is not a *learning*-enhancing one. Viewed this way, promoting *competition* between learners, for instance, is not only destructive to the social cohesion of the classroom but counterproductive in terms of the pressure it creates. For high-quality learning to take place, pressure needs to be *removed*, a calm atmosphere encouraged and space created for considered thought. There is enough stress in life for many young people, without deliberately adding to it. Holt (1990: 89) describes learners 'who see a problem as an order to start running at top speed from a given starting point, in an unknown direction, to an unknown destination'.

Task Rushing

Don't rush—take your time. Check your work carefully—make sure that it is right, please.

Mathematics teacher

How often do you ask learners to speed up?
How often do you ask learners to slow down?
How often do learners *ask you* to slow down or speed up?

Traditional wisdom is replete with warnings against haste: 'More haste; less speed', 'Haste makes waste', 'Marry in haste; repent at leisure', 'Fools rush in where angels fear to tread', 'Slow and steady wins the race'. The most popular speed for a piece of music is *andante*: a walking pace. Some learners' lives are a constant dash, from the rush-hour school-run to getting changed after PE and running down the corridor with things falling out of their bag as they try not to be late for the next lesson. Near my home, I sometimes see a small boy walking beside his father, with the father taking massive strides and the boy walking as quickly as he can but taking a few little running-jumping steps every so often to keep up. In the mathematics classroom, many learners simply cannot keep up with the teacher's pace, but that does not necessarily mean that they are poor mathematicians: it is important to be accepting of different thinking speeds and not look down on those who give problems more consideration (Sangster, 2007).

Learners may experience something of a culture shock if they are suddenly expected to take their time and think more deeply about the mathematical problems that they are given. They may feel that they are making slow progress. Encouraging learners to aim for *quality* of thinking rather than speed of answer can be helpful. Sometimes learners appear to panic and think that *any* answer is better than letting someone else get in first. In quick-fire oral work, learners have a tendency to panic and guess, saying things that they don't really think are right, just hoping that they might get lucky (Holt, 1990). This can be confusing for a teacher who tries to take learners' answers seriously ('Why on earth would they have thought that? What misconception could be buried there?'). According to Bouvier (1987: 17), it is too simplistic to categorize mistakes as 'careless', because 'since Freud, we know that the smallest "slip of the tongue" has significance'. But this may not apply when learners are simply guessing in desperation. Guessing also removes any self-checking apparatus that learners might develop—they are no longer autonomous, deciding for themselves whether something is correct; they are completely at the mercy of the teacher's authority. Gattegno (1987) describes the difference between a learner answering the question '2 plus 3?' with a querying intonation, 'Five?', rather than 'Five!', indicating that they are sure. The point isn't that they should put on a fake confident manner but that *self*-evaluation is better than *external* evaluation.

Using mini-whiteboards can be an effective way of allowing all learners to answer in their own time, avoiding knee-jerk responses; alternatively, if they are bursting to tell someone then they might be invited to tell their neighbour what they think the answer is. Asking learners to work something out 'and then think about how you could explain the way you did it' or 'and then make up a similar question' can be ways to prevent learners from thinking too soon that they have finished. Questions with multiple (infinitely many, even) possible answers can be very useful.

Task Solutions

There are no solved problems; there are only more-or-less solved problems.

Henri Poincaré

Try to find some integer values of *x*, *y* and *z* that satisfy these equations:

$$x + y = z \qquad x^2 + y^2 = z^2 \qquad x^3 + y^3 = z^3 \qquad \sqrt{x} + \sqrt{y} = \sqrt{z} \qquad \frac{1}{x} + \frac{1}{y} = \frac{1}{z}$$

Too much focus on *pace* in lessons tends to lead to a *race*. It is much better to aim for *space*—giving learners time to think carefully before answering, and encouraging this by responding to tentative-sounding answers with 'You don't sound very sure; do you want to think about it a bit more?', 'How do you know?' or 'Why do you think that?' Of course, if you do this only when they are wrong, then they will quickly take these sorts of questions to imply that they have made a mistake. So it is worth being upfront about what you are trying to achieve and saying explicitly that your questions are just questions and shouldn't be taken to mean anything. It is worth being careful what you *praise* in the classroom, as you are likely to get more of it. Praise does not automatically lead to increased confidence (Dweck, 1999). Praising learners for qualities that they believe are innate and unchangeable can be detrimental, because when learners find things difficult they begin to think that they are incapable. For such learners, struggling is a sign of not being clever. Wong and Waring (2009) highlight some dangers of using praise phrases such as 'very good' and suggest a number of practical alternatives.

12.3 Extending

Where one journey ends, another begins.

Proverb

I intend to digress ... as often as I see occasion.

Henry Fielding, *Tom Jones*

Once learners accept that the purpose of a mathematical task is not to 'get to the end' but to do something worthwhile along the way, they can become very adept at extending ideas and finding interesting mathematics to work on. Many avenues offer a combination of *acceleration* and *enrichment* (see chapter 15), leading to new mathematics for the learner at the same time as a degree of rehearsal of known ideas. Even when old ideas are being met in a different setting, valuable learning may be taking place. Of course, learners may be discouraged from self-extending tasks if they find that they are penalized for it by being asked to 'finish off' whatever they have done! One solution is to ask learners to work for a set amount of homework time, accepting that this will lead to different outcomes for different individuals.

Task Endings

If you add a zero onto the end of an integer, it makes it 10 times bigger.

$$e.g., 45 \times 10 = 450$$

What happens if you add other digits onto the end of an integer?
I can cancel down $\frac{20}{30}$ to $\frac{2}{3}$ by 'crossing off' the zeroes; why can't I 'cross off'

the fours in $\frac{24}{34}$?

Finding profitable extensions for learners takes some thought. Some changes just create *more of the same*, repeating everything all over again in an uninterestingly different situation. Sometimes, changing some feature of a problem makes it too hard. For example, a student who has successfully solved $x^2 + 17x + 30 = 0$ by factorizing is not going to get very far with $x^3 + 17x + 30 = 0$, so that would be unlikely to be an effective extension. Sometimes, changing the numbers makes the problem harder without necessarily being much more interesting, so solving $x^2 + 64x + 1008 = 0$, although it might keep the learner quiet for a little longer, becomes more about large numbers than anything much to do with quadratics. One possibility would be to introduce some negative coefficients, which they may or may not have considered. Another would be to disguise the 'quadraticness' in some way, such as offering $x = \dfrac{24}{x - 10}$, or a pseudo-real-life situation (e.g., one to do with areas of fields) that leads to a quadratic equation to solve. Another possibility would be to make the quadratic non-monic; for instance, $2x^2 + 17x + 30 = 0$, which can also be solved by factorizing. Finding monic quadratics with integer coefficients which, like this one, factorize, and which still factorize when the coefficient of x^2 is changed from 1 to 2, is itself an interesting task.

Productive extension tasks can often result from tweaks such as the following:

- try making another one;
- try using a different method;
- try doing it without a calculator;
- try making a 'harder' one;
- try it in 3D rather than 2D;
- try it on an isometric, rather than a square, grid;
- try changing the numbers/details;
- try doing it the other way round.

As learners develop in confidence, they may become more comfortable deciding for themselves how much of a task to 'bite off' and how long to spend on it. As they become accomplished at extending mathematical tasks, they will develop a greater web of interconnections in their minds, so that everything reminds them of something else.

Task Summary task

Arriving at one goal is the starting point to another.

John Dewey

How good are the learners that you teach at spontaneously modifying the tasks that you give them?
What could you do to help them to extend tasks for themselves?

Comments on mathematical tasks

Task: Factors

Below 100, there is a tie among 60, 72, 84, 90 and 96, which all have 12 factors. However, below 1000, the number 840 is the clear winner, with 32 factors. Prime factorization offers a quick way of finding the *number* of factors that a number has without finding all the factors themselves.

Task: Three equations

It is possible to approach this *by inspection* (or trial and improvement) or algebraically. Taking an algebraic approach, first,

$$(x+y+z)^2 = x^2 + y^2 + z^2 + 2(xy + yz + xz)$$

so $xy + yz + xz = 726$.
Then,

$$(x+y+z)^3 = x^3 + y^3 + z^3 + 3xy(x+y) + 3yz(y+z) + 3xz(x+z) + 6xyz$$
$$= x^3 + y^3 + z^3 + 3xy(49-z) + 3yz(49-x) + 3xz(49-y) + 6xyz$$
$$= x^3 + y^3 + z^3 + 147(xy + yz + xz) - 3xyz$$

so $xyz = 3024$. From this it follows that x, y and z are solutions of the equation $t^3 - 49t^2 + 726t - 3024 = (t-7)(t-18)(t-24) = 0$, from which $t = 7$, 18 or 24.

Task: Product

As shown in Figure 12.1, the answer is 121 932 631 112 635 269.

									1	2	3	4	5	6	7	8	9
×									9	8	7	6	5	4	3	2	1
									1	2	3	4	5	6	7	8	9
								2	4	6	9	1	3	5	7	8	0
							3	7	0	3	7	0	3	6	7	0	0
						4	9	3	8	2	7	1	5	6	0	0	0
					6	1	7	2	8	3	9	4	5	0	0	0	0
				7	4	0	7	4	0	7	3	4	0	0	0	0	0
			8	6	4	1	9	7	5	2	3	0	0	0	0	0	0
		9	8	7	6	5	4	3	1	2	0	0	0	0	0	0	0
1	1	1	1	1	1	1	1	0	1	0	0	0	0	0	0	0	0
1	2	1	9	3	2	6	3	1	1	1	2	6	3	5	2	6	9

Figure 12.1 123 456 789 × 987 654 321

Task: Solutions

Since zero is an integer, (0, 0, 0) would be a solution for the first three equations, but not the last. There is much here to explore.

Task: Endings

What happens depends on the number of factors that the digit you are adding (a) has. If the starting number is x ($\neq 0$), then the new number will be a multiple $m = \dfrac{10x + a}{x}$ times as large as x, which can be written as $m = 10 + \dfrac{a}{x}$. For values of a from 1 to 9, the numbers 6 and 8 have the most factors (four each), so, taking 6 as an example, we have:

$$1 \times 16 = 16 \qquad 2 \times 13 = 26 \qquad 3 \times 12 = 36 \qquad \text{and} \qquad 6 \times 11 = 66$$

Learners could explore adding more than one digit (e.g., adding two zeroes multiplies by 100).

Cancelling down a fraction by subtracting the same amount from the numerator and from the denominator $\left(\text{e.g., } \dfrac{a + x}{b + x} \text{ to } \dfrac{a}{b} \right)$ is a common error, which this task might help to address.

Further reading

Prestage, S. and Perks, P. (2001) *Adapting and Extending Secondary Mathematics Activities: new tasks for old*, London: David Fulton Publishers.

Watson, A. and Mason, J. (2005) *Mathematics as a Constructive Activity: learners generating examples*, Mahwah: Erlbaum.

Useful resources

Gardiner, T. (2007) *Extension Mathematics: year 7: alpha*, Oxford: Oxford University Press.

Chapter 13

Independent thinking

On the word of no one.

Motto of The Royal Society

Being in school is a temporary phase and, although we might wish students to be lifelong learners, they cannot forever be learning in a school environment. So it must be every teacher's intention to 'do themselves out of a job' in the sense of helping young people to become increasingly independent learners. So, alongside the progression that a learner makes in their mathematics, we might also look for developing social skills and independence of thought and action. If 18-year-old learners of mathematics are learning in basically the same sort of way as 11-year-old learners, then they are not learning to learn, and something is wrong.

13.1 Conformity

The nail that sticks up gets hit on the head.

Japanese proverb

To a very great extent, schools encourage and reward conformity. Bells ring and everybody moves – a clear display of authority. Almost all schools have a dress code or uniform of some kind, which in many cases the most highly-paid members of the school staff spend a great deal of time trying to enforce (Brunsma, 2004). There is frequently a continual battle in which learners seek to depart from the uniformity imposed on them and express some individuality – or at least a *different* conformity (slavishly following local and current fashions) (Meadmore and Symes, 1997). The matter is hardly trivial: repeated refusal to comply leads in some cases to school exclusion (Pomeroy, 2002).

When learners enter a classroom and immediately want to sit as near to the back as they can, they may be displaying some disaffection with the subject or just a desire not to be noticed – not to be 'picked on', as they might put it – by the teacher. By attempting to melt into the background, some learners hope to keep their heads down and thus to avoid confrontation, embarrassment or trouble. Others might be seeking privacy to pursue a contrary agenda to the teacher's. In a school culture in which being academically smart is not seen as aspirational, there may be a disincentive for learners to be enthusiastic about learning mathematics if that will draw unwanted attention in their direction. In such cases, conformity to a prevailing peer culture can be damaging, and this requires sensitive handling by the teacher, who will need to be careful not to spotlight in an embarrassing way the successes of individuals within the class. A desire not to stand out can put a premium on fitting in with the teacher's expectations and not doing anything to rock the boat, leading to learners offering 'safe' answers in lessons and avoiding asking questions that might be unwelcome. The stultifying nature of traditional school learning has been well documented; Sacks (2001), for instance, describes the contrast between his love of learning in his spare time and his depressing experience of school:

> "[A]t school, I was forced to sit in classes, to take notes and exams, to use textbooks that were flat, impersonal, deadly. What had been fun, delight, when I did it in my own way became an aversion, an ordeal, when I had to do it to order".
>
> (p. 314)

Mathematics teachers sometimes complain that learners do not appear to want to learn, but curiosity and a desire to know runs deep in human nature, and it is much more likely that the learner does not want to learn *in the way in which they perceive school learning to be currently defined.*

Learners sometimes appear passive or to lack effort in class – they may seem to be 'opting out'. It can be helpful to see this as a defensive behaviour, or *self-handicapping*, as Dweck (2000) explains:

> The reasoning behind it goes like this: If you withhold effort and do poorly, you can still think highly of your ability, and you can preserve the belief that you *could* have done well had you applied yourself. If you somehow happen to do well anyway, then this is the supreme verification of your intelligence.
>
> (p. 41)

Breaking out of this mentality is a challenge. Too often the short, closed questions offered in mathematics lessons are intended to permit only one answer, so no deviation is allowed. For instance, tasks which invite learners to 'guess the next one' in a number sequence have been criticized as fundamentally un-mathematical (Hewitt, 2008). Guessing what sequence the teacher might be thinking of is more psychology than mathematics. When learners make simplistic *empirical* generalizations based on the idea that 'obvious' patterns will necessarily continue, they are conforming to a 'keep it simple' view of mathematics. The expectation is that the teacher will not allow anything complicated to happen. By contrast, *structural* or *generic* generalizations *are* mathematical, depending on some knowledge of where the sequence has come from, such as a geometrical situation (e.g., matchstick patterns) (Küchemann, 2010). One way to rescue this sort of task is to encourage learners to find as many different possible answers as they can. Of course, absolutely any answer will do, provided the learner can give a reason or a rule to explain why they have chosen it. (See the comments at the end of the chapter for some possibilities.)

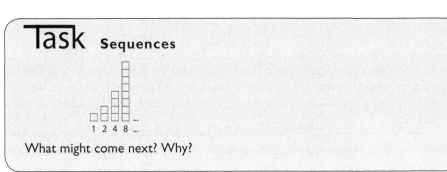

Task **Sequences**

1 2 4 8 ...

What might come next? Why?

In a similar way, finding 'the odd one out' in a list of mathematical objects can be interpreted merely as an invitation to think in the same way as the setter of the problem. Instead, it can be much more interesting to ask learners to give a reason why *each* object could be the odd one.

Task Odd one out

Give a reason why *each* of these graphs could be the odd one out.

$y = x$ $y = 2x$ $y = 3$ $y = 5 - x$ $y = x + 1$

Such a task encourages learners to think from different points of view and to examine, compare and contrast the different features. When working on such tasks, learners often seek to be the 'odd one out' themselves in giving a reason that no one else has thought of. Devising good lists of examples, with reasons why each might be the odd one out, can be a highly creative task (Watson and Mason, 2005). When mathematics teachers prize 'thinking outside the box', they may be surprised and delighted by what learners can create. The word 'educate' (Latin: *educare*) literally means to 'lead out'. The 'duc' part of the word is related to words like 'ductile' – drawing out into a fine thread – and this provides an image of education working gently with the raw material of the learner to pull together a beautiful finely-drawn thread of learning. This is in complete contrast to the idea of stuffing knowledge and skills *into* a learner (which might be termed '*in*doctrinate') (see chapter 4).

Task Conformity

Science is the belief in the ignorance of experts.

Richard Feynman

To what extent do you want learners to *conform* in your lessons?
How is this communicated?
Do you like to be surprised? Argued with?
How would you react if a learner were to change in some way a task that you had set?

Sometimes the most mathematical actions can appear to a teacher as 'bad' behaviour (Foster, 2007). Questioning assumptions and looking for exceptions, pushing an idea to the limit to see what is possible and experimenting are all common teenage preoccupations, and when applied to mathematics can be very productive. One aspect of classroom conformity is the teacher '*we*', as used in questions such as 'What do we do when we see brackets?' or 'What do we always do with fractions?'. Such questions can be mystifying to an observer watching the lesson, but learners may be trained to respond with 'Do that bit first' or 'Find a common denominator'. The teacher seeks to use the pronoun to trap learners into agreement (Mühlhäusler and Harré, 1990). Such knee-jerk responses may help learners to succeed within a narrowly defined range of problems, but would seem to have more to do with conformity to an imposed scheme than with real mathematical thinking. In a similar way, rules may be expressed as 'Mathematicians always ...', yet the mathematicians I know do not in fact, for instance, necessarily always 'show their method clearly', 'use a pencil and ruler for doing drawings' or 'write curly '*x*'s so that they don't look like multiplication signs (×)'. Presenting such advice in this way gives learners an inaccurate perception of the variety of ways of working mathematically and makes mathematical success (as defined in this classroom) contingent on behaviours that may not strictly be necessary. It risks prioritizing one conception of being a mathematician over other equally valid ones (see also page 118).

Too many classroom rules can be oppressive and counterproductive. In particular, negative rules can actually encourage the unwanted behaviour (e.g., try not to think about oranges ... what are you thinking about?). It has been reported (BBC News, 2007) that 'Women who tried to stop thinking about chocolate ate 50% more than those who were encouraged to talk about their cravings'. Too much *goal-oriented* focus on *the answer* can be distracting for learners and prevent them from engaging fully in the mathematical task at hand. Keeping the emphasis on the thinking, the ideas and the approaches taken, and stressing the value of variety and difference, can be much more useful. Learners like to be given responsibility and for their ideas to be taken seriously, and they will frequently surprise the teacher with their ingenuity when given the chance.

13.2 Independence

> Mathematics is not a careful march down a well-cleared highway, but a journey into a strange wilderness, where the explorers often get lost. Rigour should be a signal to the historian that the maps have been made, and the real explorers have gone elsewhere.
>
> W.S. Anglin

Many mathematics teachers find the *territory metaphor* a powerful one (Noyes, 2006); after all, we use the word 'area' to refer to a particular part of mathematics. There are many ways to come to know a geographical area, and a guided tour is certainly one of them. Many people view mathematics as a hostile and bewildering place and are glad of a friendly guide to show them around: it saves time to have someone point out the best places. However, Skemp (1976) contrasts an *instrumental understanding* of how to get from one location to another with a *relational understanding* consisting of a deeper sense of the local area:

> When I went to stay in a certain town for the first time, ... I learnt a limited number of fixed plans by which I could get from particular starting locations to particular goal locations. As soon as I had some free time, I began to explore the town. Now I was not wanting to get anywhere specific, but to learn my way around, and in the process to see what I might come upon that was of interest. ... These two activities are quite different. Nevertheless they are, to an outside observer, difficult to distinguish. The characteristic of a plan is that it tells him what to do at each choice point: turn right out of the door, go straight on past the church, and so on. But if at any stage

he makes a mistake, he will be lost; and he will stay lost if he is not able to retrace his steps and get back on the right path. In contrast, a person with a mental map of the town has something from which he can produce, when needed, an almost infinite number of plans by which he can guide his steps from any starting point to any finishing point, provided only that both can be imagined on his mental map. And if he does take a wrong turn, he will still know where he is, and thereby be able to correct his mistake without getting lost; even perhaps to learn from it.

(p. 25)

For Skemp, personal exploration is necessary in order to understand mathematics in any meaningful way. As Hofstadter (2000: 286) puts it, 'A gifted mathematician ... just "smells" the promising paths, and takes them immediately'. This kind of 'nose for mathematics' can only be developed if learners are 'let loose' to go off in their own directions and find things out for themselves. According to Ollerton and Watson (2001: 41), 'Independent learning in mathematics involves more than personal organization, planning, choice and evaluation skills; it also includes intellectual activity which relates to examining mathematical structures'. This cannot happen if learners are always led by the teacher.

Viewing mathematics as a *creative endeavour*, in which there are choices to be made and different paths to be followed, enables learners to develop attitudes and skills that they may associate more with other subject areas. (Schools which categorize certain subject departments – not usually mathematics – as 'creative' show an unfortunate ignorance of the true nature of mathematics.) An Association of Teachers of Mathematics working group (1991) concluded that:

There is an aspect of doing mathematics which is more like writing a poem than it is like talking. When trying to write a poem, one struggles with the possibilities and consequences of particular phrases; when trying to work at a piece of mathematics, one struggles with the possibilities and consequences of choosing certain signs or a sign-system; in both cases, one is trying to capture awarenesses.

(p. 19)

Asking learners to create meaning for symbols can be one way of offering mathematical autonomy.

Task Ratio

If 6 : 10 = 3 : 5, what might 6 : 10 be equal to? Why?
Can you extend your idea to 6 ┆ 10?

In a task such as this, there is no one expected 'right answer'. The idea is for learners to create some meaning and pursue the idea to see where it may lead. Generalizing is fundamental to mathematics: as Mason (2003: 290) comments, 'A lesson without the opportunity for learners to generalise is not a mathematics lesson'. Such tasks can generate a lot of excitement, but they can also fall quite flat sometimes, so it can be sensible to offer a choice of several different starting points. A musician might be inspired to compose a symphony by a particular photograph, but might find another photograph completely un-stimulating, so some sensitivity is required when expecting learners to be creative 'on demand'.

Whitehead (1962) describes learning that begins with what he calls *romance*, in which learners grasp the novelty of a situation, explore it and appreciate its wonder. Some mathematics teachers may not have experienced mathematics as a creative, open-ended and exploratory pursuit. They would describe their mathematical success in terms of attendance at lessons and lectures, dutiful completion of exercises and gradual mastery of given techniques. For some learners, real mathematics is done by others and 'handed down' to us mere mortals, who would see no point in reinventing the wheel and gladly accept the discovered wisdom of past ages. Such learners think that mathematics teachers know it all – or enough, at any rate – and may seek hints and direction rather than space to work it out for themselves. One way to deal with this is to avoid giving suggestions and just demonstrate genuine interest in learners' *current* thinking, asking them to explain it to you, and avoiding the temptation to try to 'move them on'. Most mathematics teachers do not want to be doing all the mathematics and providing their learners merely with recipes for doing various 'tricks' to pass an examination.

Task Independence

Which of these statements about two events A and B can be true *at the same time*?

- $p(A) = 0.4$
- $p(B) = 0.5$
- $p(A \cap B) = 0.6$
- $p(A \cup B) = 0.7$
- A and B are independent
- A and B are mutually exclusive

A task such as this encourages learners to add and subtract constraints, constantly testing for consistency at each stage. It is a good way to find the limits of what is possible and to understand the consequences of mathematical properties more fully. It may also expose misconceptions, such as that $p(A \cap B) = p(A)p(B)$ always, rather than just when A and B are independent. Another good strategy for helping learners to develop greater independence is to encourage them to *construct mathematical examples* that satisfy certain conditions (Watson and Mason, 2005). For example, this task could be modified by asking learners to specify probabilities for events A, B, C and D such that A and B are mutually exclusive, B and C are independent, etc. By generating their own mathematical examples, learners reveal what possibilities they are currently aware of, and have the opportunity to push back the boundaries to widen their *example spaces* to include previously unanticipated ideas. *Counterexamples* can be equally rich, as Klymchuk (2010) explains:

> Using counterexamples to disprove wrong statements can generate many questions for discussion. What changes will make the statement at hand correct? How can you change a counterexample and have it remain one? Can you think of other statements that your counterexample refutes?
>
> (p. 2)

Very often teachers create the examples (and counterexamples) themselves, and many pride themselves on being able to select particularly 'good' ones. The skill they show in doing this suggests the kind of deep engagement with the concepts that we want learners to develop. Learners can be challenged by being asked to give examples of pairs of fractions where the lowest common denominator is equal to one of the denominators (or isn't) or where the answer to their sum needs cancelling down (or doesn't) or could be written as a mixed number (or couldn't). The trial and error needed to construct these provides useful practice in adding fractions alongside a growing awareness of what it is that makes these things happen.

Johnston-Wilder and Lee (2010: 38) use 'the term "mathematical resilience" to describe a learner's stance towards mathematics that enables pupils to continue learning despite finding setbacks and challenges in their mathematical learning journey'. Mathematically resilient pupils will:

> resist any expectation that they should passively accept mathematical ideas but they will demand to be allowed to work at understanding them for themselves. They will reclaim their right to progress their own mathematical thinking, using existing knowledge, skills, understanding and strategies and be confident about their ability to learn new mathematics.
>
> (p. 40)

Clearly this goes beyond mathematics to embrace qualities such as adaptability and perseverance that learners will benefit from more generally in life. Borovik and Gardiner (2007: 7) describe the importance of what they call the *acceptable solution time*, by which they mean 'the time learners are prepared to spend on a problem which they cannot immediately see how to tackle'. More resilient learners might be expected to persevere for longer before making a breakthrough. Such attitudes, and the confidence that accompanies them, are vital for citizens in a participatory democracy, yet some might question whether powerful forces in society want a generation of learners who question and work things out for themselves – a public who cannot be easily deceived with dubious statistics and who will have a tendency to ask awkward questions of their leaders.

Task Thinking

What I'm really trying to do is make them think.

Mathematics teacher

What teacher behaviours in mathematics lessons do you think *discourage* learners from thinking for themselves?

Why do these occur? How could they be removed?

Learners are always thinking, but not always as autonomously as we might wish, and not always about mathematics! It is necessary for mathematics teachers to accept some responsibility for creating lazy thought habits if they typically offer mindless tasks in the classroom. According to Hofstadter (2000):

essential abilities for intelligence are certainly:

- to respond to situations very flexibly;
- to take advantage of fortuitous circumstances;
- to make sense out of ambiguous or contradictory messages;
- to recognize the relative importance of different elements of a situation;
- to find similarities between situations despite differences which may separate them;
- to draw distinctions between situations despite similarities which may link them;
- to synthesize new concepts by taking old concepts and putting them together in new ways;
- to come up with ideas which are novel.

(p. 26)

All learners can act in mathematically intelligent ways, provided that they are given tasks that are suitably complex and mathematical, and are encouraged to work on them creatively – and, importantly, are given the time necessary to do this.

Bloom's taxonomy is a system for classifying the complexity of thinking. It exists is different forms, often represented as a pyramid, but one version is the following (Krathwohl, 2002):

1. *remembering*: recognizing and recalling;
2. *understanding*: interpreting, exemplifying, classifying, summarizing, inferring, comparing and explaining;
3. *applying*: executing and implementing;
4. *analyzing*: differentiating, organizing and attributing;
5. *evaluating*: checking and critiquing;
6. *creating*: generating, planning and producing.

It can be helpful from time to time to consider to what extent learners in your lessons might have been engaged in each of these six modes. Another important scheme is the van Hieles' model of the development of geometric thinking (Burger and Shaughnessy, 1986):

0. *visualization:* learners 'saying what they see', perhaps treating a shape as a square, for instance, because it looks like it, rather than because of explicit consideration of its properties;
1. *analysis:* learners aware of properties but not reasoning on the basis of them; for example, they note that a square has four right angles and four equal sides;
2. *abstraction:* learners recognizing more formal properties and definitions; for example, they might realize that a square is an example of a rectangle because it has four right angles;

3. *deduction:* learners using more formal reasoning, based on axioms, definitions and theorems; for example, they might prove that one right angle and four equal sides, taken together, are sufficient conditions for a quadrilateral to be a square;

4. *rigor:* learners argue precisely, comparing systems operating under different axioms and not being bound by the particularities of diagrams.

These *van Hiele levels* are no longer necessarily thought of as completely discrete, and at any particular time it is possible for a learner to be operating at more than one of them (Gutiérrez *et al.*, 1991).

An independent attitude to the learning of mathematics does not develop overnight. Some learners seek repeated reassurance about what they are doing. The learner who nervously asks, 'Am I doing this right?' or 'Are these correct?' is attempting to hand over the responsibility for evaluation to the teacher. Rogers (2002: 119) contrasts the person with a mainly *external locus of self-evaluation* with someone who has a more *internal* one. When someone has an external locus of self-evaluation, they are very dependent on other people's opinions of whether they are doing well; as learners internalize their locus of self-evaluation, they become happier to decide for *themselves* how they are doing. Mathematics cannot be an authority-based subject – it has to be individually verifiable. The idea that learners should ask the teacher for help whenever they are unsure can easily lead to a helpless dependency. Some strategies for encouraging learner mathematical self-evaluation would include:

- using a calculator or spreadsheet to confirm a numerical result;
- estimating with the values given or using a rough sense of the size of an answer to identify an obviously wrong answer;
- back-substituting the solution(s) to an equation to verify that they satisfy it;
- realizing that a certain length or angle must be less or more than another (e.g., using the triangle inequality, or noticing that the hypotenuse must be the longest side when using Pythagoras's theorem, or appreciating that an angle must be less or more than $45°$ or $90°$);
- trying an alternative method to confirm the result;
- comparing a difficult problem with previous successful solutions, or modifying a problem so that you can do it and then putting the complexity back in.

When learners are stuck, it takes some thought to deal with them in ways that do not sacrifice their independence. Mathematics teachers can have a tendency to 'take over' and start giving instructions to get the learner out of the difficulty. It is more important in such circumstances to help the learner build ways of sorting out such situations themselves. Structuring learning into bite-size chunks can be compared with cutting up someone's food for them to make it easier to eat. You might do that temporarily for someone who is ill but, unless they have a long-term disability, continuing to do so would eventually lead to *learned helplessness*. As Spencer (1910: 94) puts it, 'Having by our method induced helplessness, we make the helplessness a reason for our method'. *Spoon-feeding* is a form of *scaffolding* (see chapter 4), which needs to *fade*. Learners like to be given responsibility, and frequently do things much better than they (or their teacher) might have anticipated. In the Jewish tradition (Pirkei Avot, 5:15), disciples are categorized as sponges, funnels, strainers or sieves:

> The sponge absorbs all. The funnel takes in at one end and lets it out the other. The strainer rejects the wine and retains the sediment. The sieve rejects the coarse flour and retains the fine flour.
> (www.chabad.org/library/article_cdo/aid/2099/jewish/Chapter-Five.htm)

All teachers will be familiar with the 'in one ear, out of the other' *funnels* as well as with the *strainers* who 'get the wrong end of the stick', but should we idolize *sponges*? The world needs innovators, and it is sensible to encourage learners of mathematics to be *sieves* instead, sifting what they hear discerningly. Learners must not become uncritical and gullible – they should not be believing mathematical statements simply because their teacher says that they are true. Instead, mathematics teachers must urge learners to take responsibility for checking, testing and working things out for themselves.

Spencer (1910: 125) remarks that 'The men to whom in boyhood information came in dreary tasks along with threats of punishment, and who were never led into habits of independent inquiry, are unlikely to be students in after years'. As modern life changes ever more quickly, it becomes more and more difficult to say what learners should be taught in school. For some, the idea of *learning to learn*, or *learning power*, is becoming central. Carr and Claxton (2002) argue that:

> the focus of education is shifting to a concern with the development of aptitudes and attitudes that will equip young people to function well under conditions of complexity, uncertainty and individual responsibility: to help them become, in other words, good real-life learners.
>
> (p. 9)

The teaching of mathematics has a part to play in this overall development. Someone has asked 'Why would you climb a mountain if you could persuade someone to take you up to the top in a helicopter?' There are many reasons, such as the sense of achievement in exploiting your powers to do something, the benefits from the exercise, the pleasure of the journey, and the feeling of autonomy in doing something for yourself.

Task   **Summary task**

If you give someone a fish, you feed them for just a day. But if you give them a fishing rod and teach them how to fish, they can feed themselves and their family for a lifetime.

Proverb

What could you do to create more opportunities in your classroom for learners to do their mathematics independently?

What problems might this lead to and how might you prepare for them?

Comments on mathematical tasks

Task: Sequences

Some possible continuations of our 1, 2, 4, 8, ... sequence are:

- 16, 31, 57, ...
  The maximum number of regions you can make by joining n points on the circumference of a circle by straight lines (A000127). The formula is $^nC_4 + {}^{n-1}C_2 + {}^nC_1$ (Conway and Guy, 1998; Anderson, 1995).
- 15, 26, 42, ...
  These *cake numbers* are the maximum number of pieces a cylindrical cake can be cut into using n planar cuts, and is given by $^{n+1}C_3 + n + 1$, for $n > 1$ (A000125). This is also the sequence you would obtain by assuming constant third differences (Figure 13.1).
- 16.
  The factors of 16.
- 16, 30, 60, ...
  The number of positive factors of $n!$ (A027423).
- 16, 23, 28, ...
  The sum of the digits in all the previous terms (A004207).
- 17, 39, 89, ...
  The number of n–carbon aliphatic alcohols (A000598) – see *Task: alcohol* (page 37).
- 16, 32, 64, ...
  The powers of 2.

(References in brackets indicate the sequence number in *The On-Line Encyclopedia of Integer Sequences*, http://oeis.org.)

Learners might be invited to substitute $n = 1, 2, 3, 4$ and 5 into a formula such as $\frac{1}{24}(85n^4 - 846n^3 + 2963n^2 - 4218n + 2040)$, and may be very surprised by the result $\{1, 2, 4, 8, 100\}$. Other interesting sequences to try for $n = 1, 2, 3, 4, 5$ and 6 are $\frac{1}{2}(11n^5 - 165n^4 + 935n^3 - 2475n^2 + 3016n - 1320)$, $\frac{1}{30}(-11n^5 + 195n^4 - 1290n^3 + 3930n^2 - 5404n + 2670)$ and $\frac{1}{120}(-9n^5 + 150n^4 - 935n^3 + 2730n^2 - 3496n + 1800)$, which give $\{1, 2, 3, 4, 5, 666\}$, $\{3, 1, 4, 1, 5, 9\}$ (the first six digits of π) and $\{2, 3, 5, 7, 11, 13\}$ (the first six prime numbers), respectively.

Task: Odd one out

Some possible answers would be:

- $y = x$, the only one passing through (2, 2);

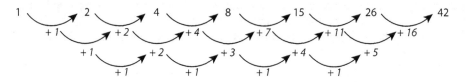

Figure 13.1 1, 2, 4, 8, 15, 26, 42, ...

- $y = 2x$, the only one steeper than 45°;
- $y = 3$, the only horizontal one;
- $y = 5 - x$, the only one that enters the fourth quadrant; and
- $y = x + 1$, the only one that intersects the negative x-axis.

There are, of course, many other possibilities.

Task: Independence

Since $p(A) + p(B) < 1$, the first two statements could be consistent with A and B being mutually exclusive, which would imply that $p(A \cap B) = 0$, rather than 0.6, and $p(A \cup B) = 0.9$, rather than 0.7. It would not be possible for A and B *also* to be independent, since $p(A)p(B) \neq p(A \cap B)$.

However, if A and B *were* independent, then $p(A \cap B) = 0.4 \times 0.5 = 0.2$, and the identity $p(A \cup B) = p(A) + p(B) - p(A \cap B)$ would be satisfied by the first, second and fourth statements, meaning that four out of six of the statements were simultaneously true.

Further reading

Johnston-Wilder, S. and Lee, C. (2010) 'Mathematical resilience', *Mathematics Teaching*, 218, 38–41.

Mason, J. (2009) 'From assenting to asserting', in O. Skovsmose, P. Velero and O.R. Christensen (eds) *University Science and Mathematics Education in Transition,* New York: Springer, pp. 17–40.

Ollerton, M. (2009) *The Mathematics Teacher's Handbook*, London: Continuum.

Chapter 14

Assessment

> Not everything that counts can be counted; not everything that can be counted counts.
>
> William Bruce Cameron

Formal assessments have the power to affect learners' lives in dramatic ways, success in external mathematics examinations acting, to a large extent, as a *gatekeeper* to many future careers and opportunities (Stinson, 2004) – see chapter 15. Internal assessments can also have important consequences for learners, especially if they result in their being sorted into different classes according to the results (see chapter 7). Assessment that is not primarily intended to help the learners' learning, but instead to evaluate what they have learned by some end point, is called *summative*. Summative assessment may be *norm-referenced*, where learners are compared with one another, or *criterion-referenced*, where they are judged against fixed benchmarks, irrespective of how anyone else does (Fairbrother, 1997). The high-stakes nature of summative assessment can lead to *backwash*, with the form of assessments largely dictating the *hidden curriculum* – those things that learners (and teachers), in practice, give weight to (Sambell and McDowell, 1998). When learners ask, 'Are we going to be tested on this?', they are enquiring as to the status of a piece of mathematics in the assessment system, so they can establish the actual hurdles that they need to jump. According to Watson (1999):

> Assessment both contributes to, and is partly formed by, the classroom culture as a whole. The mechanisms of assessment reflect what is valued by teachers and others, explicate such values, bestow status and also shape classroom activities so that valued behaviour is generated.
>
> (p. 106)

It is a two-way process: we test the things that are deemed to be important, and the things that we test acquire a kind of importance *because* they are being tested. The increasingly excessive burden of assessment in schools has been widely deplored, along with the *teaching to the test* that inevitably results (see chapter 15). Noddings (2003) describes how the experience of poetry, for instance, can be poisoned for learners when it is turned into things that can be easily tested. She comments (2003: 37) that 'Some things, even in schools, should be offered as gifts – no strings, no tests attached'.

At a more day-to-day level, *informal* assessment is impossible to escape in the mathematics classroom: learners are making judgements about their peers, the teacher, the resources and themselves, and the teacher is forming opinions about the learners. *Affective* aspects of learning mathematics are much harder to measure than simple test scores, but extremely important nonetheless. Ongoing informal assessment is termed *formative* because its purpose is to inform the teacher about how to help the learner to progress more effectively. *Assessment for Learning* (Wiliam, 2009) has sought to make assessment a more positive experience, to help learners to *self-assess* more effectively and to help teachers make better use of the information obtained.

Task Assessment

Weighing a pig doesn't make it heavier.

Anon.

In what ways are learners of mathematics assessed in your school?
Do you think that learners are *over-assessed*?

When informal assessment is understood as simply getting to know your learners mathematically, this is just a natural part of the business of teaching. In any working relationship, it is important to understand the people around you – to 'weigh them up'. Perhaps a lecturer can lecture in much the same way regardless of the individuals who make up their audience, so long as *en masse* they seem to be 'following'. But a teacher needs to know the 'audience' much more carefully, because they are not merely an 'audience' but participants. This is one reason why it is hard to be a supply teacher or to begin in a new school. Farmers do weigh their pigs, and new babies are weighed regularly, not because it *makes them* put on weight, but because it is a simple (though crude) way of picking up many problems. This is problematic only when it is carried to extremes, such as with someone who is dieting and who weighs themselves compulsively several times a day. It is biologically unreasonable to expect weight to change (either up or down) in a simple monotonic fashion at regular intervals, and it is educationally unreasonable to expect 'learning' to do so, especially as it is much harder to measure, or even to define what learning is. As the saying goes, 'a watched pot never boils'. In some schools, assessment has become all that seems to matter, with learners defined by numbers in a spreadsheet, rather than as individual human beings.

14.1 Judgements

I used to love mathematics for its own sake, and I still do, because it allows for no hypocrisy and no vagueness.

Marie-Henri Beyle (penname Stendhal), *The Life of Henri Brulard*

Mathematics teachers who are used to being confident about their mathematics may sometimes inappropriately carry over that confidence into their opinions about the learners that they teach (Watson, 2006). Colleagues sometimes expect one another to be able to give a confident summary of anyone that they teach, but people are messy and complicated. Learning mathematics takes all kinds of twists and turns, and simplistic judgements are out of place. The most dangerous aspect of this is *confirmation bias*, the subconscious tendency to look for or stress evidence which confirms your preconceived ideas and to avoid anything which might contradict it. Ruthven (1987: 248) reports that 'teachers' perceptions of pupils and expectations of their achievement are highly stable, and tend to persist even in the face of contrary evidence'. Holt (1990) questions whether teachers really want to know what their students know. He describes how surprise tests in an unfamiliar format:

> throw the automatic answer-finding machinery out of gear ... But what do we do when the result of such tests is to show that hardly any of our pupils understand anything of what we have been trying to teach them during the year?
>
> (p. 177)

He suggests that teachers prefer to set highly predictable tests because learners are more likely to succeed in them.

The *teacher-expectancy effect* refers to the self-fulfilling prophecy of learners rising (or falling) to the level that their teacher anticipates. In one famous study (Rosenthal and Jacobson, 1968), teachers were told that tests showed that certain children in their class would be 'growth spurters'. In fact, no such tests had been carried out, and the children were picked at random, yet it was those children that the teachers *believed* would improve the most who *did*, when tested at the end of the year (Babad, 1993). The same is true of negative perceptions. According to Dweck (2000: 84), 'Once you have decided that someone has innate, fixed, low intelligence (or other traits), you have also decided – in advance – what they can and cannot learn. And this may dramatically affect what and how you try to teach them'. As Ollerton and Watson (2001) put it:

> One student who asks questions might be "showing interest" where another one, asking similar questions, might be "needing reassurance". In some cases teachers can even subconsciously ignore evidence which contradicts their view, or try to explain it away as a fluke.
>
> (p. 89)

Being aware of the danger of expectancy effects can help teachers to avoid premature judgment and remain open-minded in the classroom. Deliberately resisting pressure to put learners into categories (mentally, as well as on paper or in a spreadsheet) can help to prevent them acquiring labels which can later be hard to shift. Even teachers' perceptions of brothers and sisters, or prejudices about where the learner lives, can influence a teacher's judgment of their mathematical capabilities.

Task Judgements

The boys in that class are just not interested.
It's a spatial task, so the girls are going to struggle.
He's a good worker – he just keeps his head down and gets on with it.
I wouldn't trust that one as far as I could throw him.
Not exactly the sharpest knife in the drawer, is she?
The poor kid doesn't have two brain cells to rub together.

Mathematics teachers

What common judgements or categories for learners are used in your department?
What are their benefits and dangers?

Although these sorts of comments would not be made in the classroom, learners occasionally ask teachers whether they talk about them in the staffroom – there is an awareness that teachers have private views of them which may not be articulated in their hearing. They know that it matters what their teachers think about them. Jackson (2002) remarks that:

> The very young student may be temporarily fooled by tests that are presented as games, but it doesn't take long before he begins to see through the subterfuge and comes to realize that school, after all, is a serious business. It is not only what you do there but what others think of what you do that is important.
>
> (p. 123)

Dweck (2000: 59) describes the *fallacy of assessment* as 'thinking that by measuring someone's present skills, you've measured their potential; that by looking at what they can do now, you can predict what they're capable of doing in the future'. When a learner does something incorrectly or scores a low mark in a test, this *absence of evidence of competence* is not the same as *evidence of incompetence*. Any number of factors might account for an exceptional poor performance, such as a problem at home, an ill relative or an inadequate (or missing) breakfast. Watson (1999: 109) found that 'For some teachers motivation, interest, boredom, confidence and preferred learning styles were treated as given, but other teachers regarded it as part of their job to affect these through their expectation or teaching styles'. To be a teacher is to believe that people change and that education can affect people for the better. Any judgment is useful only insofar as it helps the learner to take the next step.

The two tasks below involve difficult *mathematical* judgements.

> # Task Sand or stars
>
> I will surely bless you and make your descendants as numerous as the stars in the sky and as the sand on the seashore.
>
> > Genesis 22:17 (New International Version)
>
> Which of these two do you think is the 'bigger' promise?
> Are there more stars in the sky or is there more sand on the seashore?

Comparing two extremely large numbers can be very difficult unless you have something to relate at least one of them to.

> # Task DNA
>
>
> If you took all of the DNA from all the cells in your body, roughly how much do you think it would weigh?

This is the hardest kind of estimation problem, because there is a huge number of cells but each contains a very tiny amount of DNA. So you are trying to estimate a very small number multiplied by an extremely large number, which could make just about anything!

Heavy-handed judgements by the mathematics teacher can do a lot of damage, and teachers should certainly avoid making comparisons with other learners (especially siblings); instead, comparisons with the learner's previous work ('I remember when you used to have a lot of trouble doing that') can be useful. Mathematics teachers need to refrain from judging too much. As Holt (1990: 36) puts it, 'Only as teachers in schools free themselves from their traditional teacher tasks – boss, cop, judge – will they be able to learn enough about their students to see how best to be of use to them'.

14.2 Marking

> *I h2³ maths* (i.e., 'I hate maths')
>
> > Seen on the cover of a learner's mathematics book

Some mathematics teachers' lives are made a misery by marking. Teachers who love being in the classroom, and teach with enthusiasm and energy throughout the day, slump in their chairs and look around for distractions when the time comes for marking. Most mathematics departments will have some kind of *marking policy*, dictating how often learners' written work should be looked at and how it should be annotated. Wise managers ensure that colleagues are not over-burdened with paperwork, because in such circumstances the first thing that may be sacrificed is careful lesson preparation. Beginning teachers may spend much more time planning lessons than they do marking, but for more experienced colleagues it tends to switch the other way round, as Wiliam (2001) comments:

> In Britain, the majority of teachers spend most of their lesson preparation time in marking books, invariably doing so alone. In some other countries, the majority of lesson preparation time is spent planning how new topics can be introduced. ... This is sometimes done individually or with groups of teachers working together.
>
> (p. 275)

Black *et al.* (2003) have shown that learners do not benefit from *grades and marks* on their work, however much they might say that they want them, but from *constructive comments* about how they can improve. It seems that when grades are given *alongside* comments, the presence of the grades washes out the positive effects of the comments, so *comment-only marking* is advocated. However, teachers' comments are likely to be ineffectual unless learners are encouraged to respond to them in some way. The point of formative assessment is what happens *after* the assessment – how it is used to help learners to progress.

14.2.1 Project work

Sometimes worries about difficulties over assessment prevent interesting mathematical tasks from being carried out, which is 'the tail wagging the dog'. For instance, concern over the difficulties of identifying each learner's individual contribution to a group task should not discourage the teacher from embarking on it. However, before you start a mathematical task, it is sensible to think about your options for assessing it. Setting a task and only later thinking about the assessment is a bit like carrying out a statistical survey and not contemplating how you will analyse the data until you have acquired it all: you may find that it is in an inconvenient format, is flawed or does not quite address what you wished it to.

Pages of exercises are as tedious to mark as they are to do, and a constant diet of this offers learners little room for creativity and mathematical exploration (see chapter 6). Frequently, the book that a learner does their mathematics in acquires the name 'exercise book', cementing an understanding that any other kind of task requires an excuse (it is the end of term, the normal teacher is away, etc.). Alternatively, if learners work on more substantial open-ended tasks, then their responses will be more varied, making reading them more interesting and the whole process more worthwhile for everyone. You might be able to give learners longer to work before collecting anything in, monitoring their lesson-by-lesson progress and writing brief comments as you circulate around the room. The following would be a possible task.

Task Bouncing robots

‹—————12 metres—————›

Two identical robots face each other at opposite ends of a 12-metre-long room.

At the same moment, they begin moving towards each other, both travelling at 1 metre per second.

Whenever they bump into each other, or into the walls, they bounce off at the same speed in exactly the opposite direction.

Describe what happens.

Now suppose that one of the robots begins in the middle of the room and the other begins at the end.

What happens if the robots are *facing each other* when they start?

What happens if the robots are *facing in opposite directions* when they start?

Try starting the robots at different positions and facing in different directions.

Can you predict and describe what will happen?

As a period of project work draws to a close, some alternatives to 'writing up' would be a presentation to the rest of the class, or a poster (see pages 151–152). (The view that nothing is serious until it is written down somewhere – the notion of 'evidence' for parents or senior managers – foolishly undervalues oral work.) When marking open-ended work, ticks and banal remarks such as 'well done', 'interesting' or 'very good' would seem to be of little value. More helpful would be comments which appreciate the effort that the learner has put in and celebrate some of the results. Comments that begin 'I …' are often more genuine and appreciative than those that start 'You …'. The mathematics teacher might look out for opportunities to support literacy across the curriculum and pose some follow-up questions. Evaluative judgements might be deliberately avoided.

14.2.2 Peer marking

It is well established that learners can benefit greatly from marking their own and each other's work (Black *et al.*, 2003). There are issues of trust and confidentiality when one learner is writing comments in another learner's book, and what is possible will depend on the classroom climate currently operating. Teachers may also be concerned about the opportunity to *cheat and copy*, yet such issues are a feature of all classrooms, however

Figure 14.1 A learner getting frustrated with his error

mathematics is assessed, and may be best addressed by working on learners' sense of purpose in what they are doing. If learners are not being judged adversely on their performance, but are simply seeing where they currently are with their mathematics, what incentive would there be for falsifying their result? When learners copy mathematics from somebody else, or plagiarise from the internet, it might be supposed that they don't experience the classroom as a place of learning. When learners correct their answers (and understand why) before ticking them, this may be a signal of lacking security which may improve with time as trust builds. Learners who see the value of checking their own mathematics are frequently much harder on themselves than their teacher would be, occasionally using quite explicit language to criticize their errors! A mild example of a learner's frustration with his own sign error is shown in his marking in Figure 14.1.

14.2.3 Class tests

A test is said to be *valid* if it actually tests what it claims to test. For example, a learner who scores a low mark on a mathematics test because they cannot read the questions is not providing evidence of weakness at mathematics. Clausen-May (2001: 5) comments that 'Many aspects of the language, layout or presentation of a question paper may affect its validity. It may use language which is unfamiliar, or contexts which are confusing'. On the other hand, a test is said to be *reliable* if the same person taking the same test again (for the first time, of course!) would get the same mark. Clearly, no one can take the same test twice without the first attempt affecting the second, so reliability can never be proven. Validity and reliability are to some extent in conflict, because making a test valid might involve adapting it to some degree for different candidates, but varying the conditions is likely to undermine its reliability (Clausen-May, 2001).

When marking more procedural work, such as typical tests, it is possible to use abbreviations to direct learners' attention to particular problems (Foster, 2011b). It is more fun if you do not define these in advance but allow learners to deduce their meanings from comments that are common to several learners and from studying what they did that provoked them. An example is given in Figure 14.2. Sometimes marking tests can lead to puzzling errors that can be instructive to deal with, and it is worth being on the lookout for interesting mathematics in learners' books. If you are marking near to a photocopier, then it is easy to capture them for future use.

Task Solutions

Below, a learner attempts to find the stationary point(s) of the graph $y = 4x^2 + \dfrac{1}{x}$, and obtains two values of x, yet a sketch (Figure 14.3) suggests that there is just one – a minimum.

$$4x^2 + \frac{1}{x} = 4x^2 + x^{-1}$$

$$\frac{dy}{dx} = 8x - x^{-2}$$

$$-x^{-2} + 8x = 0$$

$$7x \neq 0 \qquad x^{-2} - 8x = 0$$

$$x = 0 \qquad x(x^{-3} - 8) = 0$$

$$x = 0 \text{ or } x^{-3} = 8$$

$$\underline{x = \frac{1}{2}}$$

Where is the problem?
How might you follow this up with this learner?

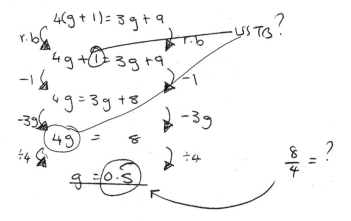

Figure 14.2 WSTB = What should this/these be?

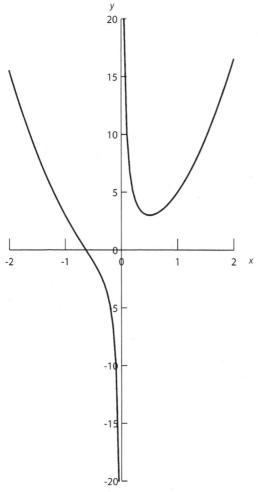

Figure 14.3 The graph $y = 4x^2 + \dfrac{1}{x}$

14.3 Communicating with parents

> I was never any good at maths when I was at school.
>
> Parent

Parents frequently complain about their children's reports – that they are hard to understand, too long, too short, too vague or report problems too late (Power and Clark, 2000). 'They don't really know my child' is a common comment. Sometimes brevity creates difficulties: does 'outstanding' work mean that it was brilliant or that it was not handed in? It is much easier to write clear and accurate reports in a reasonable amount of time if concise records of learners' mathematics have been kept. It is worth thinking about the explicit and implicit messages about the nature of mathematics, and learning mathematics, that your reports may convey (see chapter 1). Standard phrases may have pedagogical beliefs embedded in them that present, for instance, a hierarchical, sequential view of mathematics, where 'keeping up' is vital, or 'mathematics' may be equated with written work. Advice such as 'always seek help whenever you are unsure' may limit learners' opportunity to develop independent coping strategies (see chapter 13). As with face-to-face meetings, it can be helpful to phrase comments positively as much as possible.

Many schools promote the idea of a *home–school partnership* and stress the importance of the free flow of information both ways between home and school, but in practice it can sometimes be difficult. For some parents or carers, it can be extremely hard to walk into a school building and attend a parents' evening or individual meeting with a teacher. Many parents will have negative memories of their own school days, perhaps particularly of learning mathematics, and may feel that school is not a place that they would choose to go back to, and it can be difficult for a teacher who was successful at school to empathize with this. If the child is good at mathematics, the parent may feel embarrassed ('My daughter is way beyond me now'), whereas if the child is struggling the parent may feel guilty ('I'm afraid he takes after me'). It is important that the mathematics teacher is sensitive to the feelings that the parent may bring and is reassuring.

Many parents will want to support their child but may not feel that they know how to or are able to when it comes to mathematics. Homework (especially in mathematics) frequently leads to conflict in the home (Hughes and Greenhough, 2008). BECTA (2010) reports that:

> Almost a quarter (22 per cent) of parents say they are frequently unable to provide support. Dads are most likely to struggle – more than one in three (35 per cent) finding it difficult to engage with their child's learning, compared to one in eight (12 per cent) of mums. ... More than half (58 per cent) of children say their parents often confuse them when they try to help with homework because they explain things differently to the teacher.

When surveyed, 37% of parents said that mathematics was the subject that they find it most difficult to help their child with, and 31% of children said that mathematics was the subject that their parents were least able to help them with. Noddings (2003), however, questions the wisdom of enlisting parents' help with children's homework:

> The practice of involving parents in their children's homework may, for example, actually reduce the parents' enthusiasm for informal learning. Forced to act as taskmasters, parents may begin to feel that their proper role is to enforce formal learning instead of enjoying moments of shared experience with their children.
>
> (p. 156)

Mathematics teachers do not always feel that the requirement to set frequent homework is beneficial. Ollerton (2003a) confesses that:

> All too often I felt I had to set homework, not to enhance students' learning, but because this was the school policy or because a parent had complained to the headteacher about their child not having any homework for a period of time.
>
> (p. 172)

Given the amount of time that learners spend in school over the years, it is questionable why schoolwork has to extend into the evenings, when there are so many other valuable things for children to do. Cynics might argue that the system is an attempt to normalize the taking of work home, so that when children are adults they are less likely to question their boss giving them paperwork to complete before the next day. Homework can easily become an issue of conflict for the teacher too, if it is not completed on time or appears to be rushed or of poor quality.

However, it is possible to view homework positively, as an opportunity for learners to work more independently and continue their mathematical thinking away from the confines of the classroom. Homeworks which appear to be set 'for the sake of it' or which involve 'finishing off' can be problematic, with some learners expected to spend an unreasonable amount of time 'catching up'. 'Holiday homework' can be particularly unpopular, and might seem to be a contradiction in terms. On the other hand, a homework task which invites a learner to spend a specified amount of time on extending a piece of class work, or which involves a puzzle or other open-ended activity, may be more acceptable. Other possibilities are finding something out or preparing something to present or report back on in the next lesson. A lot of stress can be created at home because parents feel that homework must be perfect, otherwise it reflects badly on them. Noddings (2003) remarks that:

> As a math teacher, I believed that homework should be an opportunity to learn – to practice, but also try things out. There is no expectation that students would (or should) get everything right, and it is often fun to hear the variety of solutions attempted.
>
> (p. 257)

Task Parents

She's got to the point where we can't help her at home anymore.

He's never going to be a mathematician but he's got to get through his exams because maths is important.

Half the stuff you do in maths you never use, do you? I mean, I never have!

Parents

How might you respond to remarks like these?

Parents who want to help their children with their mathematics homework can be encouraged to ask questions and to listen rather than to lecture. Empowering parents might involve encouraging them to use their ignorance to their advantage by asking questions and learning together, exploiting strategies to use when stuck. They may be reassured that they will not do irreparable damage to their children by sharing different calculation methods (a common concern), since it can be very helpful for learners to see and understand alternative approaches (see chapter 12). There are some excellent books (e.g., Eastaway and Askew, 2010) and some helpful information and advice at www.nctm.org/resources/families.aspx. Websites such as www.nrich.maths.org.uk and DVDs such as *The Story of Maths* (du Sautoy, 2008) can also be of great benefit.

Task Summary task

How could you improve the mathematical assessment of your learners?
Do you think that there is too much of it? Is it of the wrong kind?
How are the findings used to help learners to develop?

Comments on mathematical tasks

Task: Sand or stars

It is extremely hard to tell. There are thought to be around 10^{20} grains of sand on the earth but something like 10^{22} stars in the universe, but both estimates are so imprecise that it is difficult to be sure (Archimedes, 1960). However, most sources (e.g., Sagan, 1981) seem to think that there are more stars in the universe than grains of sand on the earth.

Task: DNA

The answer is probably of the order of 10 grams.

Task: Bouncing robots

Sketches (or accurate drawings) of travel graphs may be helpful here. It may be possible to find battery-operated toys that will mimic this process.

Task: Solutions

Everything is correct up to $x^{-2} - 8x = 0$, but in the next step, where she 'factorizes', she effectively divides by x, which could be zero, thereby introducing a spurious solution of $x = 0$. A better way to proceed would be to multiply through by x^2:

$$\frac{1}{x^2} - 8x = 0$$

$$1 - 8x^3 = 0$$

leading to a single solution, $x = \frac{1}{2}$. The learner might be invited to construct other situations in which something of this nature happens, or to make a 'warning' poster (perhaps a humorous one) for the classroom wall about this sort of 'hazardous situation'.

Further reading

Wiliam, D. (2009) *Assessment for Learning: why, what and how?*, London: University of London, Institute of Education.

Morgan, C. and Watson, A. (2002) 'The interpretative nature of teachers' assessment of students' mathematics: issues for equity', *Journal for Research in Mathematics Education*, 33(2), 78–110.

Watson, A. (2006) *Raising Achievement in Secondary Mathematics*, Maidenhead: Open University Press.

Chapter 15

Constraints

For every ailment under the sun
There is a remedy, or there is none;
If there be one, try to find it;
If there be none, never mind it.

Mother Goose rhyme

15.1 Procedures

Once the class are in and I close the door, they're mine and I can do what I like.
Mathematics teacher

Despite this teacher's feeling of autonomy, mathematics teaching does not take place in a vacuum: the mathematics teacher is under all sorts of pressures from school management, learners, parents and government. Teachers are expected to be familiar with and abide by an ever-increasing list of school policies, and when there are tight controls on what teachers can do this pressure can easily be passed on to learners, resulting in attempts to micro-manage every aspect of their learning (Pelletier and Sharp, 2009).

In enlightened schools and mathematics departments, systems are in place to involve classroom teachers in shaping policy. Different members of the mathematics department might take responsibility for schemes of work for particular year groups, or devising sequences of lessons. Or an enthusiastic mathematics teacher might look into forging greater cross-curricular links with other departments, setting up a mathematics club or organizing a mathematics trip. It is more constructive to suggest or volunteer to set up alternatives rather than merely to criticize what is already in place. However, there will be times when there are serious conflicts between what is expected and what the conscientious mathematics teacher wants to do. Noddings (2003: 230) describes how some people 'give way out of fear and adopt ends or means they have moral reason to reject. Others manage to rationalize practices that should make them deeply unhappy'. Ball (1997: 239) refers to the politics of education centring on *'the taming of teachers'*, arguing that the focus of much education policy 'has been to control and discipline teachers. The work of teaching has become increasingly over-determined and over-regulated'. By contrast, he calls instead for teachers to be *'public intellectuals'*. Russell (2009: 110) remarks that 'A feeling of intellectual independence is essential to the proper fulfilment of the teacher's functions'.

> # Task Tables
>
> A new mathematics teacher wants to rearrange the tables in their classroom to encourage group discussion in their lessons. Their departmental colleagues are unconvinced of the value of this, and find it inconvenient when they have to use the room, complaining that it leads to unwanted 'chattiness' among their learners.
>
> Should the new teacher toe the line or risk rocking the boat?

In such situations a compromise can often be found, such as learners moving the furniture at the end of one lesson ready for the next class. There also might be some opportunity for discussion about the different styles of lesson, or mutually supportive lesson observations. Learners who initially misuse opportunities to talk about mathematics might develop a better mathematical focus with time, if given interesting enough tasks to work on (see chapter 11). Where mathematics teachers come into conflict over school procedures with regard to rewards and sanctions, for instance, they must carefully weigh up their principles against the possible repercussions. A colleague running a detention may think that a mathematics textbook will provide a suitable set of exercises to use as a punishment, but the mathematics department may feel that this would undermine their efforts to present mathematics as a meaningful, purposeful and enjoyable pursuit.

> # Task Consistency
>
> *A foolish consistency is the hobgoblin of little minds.*
>
> Ralph Waldo Emerson
>
> Do you agree? Do attempts to foster consistency inevitably lead to *dumbing down* or can they have a positive purpose?
>
> Suppose that a colleague regards as 'silly' a school rule about learners using teachers' surnames rather than first names and intends to disregard it. What possible problems might arise?

Daring to be different and adopting a slightly subversive approach in the classroom (Postman and Weingartner, 1971) can be noble for the teacher with principles, and mark them out as a lovable eccentric (McCulloch, 2009), but on the other hand procedures tend to exist for a reason. It would be unwise, and perhaps unprofessional, to take such a course of action without discussing it with senior managers first. For an excellent example of how this can work, see Ollerton (2004).

Task Pentagon

An interesting *mathematical* constraint comes from the commonly-used ISO paper sizes, such as A4, where sides are in the ratio $1:\sqrt{2}$.

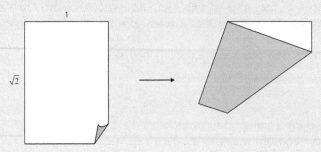

Take a piece of A4 paper and fold it corner-to-opposite-corner.
Make some conjectures about the resulting pentagon.
Can you prove your ideas?
Taking the shorter side of the A4 paper as 1 unit, find the area and perimeter of the pentagon produced.
What happens if you start with a different shaped rectangle (not ISO size)?

15.2 Examinations

> It's just exams, exams, exams – there's no time to do any actual teaching!
>
> Frustrated mathematics teacher

There is no denying that in recent years high-stakes mathematics examinations have assumed a greater importance than ever within schools, with an injurious effect on mathematics teaching (Watson, 2007). This is not an entirely new phenomenon, however. Orwell (2008: 74), describing his own school days in the early years of the twentieth century, comments that he and his peers 'were crammed with learning as cynically as a goose is crammed for Christmas'. His description of a narrow focus on what might be expected to appear in the examinations, and endless past paper practice, sounds sadly familiar to the modern ear (Nichols and Berliner, 2007). Holt (1990) takes a more cynical line:

> the test–examination–marks business is a gigantic racket, the purpose of which is to enable students, teachers, and schools to take part in a joint pretense that the students know everything they are supposed to know, when in fact they know only a small part of it – if any at all. Why do we always announce exams in advance, if not to give students a chance to cram for them? Why do teachers ... always say quite specifically what the exam will be about, even telling the type of questions that will be given? Because otherwise too many students would flunk.
>
> (p. 232)

When observing learners in public examinations, I often notice that, as soon as they are told that they can begin, the candidates open their booklets and almost immediately begin writing. I don't get the impression that this is a panicky reaction to the stress of the situation, but exactly what they are expected to do. This would seem to suggest that little thinking time is provided or required, and that the paper, at least in places, is testing little more than factual recall.

Task Examination questions

If someone can answer a question immediately then the question wasn't worth asking.

Mathematics teacher

What do you think about this?
What makes a good question in a mathematics examination?
Is it different from what makes a good question in a mathematics lesson?

Recent developments in post-16 examinations in the UK illustrate the constant change that has become endemic (Porkess, 2011). A great deal of energy and financial resources are consumed in updating teachers' knowledge of examination requirements, taking away precious time from thinking about mathematics teaching itself. Meeting the needs of the examinations while providing learners with valuable mathematical opportunities in the classroom has become a major challenge. *'Coverage'* of the requirements has become, in many eyes, the teacher's primary responsibility.

Task Cover the spot

It's been such a rush this term; I just hope I've covered everything!

Mathematics teacher

A carnival game invites punters to place five identical circular discs so that they completely cover a painted red circle. You have to put down the discs one at a time – and, once positioned, they may not be moved.

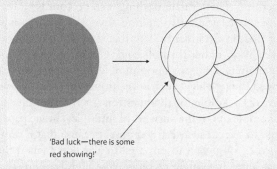

'Bad luck—there is some red showing!'

How large should the discs be in relation to the red painted spot?

The detailed specifications provided by awarding bodies tend to encourage teachers to think in terms of 'delivery' and 'coverage' of material rather than learners' capabilities, confidence and understanding. One approach is to focus on normal 'proper' teaching most of the time, switching into focused preparation when the examinations appear on the horizon (Boaler, 1997). Mason and Johnston-Wilder (2004) comment that:

> Certainly prior to an examination, practice is valuable in getting up speed, which means reducing the amount of focused attention required to perform the technique so that you can be on the look out for slips and wrinkles, and maintain a direction towards the solution of the problems.
>
> (pp. 174–5)

Unfortunately, this separation is harder to achieve in modular courses, where teachers can feel that learners are always doing important examinations – or preparing for them or reviewing how they went – and the amount of 'normal' teaching shrinks alarmingly. Indeed, it is so bad that some teachers might have lost touch with what 'normal' means, and see nothing unusual or problematic about living on a constant examination treadmill. When this happens, learners can end up doing little more in school than 'practising the finished product' (Prestage and Perks, 2006). Sometimes the process of *revision*, which literally means 'looking again' at ideas, turns into learning previous examination papers in meticulous detail and practising cloned questions (Foster, 2005). As Holt (1990) puts it:

> Before every test we had a big cram session of practice work, politely known as "review." When they failed the exam, we had postmortems, then more review, then a makeup test (always easier than the first), which they almost always failed again.
>
> (p. 14)

The increasing prevalence of high-stakes examinations can lead to a *hidden curriculum* in which scoring points assumes greater importance in practice than learning mathematics (see chapter 14). Some of the principles of *examination technique* can hinder *relational learning* (Skemp, 1976). For instance, when you are trying to score marks in an examination, the worst thing that you can do is leave a question unanswered: guess if you have to; you have nothing to lose. In examinations, you should never express doubt or ignorance, but in the classroom admitting to being unsure can be a very positive step. Offering a wild guess because 'something is better than nothing' can be confusing for the teacher who is trying to make sense of the learner's thinking. Even beyond an educational setting, it would be better if a doctor, for instance, said that they did not know the details of some treatment and looked it up rather than guessed! Guessing is fine in pub quizzes, but in anything that really matters it is not a good idea. When coached for examinations, candidates are encouraged to use 'clues', such as the topics that have come up in recent years, or the number of marks available for the question (or the amount of space provided) to gain an idea of the complexity of the answer. In multiple-choice papers, there are reports of learners being told to select the *longest* response, because that is thought to be the most likely one to be correct, or always to put a particular letter when they don't know the answer, because that letter is thought to be correct slightly more often than the others. Those who set multiple-choice tests often do so naïvely (Burton, 2005), and when teachers hear that colleagues, perhaps at other schools, are 'preparing' learners in this way, it can be hard for them to stick to their principles for fear of disadvantaging their learners. The approaches in examination marking of *error-carried-forward* and *ignore-subsequent-working* can give a false impression of competence. For example, when a learner correctly simplifies an expression to $5a + 2b$ but then *incorrectly* 'simplifies' this to $7ab$, choosing to recognize what is correct but ignore clear evidence of a misconception would seem to be simply dishonest.

Task Facts

Teach these boys and girls nothing but Facts. Facts alone are wanted in life. Plant nothing else, and root out everything else. You can only form the minds of reasoning animals upon Facts: nothing else will ever be of any service to them.

Dickens (2000: 3)

How important do you think it is to teach *mathematical facts*? Why?
How do you help learners to remember them?

Many mathematics teachers would say that there is a place for learning key facts. Knowing multiplication tables helps with factorizing: $72 = 8 \times 9 = 2^3 \times 3^2$, although modern calculators can do this at the touch of a few buttons. Memorizing trigonometric identities, such as $\sin(A \pm B) \equiv \sin A \cos B \pm \cos A \sin B$, can enable learners, for instance, to spot that $\sin 30° \cos 45° + \cos 30° \sin 45°$ is just $\sin 75°$, saving a lot of calculation. The assumption that rote learning and learning for understanding are mutually exclusive has been challenged as a Western way of thinking (Kember, 2000). Ollerton and Watson (2001) point out that:

> Sometimes mechanical knowledge, such as rote-learnt methods, can lead to insight about meanings and understanding. For example, knowing the rhythms of the eleven-times table can help students become curious about its structure, and can offer a way to learn more about place value when the rhythm breaks down for larger numbers.
>
> (p. 7)

When you have a poem 'committed to heart', you may be better positioned to appreciate some of its qualities; in a similar way, when you know the first so-many square numbers, without having to worry about working them out, you may be more likely to notice that none of them ends in 2, 3, 7 or 8. Noddings (2003: 123) advises that 'Drill should be used judiciously – to routinize skills that will make the learning of important concepts easier and more enjoyable'.

When fluency is being developed, practice may indeed 'make perfect'. However, as Holt (1990) puts it:

> the notion that if a child repeats a meaningless statement or process enough times it will become meaningful is as absurd as the notion that if a parrot imitates human speech long enough it will know what it is talking about.
>
> (p. 193)

Textbooks and revision guides can encourage an over-dependence on *mnemonics* and 'tricks' for short-term 'success', rather than promote the development of deeper understanding. In some mathematics lessons, following and attempting to remember given facts and techniques can completely take over. Some mathematics classroom walls are plastered with memory aids such as SOHCAHTOA for trigonometry or BODMAS (or similar) for the priority of operations. According to Ariely (2010), acronyms are popular because they:

> confer a kind of secret insider knowledge; they give people a way to talk about an idea in shorthand. They increase the perceived importance of ideas, and at the same time they also help keep other ideas from entering the inner circle.
>
> (p. 120)

Adams (1962: 269) found that 'the mnemonic device did not appear to help either rote or meaningful learning'; however, Scruggs and Mastropieri (2000) disagree. For some mathematics teachers, an ACRONYM may simply be *A Cruel Reminder Of Needing Your Memory*, and BODMAS may also be satirized as *Beware Of Dubious Memory-Assistance Schemes*! When such things are imposed by the teacher, they may just become extra baggage for learners to carry around. However, when learners are involved in creating them, then even something as apparently unwieldy as remembering the word 'tectonics' by using 'thick earth crust, the oceanic, nudged in currents, subducted' might work (Brown, 2009: 46)! Constructing a *mind map* (*mind association diagram*) may be useful for a learner, whereas using (still less, copying out) somebody else's is probably less so. However, a concern with all such memory work is how permanent it will be. Holt (1990: 289) comments that 'The only difference between bad and good students ... is that the bad students forget right away, while the good students are careful to wait until after the exam'.

Task Memory

MNEMONICS: Mnemonics Neatly Eliminate Man's Only Nemesis – Insufficient Cerebral Storage

Anon.

TIIAF = twelve inches in a foot
SDIAW = seven days in a week
Make up some other ones and see if someone else can decode them.

Gattegno (1987) coined the term *ogden* to represent one unit of 'memorizing energy' needed to remember 'one fact', and calculated the number of ogdens needed, for instance, in order to know the number names up to, say, 100 (Gattegno, 2010). Because of the redundancy in these words, it costs relatively few ogdens. It is possible to look at the mathematics curriculum as a mixture of the *arbitrary* and the *necessary* (Hewitt, 2001). Things that are arbitrary (e.g., that there are 360° in one revolution) must be communicated to learners somehow and remembered, whereas things that are necessary (e.g., that the total interior angle of a plane triangle is the same as that of half a revolution) can be found out and, if forgotten, can be worked out again (see page 134). It is interesting to consider what makes something memorable or not. Even a mathematics teacher who knows the first 50 digits of π may struggle to remember their four-digit security PIN. It is not simply how important the person perceives it to be, how recently it was learned or how often it was rehearsed. It may be that *remembering* feels like a natural process whereas *memorizing* feels artificial. The forced repetition of methods or processes that are not meaningful to a learner is oppressive (think of brain-washing cults), and it is a more positive approach to try to create *memorable learning experiences* than to find ways of making the forgettable stick. The brain has natural defences against becoming overloaded with the wash of sense data that we meet in our daily lives, and it may be unwise to try to circumvent this too often.

Feynman *et al.* (2011) point out that experts may remember far less than learners think that they do. Feynman comments that when learning any mathematical subject the teacher gives a proof:

> in such form that it can be written quickly and easily on the chalkboard or on paper, and so that it will be as smooth-looking as possible. Consequently, the proof may look deceptively simple, when in fact, the author might have worked for hours trying different ways of calculating the same thing until he has found the neatest way. ... It is certain that in all the demonstrations that are made in a course such as this, not one has been remembered from the time when the author studied. ... Quite the contrary: he merely remembers that such and such is true, and to explain how it can be shown he invents a demonstration at the moment it is needed. Anyone who has really learned a subject should be able to follow a similar procedure, but it is no use remembering the proofs.
>
> (p. 14-1)

The days when learners memorized, line-by-line, geometrical proofs that neither they nor their teachers understood are happily past, but it is far from clear that modern learners of mathematics are any better prepared to invent 'a demonstration at the moment it is needed', as Feynman puts it.

Hogben (1938) believes:

> that the teacher who ... takes the trouble to stimulate his pupils by devoting a substantial part of his time to topics which lie quite outside the syllabus will get better examination results than the teacher who keeps one eye glued on the syllabus.
>
> (p. 113)

Another approach would be to get involved with writing questions, or marking papers, for an awarding body. You may gain some valuable experience, earn a little extra money and eventually be in a position to improve things from the inside. Holt (1990: 167) comments that 'when learning happens, the school and teachers take the credit; when it doesn't, the students get the blame. ... Only when the results are good will schools and teachers accept the responsibility for what they do'. Rather than blaming examiners for what they do, a more positive response is to participate in the process.

15.3 Career

> Be nice to those you meet on the way up. They're the same folks you'll meet on the way down.
>
> Walter Winchell

For some people, to categorize teaching as a 'career' is to downgrade it from what they prefer to see as a 'vocation'. Many mathematics graduates will be well aware that they could earn far more money in other professions and have consciously turned their backs on high salaries in order to do something that they enjoy or believe is important. Such teachers may not be as motivated for promotion as their colleagues, especially if that entails less classroom teaching, so it should not be assumed that all enthusiastic mathematics teachers want to lead a department or become a senior manager or head. Some will want to, however, or to seek further challenges on the pastoral side of school as a year head or equivalent, or in special educational needs. Others will feel that their strengths lie in the classroom and that they would be wasted sitting behind a desk sending emails and organizing spreadsheets.

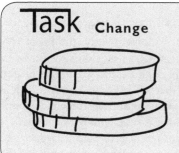

Task Change

According to a newspaper (Wheal, 2010), a survey claimed that people in the UK find £57 million of lost change every year.

How do you think this figure could have been arrived at?
Is it a plausible amount?

Change will be a part of every teacher's career, and some aspects are considered under the following three headings.

15.3.1 Open-mindedness

> To every action, there is a corresponding over-reaction.
>
> Newton's third law of management (Anon.)

It is wise to take and make opportunities at work to try different things so that you can see what you enjoy and are successful at. Spending time in different schools or in other places where mathematics teachers work can be eye-opening.

Task Schools

Think about the different schools that you have experience of.

What are their similarities and differences?
What different approaches to teaching mathematics have you seen?
Might you be able to arrange to see a school in another area or another country?

Not every mathematics teacher will want to visit a school during their holidays, but some might. Sometimes funding is available to support a teacher who wants to travel in order to develop their practice or do some research. Comparative studies between mathematics lessons in different settings can be fascinating (Andrews and Sayers, 2006). Helping with extracurricular activities (either in school or at a local youth group) can give you a wider perspective on young people, and most schools will have sporting, drama or musical activities where an additional member of staff will be much appreciated. You might notice a gap in what is offered and be able to contribute something different.

15.3.2 Colleagues

I never repeat gossip – so please listen carefully the first time.

Sign seen in a school office

Developing a reputation among colleagues as a professional and trusted equal is as important as being respected among learners. Opportunities may open up for people who are a pleasure to work with, and volunteering to chair a working group or lead a trip can be a good way to test out whether you enjoy leading colleagues. When you are applying for a job, such experiences are useful to talk about at interview, and give whoever is writing your reference something interesting to say. Being professional and reliable marks you out as useful to have around. Schools can be frantic places, with people rushing from place to place amid a variety of stresses. Among this, those teachers who somehow manage to find time to listen to colleagues and take interest in them, whether it is stopping to help someone when the photocopier has jammed or listening when someone has had a 'bad' lesson, are wonderful. Spending time chatting to colleagues at break times, rather than rushing off to get something done, can be time very well spent, and help both you and them to avoid burning out.

15.3.3 Moving forwards

The future isn't what it used to be.

Yogi Berra

The *Pareto principle* suggests that most people spend a lot of time on things that, in the long run, don't matter very much. Deciding which things are genuinely worth focusing time and energy on and which things aren't is anything but easy. For most mathematics teachers, learning more mathematics and improving our teaching of mathematics is both enjoyable and clearly a priority, though it may lack the urgency of other matters!

Task Special lesson

Suppose that somebody is coming to watch one of your mathematics lessons, or you are doing a lesson as part of a job interview.

Would you do anything differently from normal?
Do you have a 'best' lesson? If so, what makes it special for you?
If you had to teach a 'show-off' lesson (e.g., for an interview), and had completely free choice, what would you do?

Many teachers have 'party piece' lessons, which often involve a great deal of preparation or consume a lot of teacher energy to 'perform'. These get wheeled out when there are visitors or inspectors in the classroom. Colleagues can feel intimidated when they watch a lesson like this, whether in real life or on film, because it may seem in another league completely from the sorts of lessons they routinely teach, but they forget that such lessons are exceptional. Teachers in recordings used for professional development, for instance, are likely to have been chosen (or volunteered) because someone thinks that they are particularly good, and they are unlikely to be working off-the-cuff. A lot can be learned from outstanding lessons, but it is important to realize that they do not represent ordinary daily life. Just as newspaper stories of terrible crimes should not lead us to believe that criminals are everywhere, similarly one-off all-singing-all-dancing lessons should not make us feel that every teacher should be doing that all the time.

Task Aging teacher

A mathematics teacher says: 'I am 10^n seconds old, where n is an integer!' What is the value of n?

The best way to develop is in partnership with other interested and like-minded colleagues. Belonging to a local branch of a professional association such as the *Association of Teachers of Mathematics* or the *Mathematical Association*, or signing up for an Master's qualification with a local higher education institution, or working towards *Chartered Mathematics Teacher* status, can give a focus to your development. All teachers should also belong to a trade union, and these also have useful publications and courses for professional development.

Enthusiastic and expert mathematics teachers are a vital part of a school and of society. I hope that this book has helped you along your journey and I wish you the very best in your career.

Task Summary task

God grant me the serenity
To accept the things I cannot change;
The courage to change the things I can
And the wisdom to know the difference.

Reinhold Niebuhr

What do you see as the main constraints at the moment that frustrate you as a mathematics teacher?

To what extent are they shared by your colleagues?

Do you think that they are surmountable in some way or are they immovables that you must learn to live with?

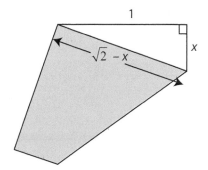

Figure 15.1 Creating a pentagon

Comments on mathematical tasks

Task: Pentagon

The pentagon has two sides of unit length and, by symmetry, the two shorter lengths must be equal. If we call these lengths x, then we can label as shown in Figure 15.1.

Using Pythagoras's theorem in the right-angled triangle reveals that $x = \dfrac{\sqrt{2}}{4}$, so the fold has split the long side of the A4 paper in the ratio 1:3. Further calculation leads to the pentagon perimeter being $\dfrac{1}{2}(4 + \sqrt{2} + \sqrt{6})$ and the area $\dfrac{5\sqrt{2}}{8}$; making it $\dfrac{5}{8}$ of the area of the original paper. A nice feature of working in this way is that you can verify that your length calculations are approximately correct by scaling up by a factor of 21 cm (the length of the unit side of a piece of A4 paper) and measuring your folded sheet to see that you are about right. For more problems of this kind, see Foster (2008).

Task: Cover the spot

Implicit in the question is the idea that the task should be *difficult but possible*. It is *just* possible with the discs shown, where the ratio of disc diameter to spot diameter is 1:1.62 (Figure 15.2). In practice, though, the discs probably need to be slightly larger than this, to give the players a sporting chance! The 'magic number' is just slightly less than the golden ratio 1.61803... (Neville, 1915). With fewer than five discs, it is possible to calculate the critical ratio exactly; with more than five discs, values have been found from computer simulation. Covering other shapes with circles has also been studied (Galiev and Karpova, 2010).

Task: Aging teacher

Only $n = 9$ is realistic!

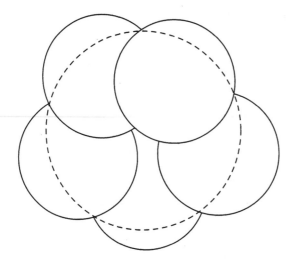

Figure 15.2 Just *covering the spot*

Further resources

Membership of the *Association of Teachers of Mathematics* and the *Mathematical Association* will give you access to fantastic journals, annual conferences and perhaps local groups of mathematics teachers near where you live or work. A school would be very well advised to pay the fees for interested members of their mathematics department.
www.atm.org.uk
www.m-a.org.uk

References

Abraham, J. (2008) 'Pupils' perceptions of setting and beyond—a response to Hallam and Ireson', *British Educational Research Journal*, 34(6), 855–63.

Acheson, D. (2010) *1089 and All That: a journey into mathematics*, Oxford: Oxford University Press.

Adams, P.E. and Krockover, G.H. (1997) 'Concerns and perceptions of beginning secondary science and mathematics teachers', *Science Education*, 81:29–50.

Adams, S. (1962) 'How good is a prescribed mnemonic device in learning textbook content?', *Journal of Educational Research*, 55(6), 267–71.

Ainley, J. (1988) 'Perceptions of teachers' questioning styles', in A. Borbás (ed.) *Proceedings of the 12th Annual Meeting of the International Group for the Psychology of Mathematics Education*, Veszprém, Hungary, pp. 92–9.

Ainley, J., Pratt, D. and Hansen, A. (2006) 'Connecting engagement and focus in pedagogic task design', *British Educational Research Journal*, 32(1), 23–38.

Anderson, J. (1995) 'Patterns which aren't, are!', *Mathematics in School*, 24(2), 20–2.

Andrews, P. (1998) 'Peddling the myth', *Mathematics in School,* 27(2), 2–4.

Andrews, P. and Sayers, J. (2006) 'Mathematics teaching in four European countries', *Mathematics Teaching Incorporating Micromath*, 196, 34–8.

Archimedes (1960) 'The sand reckoner' in J.R. Newman (ed.) *The World of Mathematics*, vol. I, London: George Allen and Unwin Ltd, pp. 420–9.

Ariely, D. (2010) *The Upside of Irrationality: the unexpected benefits of defying logic at work and at home*, London: HarperCollins.

Armstrong, T. (2009) *Multiple Intelligences in the Classroom*, Alexandria, Virginia: Association for Supervision and Curriculum Development.

Askew, M. (2008) 'Social identities as learners and teachers of mathematics', in A. Watson and P. Winbourne (eds) *New Directions for Situated Cognition in Mathematics Education,* New York: Springer, pp. 59–78.

Association of Teachers of Mathematics (1991) *Language and Mathematics*, Derby: Association of Teachers of Mathematics.

Babad, E. (1993) 'Pygmalion—25 years after interpersonal expectations in the classroom', in P.D. Blanck (ed.) *Interpersonal Expectations: theory, research, and application*, New York: Cambridge University Press, pp. 125–53.

Ball, D.L. (1992) 'Magical hopes: manipulatives and the reform of mathematics education', *American Educator*, 16(2), 46–7.

Ball, S.J. (1997) 'Better read: theorising the teacher', in J. Dillon and M. Maguire (eds) *Becoming a Teacher: issues in secondary teaching*, Buckingham: Open University Press, pp. 239–50.

Banwell, C.S., Saunders, K.D. and Tahta, D.S. (1986) *Starting Points for Teaching Mathematics in Middle and Secondary Schools*, Norfolk: Tarquin Publications.

Bauersfeld, H. (1995) '"Language games" in the mathematics classroom: their function and their effects', in P. Cobb and H. Bauersfeld (eds) *The Emergence of Mathematical Meaning: interaction in classroom cultures*, Hove: L. Erlbaum Associates.

Baxter, J.A. and Williams, S. (2010) 'Social and analytic scaffolding in middle school mathematics: managing the dilemma of telling', *Journal of Mathematics Teacher Education*, 13, 7–26.

BBC News (2007) 'Food cravings battle "pointless"', Monday 22 October, *BBC News*. Online. Available HTTP: <http://news.bbc.co.uk/1/hi/7056330.stm> (accessed 12 December 2011).

BECTA (2010) *'I'm stuck, can you help me?': a report into parents' involvement in school work at home*, BECTA. Online. Available HTTP: <http://webarchive.nationalarchives.gov.uk/20101102103713/http://publications.becta.org.uk/download.cfm?resID=42205> (accessed 1 November 2011).

Beswick, K. (2007) 'Teachers' beliefs that matter in secondary mathematics classrooms', *Educational Studies in Mathematics*, 65(1), 95–120.

Bills, C., Bills, L., Watson, A. and Mason, J. (2004) *Thinkers: a collection of activities to provoke mathematical thinking*, Derby: Association of Teachers of Mathematics.

Bird, R. (2007) *The Dyscalculia Toolkit: supporting learning difficulties in maths*, London: Paul Chapman.

Black, P., Harrison, C., Lee, C., Marshall, B. and Wiliam, D. (2003) *Assessment for Learning: putting it into practice*, Maidenhead: Open University Press.

Boaler, J. (1993) 'The role of contexts in the mathematics classroom: do they make mathematics more "real"?', *For the Learning of Mathematics*, 13(2), 12–17.

Boaler, J. (1997) *Experiencing School Mathematics: teaching styles, sex and setting*, Buckingham: Open University Press.

Boaler, J. (2005) 'Setting by ability does not work', Thursday 10 February, *The Independent*. Online. Available HTTP: <http://www.independent.co.uk/news/education/education-news/jo-boaler-setting-by-ability-does-not-work-482628.html> (accessed 12 December 2011).

Boaler, J. (2010) *The Elephant in the Classroom: helping children learn and love maths*, London: Souvenir Press Ltd.

Boaler, J., Wiliam, D. and Brown, M. (2000) 'Students' experiences of ability grouping—disaffection, polarisation and the construction of failure', *British Educational Research Journal*, 26(5), 631–48.

Boole, M.E. (1931) 'Teacher-lust', in E.M. Cobham (ed.) *Mary Everest Boole: collected works*, volume 4, London: C.W. Daniel, pp. 1411–13.

Boorman, P. (1997) 'Believing is seeing', *Mathematics Teaching*, 160, 38–43.

Borovik, A.V. and Gardiner, T. (2007) 'Mathematical Abilities and Mathematical Skills', World Federation of National Mathematics Competitions, Conference 2006, Cambridge, England, 22–28 July 2006. Online. Available HTTP: <http://www.maths.manchester.ac.uk/~avb/pdf/abilities2007.pdf> (accessed 13 November 2011).

Bouvier, A. (1987) 'The right to make mistakes', *For the Learning of Mathematics*, 7(3), 17–25.

Brooke, M. (1980) 'Limerick-gimerick', *Word Ways*, (13)1, 10.

Brown, K. (2009) *Classroom Starters and Plenaries: creative ideas for use across the curriculum*, London: Continuum International Publishing Group Ltd.

Brown, L. and Coles, A. (2008) *Hearing Silence: learning to teach mathematics*, London: Black Apollo Press.

Brown, L., Hewitt, D. and Tahta, D. (eds) (1989) *A Gattegno Anthology: selected articles by Caleb Gattegno reprinted from Mathematics Teaching*, Derby: Association of Teachers of Mathematics.

Bruner, J.S. (1966) *Towards a Theory of Instruction*, New York: Norton.

Bruner, J.S. (1986) *Actual Minds: possible worlds*, London: Harvard University Press.

Bruner, J.S. (1999) *The Process of Education*, Cambridge, MA: Harvard University Press.

Bruner, J.S. (2002) 'Tenets to understand a cultural perspective on learning', in B. Moon, A.S. Mayes and S. Hutchinson (eds) *Teaching, Learning and the Curriculum in Secondary Schools*, London: RoutledgeFalmer, pp. 10–24.

Brunsma, D.L. (2004) *The School Uniform Movement and What it Tells us About American Education: a symbolic crusade*, Oxford: Scarecrow Education.

Burger, W.F. and Shaughnessy, J.M. (1986) 'Characterizing the Van Hiele levels of development in geometry', *Journal for Research in Mathematics Education*, 17, 31–48.

Burton, R.F. (2005) 'Multiple choice and true/false tests: myths and misapprehensions', *Assessment & Evaluation in Higher Education*, 30(1), 65–72.

Candela, A. (1998) 'Students' power in classroom discourse', *Linguistics and Education*, 10(2), 139–63.

Carr, M. and Claxton, G. (2002) 'Tracking the development of learning dispositions', *Assessment in Education: principles, policy and practice*, 9(1), 9–37.

Casement, P. (1990) *Further Learning from the Patient*, London: Routledge.

Chapman, D.W. and Lowther, M.A. (1982) 'Teachers' satisfaction with teaching', *The Journal of Educational Research*, 75(4), 241–7.

Chesterton, G.K. (2006) *The Complete Father Brown Stories*, London: Wordsworth Classics.

Chinn, S.J. (2004) *The Trouble with Maths: a practical guide to helping learners with numeracy difficulties*, London: RoutledgeFalmer.

Chinn, S.J. (2010) *Addressing the Unproductive Classroom Behaviours of Students with Special Needs*, London: Jessica Kingsley.

Clausen-May, T. (2001) *An Approach to Test Development*, Berkshire: National Foundation for Educational Research.

Clausen-May, T. (2005) *Teaching Maths to Pupils with Different Learning Styles*, London: Paul Chapman.

Claxton, G. (2005) *An Intelligent Look at Emotional Intelligence: a publication commissioned by the Association of Teachers and Lecturers*, London: Association of Teachers and Lecturers.

Clayton, M.K. and Forton, M.B. (2001) *Classroom Spaces That Work*, Greenfield, MA: Northeast Foundation for Children.

Cohen, G.A. (2001) *If You're an Egalitarian, How Come You're So Rich?*, Cambridge, MA: Harvard University Press.

Collins, A., Brown, J.S. and Holum, A. (1991) 'Cognitive apprenticeship: making thinking visible', *American Educator*, 15(3), 6–11, 38–46.

Conway, J.H. and Guy, R.K. (1998) *The Book of Numbers*, New York: Copernicus Press.

Cooper, B. and Harries, A.V. (2002) 'Children's responses to contrasting "realistic" mathematics problems: just how realistic are children ready to be?', *Educational Studies in Mathematics*, 49(1), 1–23.

Cooper, B. and Harries, A.V. (2003) 'Children's use of realistic considerations in problem solving: some English evidence', *Journal of Mathematical Behavior*, 22(4), 451–65.

Cooper, B. and Harries, T. (2005) 'Making sense of realistic word problems: portraying working class "failure" on a division with remainder problem', *International Journal of Research & Method in Education*, 28(2), 147–69.

Cooper, C.L. and Travers, C. (1996) *Teachers Under Pressure: stress in the teaching profession*, London: Routledge.

Corey, S.M. (1940) 'The teachers out-talk the pupils', *The School Review*, 48(10), 745–52.

Cosforda, B. and Drapera, J. (2002) '"It's almost like a secondment": parenting as professional development for teachers', *Teacher Development: an international journal of teachers' professional development*, 6(3), 347–62.

David, M. and Watson, A. (2008) 'Participating in what? Using situated cognition theory to illuminate differences in classroom practices', in A. Watson and P. Winbourne (eds) *New Directions for Situated Cognition in Mathematics Education*, New York: Springer, pp. 31–56.

Davis, B. (2001) 'Why Teach Mathematics to All Students?', *For the Learning of Mathematics*, 21(1), 17–24.

Dean, B. and Joldoshalieva, R. (2007) 'Key strategies for teachers new to controversial issues', in H. Cialre and C. Holden (eds) *The Challenge of Teaching Controversial Issues*, Stoke-on-Trent: Trentham Books, pp. 175–87.

Dewey, J. (1991) *How We Think*, Buffalo, NY: Prometheus Books.

Dickens, C. (2000) *Hard Times*, Hertfordshire: Wordsworth Editions Limited.

Dillon, J.T. (1988) 'The remedial status of student questioning', *Journal of Curriculum Studies*, 20(3), 197–210.

Dudeney, H.E. (1970) *Amusements in Mathematics*, New York: Dover Publications.

du Sautoy, M. (2008) *The Story of Maths* (DVD), The OpenLearn team, The Open University. Online. Available HTTP: <http://www.open.ac.uk/openlearn/whats-on/ou-on-the-bbc-the-story-maths-the-language-the-universe?page=2> (accessed 6 November 2011).

Dweck, C.S. (1999) 'Caution—praise can be dangerous', *American Educator*, 23(1), 4–9.

Dweck, C.S. (2000) *Self-Theories: their role in motivation, personality, and development*, Philadelphia: Taylor & Francis.

Dweck, C. (2010) 'Mind-sets and equitable education', *Principal Leadership*, 10(5), 26–9. Online. Available HTTP: <http://www.my-ecoach.com/online/resources/3865/Equitable_Mindsets.pdf> (accessed 18 October 2011).

Eastaway, R. and Askew, M. (2010) *Maths for Mums and Dads*, London: Square Peg.

Edwards, D. and Mercer, N. (1987) *Common Knowledge: the development of understanding in the classroom*, London: Methuen.

Elton, L. (2004) 'Goodhart's law and performance indicators in higher education', *Evaluation & Research in Education*, 18(1–2), 120–8.

Ernest, P. (1986) 'Games: a rationale for their use in the teaching of mathematics in school', *Mathematics in School*, 15(1), 2–5.

Ernest, P. (1999) 'Forms of knowledge in mathematics and mathematics education: philosophical and rhetorical perspectives', *Educational Studies in Mathematics*, 38, 67–83.

Ernest, P. (2000) 'Why teach mathematics?', in J. White and S. Bramall (eds) *Why Learn Maths?*, London: London University Institute of Education, pp. 1–14. Online. Available HTTP: <http://webdoc.sub.gwdg.de/edoc/e/pome/why.htm> (accessed 20 May 2011).

Ernest, P. (2011a) *Mathematics and Special Educational Needs*, Saarbrucken, Germany: Lambert Academic Publishing.

Ernest, P. (2011b) *The Psychology of Learning Mathematics*, Saarbrucken, Germany: Lambert Academic Publishing.

Fairbrother, B. (1997) 'Assessing pupils', in J. Dillon and M. Maguire (eds) *Becoming a Teacher: issues in secondary teaching*, Buckingham: Open University Press, pp. 160–74.

Feynman, R.P. (1992) *Surely You're Joking, Mr Feynman!*, London: Vintage.

Feynman, R.P., Leighton, R.B. and Sands, M. (2011) *Feynman Lectures on Physics: mainly mechanics, radiation, and heat: volume 1*, New York: Basic Books.

Fleming, N. and Baume, D. (2006) 'Learning styles again: VARKing up the right tree!', *Educational Developments*, SEDA Ltd, 7(4), 4–7. Online. Available HTTP: <http://www.vark-learn.com/documents/Educational%20Developments.pdf> (accessed 6 November 2011).

Forster, E.M. and Gardner, P. (1988) *Commonplace Book*, London: Scolar Press.

Foster, C. (2005) 'Another look at revision', *Mathematics Teaching*, 191, 6–7.

Foster, C. (2007) 'Mathematical behaviour', *Mathematics Teaching*, 202, 12–13.

Foster, C. (2008) *50 Mathematics Lessons: rich and engaging ideas for secondary mathematics*, London: Continuum.

Foster, C. (2009) *Mathematics for Every Occasion*, Derby: Association of Teachers of Mathematics.

Foster, C. (2011a) 'Productive ambiguity in the learning of mathematics', *For the Learning of Mathematics*, 31(2), 3–7.

Foster, C. (2011b) 'Marking time', *Mathematics Teaching*, 222, 3–6.

Fox, D. (1983) 'Personal theories of teaching', *Studies in Higher Education*, 8(2), 151–63.

Galiev, S. and Karpova, M. (2010) 'Optimization of multiple covering of a bounded set with circles', *Computational Mathematics and Mathematical Physics*, 50(4), 721–32.

Gardiner, A. (2004) 'What is mathematical literacy?', paper presented at the lecture given at the ICME-10 conference in Copenhagen, Denmark, July, 2004.

Gardner, H. (2006) *Multiple Intelligences: new horizons*, New York: Basic Books.

Gardner, M. (2005) *The Colossal Book of Short Puzzles and Problems*, London: W. W. Norton & Co.

Gattegno, C. (1987) *The Science of Education*, New York: Educational Solutions.

Gattegno, C. (2010) *What We Owe Children*, New York: Educational Solutions Worldwide Inc.

Gawande, A. (2003) *Complications: a surgeon's notes on an imperfect science*, London: Profile Books Ltd.

Gilligan, C. (1982) *In a Different Voice*, Cambridge, MA: Harvard University Press.

Glasersfeld, E. von (1995) *Radical Constructivism: a way of knowing and learning*, London: The Falmer Press.

Goldacre, B. (2006) 'Brain gym exercises do pupils no favours', Saturday 18 March, *The Guardian*. Available HTTP: <http://www.guardian.co.uk/commentisfree/2006/mar/18/comment.badscience> (accessed 13 November 2011).

Goos, M. (2004) 'Learning mathematics in a classroom community of inquiry', *Journal for Research in Mathematics Education*, 35(4), 258–91.

Gore, J., Williams, C. and Ladwig, J. (2006) 'On the place of pedagogy in the induction of early career teachers', Paper prepared for presentation at the Australian Association for Research in Education Annual Conference, Adelaide. Online. Available HTTP: <http://aare.edu.au/06pap/gor06387.pdf> (accessed 12 December 2011).

Goulding, M., Rowland, T. and Barber, P. (2002) 'Does it matter? Primary teacher trainees' subject knowledge in mathematics', *British Educational Research Journal*, 28(5), 689–704.

Grambs, J.D. (1952) 'The sociology of the "born teacher"', *Journal of Educational Sociology*, 25(9), 532–41.

Greenwood, R.E. (1977) 'The numbers of isomers of the alkanes and the aliphatic alcohols', *The Mathematical Gazette*, 61(417), 220–3.

Grosholz, E. (2007) *Representation and Productive Ambiguity in Mathematics and the Sciences*, Oxford: Oxford University Press.

Grugnetti, L. and Rogers, L. (2000) 'Philosophical, multicultural and interdisciplinary issues', in J. Fauvel and J. van Maanen (eds) *History in Mathematics Education: the ICMI study*, Dordrecht: Kluwer Academic Publishers, pp. 39–62.

Guardino, C.A. and Fullerton, E. (2010) 'Changing behaviors by changing the classroom environment', *Teaching Exceptional Children*, 42(6), 8–13.

Gutiérrez, A., Jaime, A. and Fortuny, J.M. (1991) 'An alternative paradigm to evaluate the acquisition of the Van Hiele levels', *Journal for Research in Mathematics Education*, 21(3), 237–51.

Hallam, S. (2002) *Ability Grouping in Schools: a literature review: perspectives on education policy*, London: Institute of Education, University of London.

Hamming, R.W. (1980) 'The unreasonable effectiveness of mathematics', *The American Mathematical Monthly*, 87(2), 81–90.

Hamming, R.W. (1998) 'Mathematics on a Distant Planet', *The American Mathematical Monthly*, 105(7), 640–50.

Hanna, G. (1990) 'Some pedagogical aspects of proof', *Interchange*, 2(1), 6–13.

Hanna, G. (2003) 'Reaching gender equity in mathematics education', *Educational Forum*, 67(3), 204–14.

Harré, R. and van Langenhove, L. (1998) 'The dynamics of social episodes', in R. Harré and L. van Langenhove (eds) *Positioning Theory: moral contexts of intentional action*, Oxford: Blackwell, pp. 1–13.

Hart, K.M. (2005) *Children's Understanding of Mathematics: 11–16*, Eastbourne: Antony Rowe Publishing Services.

Hewitt, D. (2001) 'Arbitrary and necessary: a way of viewing the mathematics curriculum', in L. Haggarty (ed.) *Teaching Mathematics in Secondary Schools: a reader*, London: Routledge Falmer, pp. 47–63.

Hewitt, D. (2008) 'A function machine', *Mathematics Teaching Incorporating Micromath*, 211, 3–6.

Heymann, H.W. (2003) *Why Teach Mathematics?: a focus on general education*, London: Kluwer Academic Publishers.

Hines, T. (1987) 'Left brain/right brain mythology and implications for management and training', *The Academy of Management Review*, 12(4), 600–6.

Hodgen, J. (2007) 'Setting, streaming and mixed-ability teaching', in J. Dillon and M. Maguire (eds) *Becoming a Teacher: issues in secondary teaching*, 3rd edn, Maidenhead: Open University Press, pp. 201–12.

Hofstadter, D.R. (2000) *Gödel, Escher, Bach: an eternal golden braid*, London: Penguin.

Hogben, L. (1938) 'Clarity is not enough', *The Mathematical Gazette*, 22(249), 105–22.

Holt, J. (1967) *How Children Learn*, New York: Pitman.

Holt, J. (1990) *How Children Fail*, London: Penguin.

Hough, S. and Gough, S. (2007) 'Realistic mathematics education', *Mathematics Teaching Incorporating Micromath*, 203, 34–8.

Houssart, J. (2009) 'Unofficial talk in mathematics classrooms', in J. Houssart and J. Mason (eds) *Listening Counts: listening to young learners of mathematics*, Stoke-on-Trent: Trentham Books.

Huckstep, P. (2003) 'Why should I learn algebra?... I've no intention of going there!', *Mathematics in School*, 32(4), 16–18.

Hughes, M. and Greenhough, P. (2008) '"We do it a different way at my school": mathematics homework as a site for tension and conflict', in A. Watson and P. Winbourne (eds) *New Directions for Situated Cognition in Mathematics Education,* New York: Springer.

Hutchings, M. (1996) 'What will you do when you grow up?: the social construction of children's occupational preferences', *Citizenship, Social and Economics Education*, 1(1), 15–30.

Hyatt, K.J. (2007) 'Brain gym®: building stronger brains or wishful thinking?', *Remedial and Special Education*, 28(2), 117–24.

Inan, H.Z. (2009) 'The third dimension in preschools: preschool environments and classroom design', *European Journal of Educational Studies*, 1(1), 55–66.

Jackson, P. (2002) 'Life in classrooms', in B. Moon, A.S. Mayes and S. Hutchinson (eds) *Teaching, Learning and the Curriculum in Secondary Schools*, London: RoutledgeFalmer, pp. 119–23.

Jarvis, M. (2002) 'Teacher stress', *Stress News*, 2002, 14(1). Online. Available HTTP: <http://teachersupport.info/news/well-being/teacher-stress.php> (accessed 12 December 2011).

Johnston-Wilder, P. (2010) 'Using research evidence to innovate, change and improve learning', in S. Johnston-Wilder and C.S. Lee (eds) *Leading Practice and Managing Change in the Mathematics Department: a resource book for subject leaders in mathematics*, St Albans: Tarquin Publications.

Johnston-Wilder, S. and Lee, C. (2010) 'Mathematical resilience', *Mathematics Teaching*, 218, 38–41.

Kaluza, R. (2005) *Through a Reporter's Eyes: the life of Stefan Banach*, Boston: Birkhauser.

Kember, D. (2000) 'Misconceptions about the learning approaches, motivation and study practices of Asian students', *Higher Education*, 40, 99–121.

Khisty, L.L. and Chval, K.B. (2002) 'Pedagogic discourse and equity in mathematics: when teachers' talk matters', *Mathematics Education Research Journal*, 14(3), 154–68.

King, A. (1993) 'From sage on the stage to guide on the side', *College Teaching*, 41(1), 30–5.

Kline, M. (1956) 'Mathematics texts and teachers: a tirade', *Mathematics Teacher*, 49(3), 162–72.

Kline, M. (1976) *Why Johnny Can't Add: failure of the new mathematics*, London: St James Press.

Klymchuk, S. (2010) *Counterexamples in Calculus*, Washington, DC: The Mathematical Association of America, Inc.

Kounin, J.S. (1970) *Discipline and Group Management in Classrooms*, New York: Holt, Rinehart and Winston.

Krathwohl, D.R. (2002) 'A revision of Bloom's taxonomy: an overview', *Theory into Practice*, 41(4), 212–8.

Küchemann, D. (2010) 'Using patterns generically to see structure', *Pedagogies: an international journal*, 5(3), 233–50.

Lave, J. (1988) *Cognition in Practice: mind, mathematics and culture in everyday life*, Cambridge: Cambridge University Press.

Lave, J. and Wenger, E. (1991) *Situated Learning: legitimate peripheral participation*, Cambridge: Cambridge University Press.

Leder, G. and Forgasz, H. (2003) 'Achievement self-rating and the gender stereotyping of mathematics', in L. Bragg, C. Campbell, G. Herbert and J. Mousley (eds) *Mathematics Education Research: innovation, networking, opportunity* (Sydney, MERGA), pp. 476–83.

Lepper, M.R. (1988) 'Motivational considerations in the study of instruction', *Cognition and Instruction*, 5(4), 289–309.

Little, C. (2011a) 'How "real" are real-world contexts in A level mathematics problems?', *Mathematics in School*, 40(1), 13–15.

Little, C. (2011b) 'What makes a context for an A/AS mathematics question real?', *Mathematics in School*, 40(3), 11–13.

Litwiller, B.H. and Duncan, D.R. (1981) 'Length, perimeter and area: comparisons on rectangular and isometric graph paper', *Mathematics in School*, 10(1), 23–5.

Loewenstein, G. and Small, D.A. (2007) 'The scarecrow and the tin man: the vicissitudes of human sympathy and caring', *Review of General Psychology*, 11, 112–26.

Lotan, R. (2003) 'Group-worthy tasks', *Educational Leadership*, 60(6), 72–5.

Lucas, J.R. (1980) *On Justice*, Oxford: Oxford University Press.

McCallum, B., Hargreaves, E. and Gipps, C. (2000) 'Learning: the pupil's voice', *Cambridge Journal of Education*, 30(2), 275–89.

McCulloch, G. (2009) 'The moral universe of Mr Chips: veteran teachers in British literature and drama', *Teachers and Teaching: theory and practice*, 15(4), 409–20.

McNamara, D. (1991) 'Subject knowledge and its application: problems and possibilities for teacher educators', *Journal of Education for Teaching*, 17(2), 113–28.

McNiff, J. (2002) *Action Research for Professional Development: concise advice for new action researchers*, 3rd edn. Online. Available HTTP: <http://www.jeanmcniff.com/ar-booklet.asp> (accessed 25 October 2011).

Maguire, M. and Dillon, J. (1997) 'Teacher education', in J. Dillon and M. Maguire (eds) *Becoming a Teacher: issues in secondary teaching*, Buckingham: Open University Press, pp. 29–38.

Mahon, M. (1992) *Foucault's Nietzschean Genealogy: truth, power and the subject*, Albany: SUNY.

Martin, C. (2011) *Big Ideas: a holistic scheme for pupils aged 11–12*, Derby: Association of Teachers of Mathematics.

Mason, A.P. and Murphy, B. (1999) 'Triplets', *Mathematics in School*, 28(1), 29.

Mason, J. (1999) *Learning and Doing Mathematics*, 2nd edn, York: QED.

Mason, J. (2000) 'Asking mathematical questions mathematically', *International Journal of Mathematical Education in Science and Technology*, 31, 97–111.

Mason, J. (2001) *Researching Your Own Practice: the discipline of noticing*, London: RoutledgeFalmer.

Mason, J. (2002) 'Minding your Qs and Rs: effective questioning and responding in the mathematics classroom', in L. Haggarty (ed.) *Aspects of Teaching Secondary Mathematics*, London: RoutledgeFalmer.

Mason, J. (2003) 'Seeing worthwhile things', *Journal of Mathematics Teacher Education*, 6(3), 281–93.

Mason, J. (2009) 'From assenting to asserting', in O. Skovsmose, P. Velero and O.R. Christensen (eds) *University Science and Mathematics Education in Transition*, New York: Springer, pp. 17–40.

Mason, J. and Johnston-Wilder, S.J. (2004) *Fundamental Constructs in Mathematics Education*, London: RoutledgeFalmer.

Mason, J. and Johnston-Wilder, S.J. (2006) *Designing and Using Mathematical Tasks*, St Albans: Tarquin Publications.

Mason, J., Burton, L. and Stacey, K. (2010) *Thinking Mathematically*, 2nd edn, Harlow: Pearson Education Limited.

Mazur, B. (2008) 'Mathematical Platonism and its opposites', *European Mathematical Society Newsletter*, 68, 19–21. Online. Available HTTP: <http://www.math.harvard.edu/~mazur/papers/plato4.pdf> (accessed 12 December 2011).

Meadmore, D. and Symes, C. (1997) 'Keeping up appearances: uniform policy for school diversity?', *British Journal of Educational Studies*, 45(2), 174–86.

Mendick, H. (2002) 'A mathematician goes to the movies', *Proceedings of the British Society for Research into Learning Mathematics*, 24(1), 43–8.

Mercer, N. (1995) *The Guided Construction of Knowledge: talk amongst teachers and learners*, Clevedon: Cromwell Press.

Mercer, N. (2000) *Words and Minds: how we use language to think together*, Oxford: Routledge.

Middleton, J.A. and Spanias, P.A. (1999) 'Motivation for achievement in mathematics: findings, generalizations, and criticisms of the research', *Journal for Research in Mathematics Education*, 30(1), 65–88.

Mlodinow, L. (2001) *Euclid's Window: the story of geometry from parallel lines to hyperspace*, London: Penguin.

Molina, M. and Mason, J. (2009) 'Justifications-on-demand as a device to promote shifts of attention associated with relational thinking in elementary arithmetic', *Canadian Journal of Science, Mathematics and Technology Education*, 9(4), 224–42.

Moon, B. and Bourne, J. (2002) 'Ability, intelligence and attainment in secondary schools', in B. Moon, A.S. Mayes and S. Hutchinson (eds) *Teaching, Learning and the Curriculum in Secondary Schools*, London: RoutledgeFalmer, pp. 25–30.

Movshovitz-Hadar, N. (1988) 'School mathematics theorems: an endless source of surprise', *For the Learning of Mathematics,* 8(3), 34–40.

Mühlhäusler, P. and Harré, R. (1990) *Pronouns and People: the linguistic construction of social and personal identity*, Oxford: Basil Blackwell.

Murphy, M.C. and Dweck, C.S. (2010) 'A culture of genius: how an organization's lay theory shapes people's cognition, affect, and behavior', *Personality and Social Psychology Bulletin*, 36(3), 283–96.

Neville, E.H. (1915) 'On the solution of numerical functional equations, illustrated by an account of a popular puzzle and of its solution', *Proceedings of the London Mathematical Society*, 14, 308–26.

Newman, J.R. (1960) 'Srinivasa Ramanujan', in J.R. Newman (ed.) *The World of Mathematics*, vol. I, London: George Allen and Unwin Ltd, pp. 368–80.

Nichols, S.L. and Berliner, D.C. (2007) *Collateral Damage: how high-stakes testing corrupts America's schools*, Cambridge, MA: Harvard Education Press.

Noddings, N. (2003) *Happiness and Education*, Cambridge: Cambridge University Press.

Noddings, N. (2010) 'Teaching themes of care', in E.F. Provenzo Jr (ed.) *The Teacher in American Society: a critical anthology*, London: SAGE, pp. 135–45.

Noss, R. (1994) 'Structure and ideology in the mathematics curriculum', *For the Learning of Mathematics*, 14(1), 2–10.

Noyes, A. (2006) 'Using metaphor in mathematics teacher preparation', *Teaching and Teacher Education*, 22, 898–909.

Noyes, A. (2007) *Rethinking School Mathematics*, London: SAGE Publications Ltd.

O'Brien, T.C. (2007) 'The old and the new', *Phi Delta Kappan*, 88(9), 664–8.

Oldknow, A., Taylor, R. and Tetlow, L. (2010) *Teaching Mathematics Using ICT*, London: Continuum International Publishing Group.

Ollerton, M. (1995) 'Mind the gap', *Mathematics Teaching*, 152, 35–6.

Ollerton, M. (2002) *Learning and Teaching Mathematics Without a Textbook*, Derby: Association of Teachers of Mathematics.

Ollerton, M. (2003a) *Getting the Buggers to Add Up*, London: Continuum.

Ollerton, M. (2003b) *Everyone is Special*, Derby: Association of Teachers of Mathematics.

Ollerton, M. (2004) *Creating Positive Classrooms*, London: Continuum.

Ollerton, M. (2005) *100 Ideas for Teaching Mathematics*, London: Continuum.

Ollerton, M. (2009) *The Mathematics Teacher's Handbook*, London: Continuum.

Ollerton, M. and Watson, A. (2001) *Inclusive Mathematics 11–18*, London: Continuum.

Ollerton, M. and Watson, A. (2003) 'I teach them but they don't learn', *Equals*, 9(1), 17–18.

Orwell, G. (2008) *Books v. Cigarettes*, London: Penguin Books.

Papert, S. (1993) *Mindstorms: children, computers, and powerful ideas*, 2nd edn, London: Harvester Wheatsheaf.

Pashler, H., McDaniel, M., Rohrer, D. and Bjork, R. (2008) 'Learning styles: concepts and evidence', *Psychological Science in the Public Interest*, 9(3), 105–19.

Patrick, H., Turner, J., Meyer, D.K. and Midgley, C. (2003) 'How teachers establish psychological environments during the first days of school: associations with avoidance in mathematics', *Teachers College Record*, 105(8), 1521–58.

Pelletier, L.G. and Sharp, E.C. (2009) 'Administrative pressures and teachers' interpersonal behaviour in the classroom', *Theory and Research in Education,* 7(2), 174–83.

Peter, L.J. and Hull, R. (1969) *The Peter Principle*, London: Souvenir.

Picker, S.H. and Berry, J.S. (2000) 'Investigating pupils' images of mathematicians', *Educational Studies in Mathematics*, 43(1), 65–94.

Piggott, J. (2004) 'Mathematics enrichment: what is it and who is it for?', paper presented at the BERA annual conference at the University of Manchester, 15–18 September 2004. Available HTTP: <http://www.leeds.ac.uk/educol/documents/00003649.htm> (accessed 13 November 2011).

Pollard, A. (2006) *Reflective Teaching: evidence-informed professional practice*, 2nd edn, London: Continuum.

Pólya, G. (1990) *How to Solve It: a new aspect of mathematical method*, London: Penguin.

Pomeroy, E. (2002) 'The teacher–student relationship in secondary school: insights from excluded students', in B. Moon, A.S. Mayes and S. Hutchinson (eds) *Teaching, Learning and the Curriculum in Secondary Schools*, London: RoutledgeFalmer, pp. 91–106.

Porkess, R. (2011) 'Modular A levels in mathematics', *Mathematics in School*, 40(3), 2–10.

Postman, N. and Weingartner, C. (1971) *Teaching as a Subversive Activity*, London: Pitman.

Povey, H. (2002) 'Promoting social justice in and through the mathematics curriculum: exploring the connections with epistemologies of mathematics', *Mathematics Education Research Journal,* 14(3), 190–201.

Povey, H. (2003) 'Teaching and learning mathematics: can the concept of citizenship be reclaimed for social justice?', in L. Burton (ed.) *International Perspectives on Mathematics Education,* Westport, Connecticut: Praeger Publishers, pp. 51–64.

Power, S. and Clark, A. (2000) 'The right to know: parents, school reports and parents' evenings', *Research Papers in Education,* 15(1), 25–48.

Prestage, S. and Perks, P. (2001) *Adapting and Extending Secondary Mathematics Activities: new tasks for old*, London: David Fulton Publishers.

Prestage, S. and Perks, P. (2006) 'Doing maths or practising the finished product', in D. Hewitt (ed.) *Proceedings of the British Society for Research into Learning Mathematics,* 26(1), 65–70.

Ramsden, J. (2009) *Whoever Thought of That?: short biographies of some contributors to the history of mathematics*, Leicester: The Mathematical Association.

Reeves, D.J., Boyle, W.F. and Christie, T. (2001) 'The relationship between teacher assessments and pupil attainments in standard test tasks at key stage 2, 1996–98', *British Educational Research Journal,* 27(2), 141–60.

Rensaa, R.J. (2006) 'The image of a mathematician', *Philosophy of Mathematics Education Journal*, 19. Online. Available HTTP: <http://people.exeter.ac.uk/PErnest/pome19/Rensaa%20-%20 The%20Image%20of%20a%20Mathematician.doc> (accessed 12 December 2011).

Richardson, P.W. and Watt, H.M.G. (2005) '"I've decided to become a teacher": influences on career change', *Teaching and Teacher Education*, 21(5), 475–89.

Richmond, V.P. and McCroskey, J.C. (eds) (1992) *Power in the Classroom: communication, control, and concern*, New Jersey: Routledge.

Robitaille, D. and Dirks, M. (1982) 'Models for the mathematics curriculum', *For the Learning of Mathematics*, 2(3), 3–21.

Rogers, C. (2002) *On Becoming a Person: a therapist's view of psychotherapy*, London: Constable.

Rogers, C. (2007) *Counseling and Psychotherapy*, Cambridge, MA: The Riverside Press.

Rosenthal, R. and Jacobson, L. (1968) *Pygmalion in the Classroom*, New York: Holt, Rinehart and Winston.

Rowland, T. (1995) 'Hedges in mathematics talk: linguistic pointers to uncertainty', *Educational Studies in Mathematics*, 29(4), 327–53.

Rowland, T. (2000) *The Pragmatics of Mathematics Education: vagueness in mathematical discourse*, London: Falmer Press.

Rowland, T., Huckstep, P. and Thwaites, A. (2005) 'Elementary teachers' mathematics subject knowledge: the knowledge quartet and the case of Naomi', *Journal of Mathematics Teacher Education*, 8(3), 255–81.

Rowlands, R. and Davies, A. (2006) 'Mathematics masterclass: is mathematics discovered or invented?', *Mathematics in School*, 35(2), 2–6.

Rowlands, S., Graham, T. and Berry, J. (2001) 'An objectivist critique of relativism in mathematics education', *Science & Education*, 10(3), 215–41.

Rowlands, S., Graham, T. and Berry, J. (2011) 'Problems with fallibilism as a philosophy of mathematics education', *Science & Education*, 20, 625–54.

Russell, B. (2009) *Unpopular Essays*, London: Routledge.

Ruthven, K. (1987) 'Ability stereotyping in mathematics', *Educational Studies in Mathematics*, 18(3), 243–53.

Sacks, O. (2001) *Uncle Tungsten: memories of a chemical boyhood*, London: Picador.

Sacks, O. (2007) *The Man who Mistook his Wife for a Hat*, London: Picador.

Sagan, C. (1981) *Cosmos*, London: Macdonald Futura.

Sambell, K. and McDowell, L. (1998) 'The construction of the hidden curriculum: messages and meanings in the assessment of student learning', *Assessment and Evaluation in Higher Education*, 23(4), 391–402.

Sangster, M. (2007) 'Reflecting on pace', *Mathematics Teaching Incorporating Micromath*, 204, 34–6.

Sarukkai, S. (2005) 'Revisiting the "unreasonable effectiveness" of mathematics', *Current Science*, 88(3), 415–23. Online. Available HTTP: <http://www.ias.ac.in/currsci/feb102005/415.pdf > (accessed 21 May 2011).

Schön, D. (1983) *The Reflective Practitioner: how professionals think in action*, New York: Basic Books.

Scruggs, T.E. and Mastropieri, M.A. (2000) 'The effectiveness of mnemonic instruction for students with learning and behavior problems: an update and research synthesis', *Journal of Behavioral Education*, 10(2), 163–73.

Sfard, A., Nesher, P., Streefland, L., Cobb, P. and Mason, J. (1998) 'Learning mathematics through conversation: is it as good as they say?', *For the Learning of Mathematics,* 18(1), 41–51.

Shulman, L. (1986) 'Those who understand: knowledge growth in teaching', *Educational Researcher*, 15(2), 4–14.

Silver, E.A. (1986) 'Using conceptual and procedural knowledge: a focus on relationships', in J. Hiebert (ed.) *Conceptual and Procedural Knowledge: the case of mathematics*, Hillsdale, NJ: Erlbaum, pp. 181–98.

Simon, B. (1981) 'Why no pedagogy in England?', in B. Simon and W. Taylor (eds) *Education in the Eighties,* London: Batsford.

Simon, M.A. (1995) 'Reconstructing mathematics pedagogy from a constructivist perspective', *Journal for Research in Mathematics Education,* 26(2), 114–45.

Simon, M.A. and Blume, G.W. (1996) 'Justification in the mathematics classroom: a study of prospective elementary teachers', *Journal of Mathematical Behavior,* 15(1), 3–31.

Sinclair, J.H. and Coulthard, M. (1975) *Towards an Analysis of Discourse: the English used by teachers and pupils,* London: Oxford University Press.

Singh, S. (2002) *Fermat's Last Theorem: the story of a riddle that confounded the world's greatest minds for 358 years,* London: Fourth Estate.

Skemp, R.R. (1971) *The Psychology of Learning Mathematics,* Middlesex: Penguin Books Ltd.

Skemp, R.R. (1976) 'Relational understanding and instrumental understanding', *Mathematics Teaching,* 77, 20–6.

Small, D. (2010) 'Reference-dependent sympathy', *Organizational Behavior and Human Decision Processes,* 112, 151–60.

Spencer, H. (1910) *Education: intellectual, moral, and physical,* London: Williams and Norgate.

Stanley, D., Treisman, U. and Shultz, H.S. (1991) 'Paired weighings: different approaches', *Mathematics in School,* 20(5), 12–14.

Stephenson, P. (1998) 'Grab and the fizz-buzz frieze', *Mathematics in School,* 27(2), 12–13.

Stewart, I. (2010) *Professor Stewart's Hoard of Mathematical Treasures,* London: Profile Books.

Stinson, D.W. (2004) 'Mathematics as "gate-keeper" (?): three theoretical perspectives that aim toward empowering all children with a key to the gate', *The Mathematics Educator,* 14(1), 8–18.

Stylianides, G.J. and Stylianides, A.J. (2008) 'Proof in school mathematics: insights from psychological research into students' ability for deductive reasoning', *Mathematical Thinking and Learning,* 10, 103–33.

Swain, J. and Swan, M. (2007) *Thinking Through Mathematics Research Report,* London: National Research and Development Centre for Adult Literacy and Numeracy.

Swan, M. (2006) *Collaborative Learning in Mathematics: a challenge to our beliefs and practices,* London: National Institute for Advanced and Continuing Education (NIACE) for the National Research and Development Centre for Adult Literacy and Numeracy (NRDC).

Syed, M. (2011) *Bounce: the myth of talent and the power of practice,* London: Fourth Estate.

Tahta, D. (1981) 'Some thoughts arising from the new Nicolet films', *Mathematics Teaching,* 94, 25–9.

Tanner, H., Jones, S., Kennewell, S. and Beauchamp, G. (2005) 'Interactive whole class teaching and interactive white boards', paper presented at the Mathematics Education Research Group of Australia Conference (MERGA 28), Melbourne, Australia. Online. Available HTTP: <www.merga.net.au/documents/RP832005.pdf> (accessed 12 December 2011).

Tyminski, A. (2010) 'Teacher lust: reconstructing the construct for mathematics instruction', *Journal of Mathematics Teacher Education,* 13(4), 295–311.

Ulam, S.M. (1991) *Adventures of a Mathematician,* London: University of California Press.

Uttal, D.H., Scudder, K.V. and DeLoache, J.S. (1997) 'Manipulatives as symbols: a new perspective on the use of concrete objects to teach mathematics', *Journal of Applied Developmental Psychology,* 18, 37–54.

Varma-Joshi, M. (2007) 'Speak no evil, see no evil: the controversy about saying "hate" in mainly white classrooms', in H. Cialre and C. Holden (eds) *The Challenge of Teaching Controversial Issues,* Stoke-on-Trent: Trentham Books, pp. 161–73.

Vygotsky, L.S. (1978) *Mind in Society: the development of higher psychological processes,* London: Harvard University Press.

Walshaw M. and Anthony, G. (2008) 'The teacher's role in classroom discourse: a review of recent research into mathematics classrooms', *Review of Educational Research,* 78(3), 516–51.

Walther, G. (1984) 'Action Proof vs Illuminating Examples?', *For the Learning of Mathematics*, 4(3), 10–12.

Ward-Penny, R. (2010) 'Context or con? How might we better represent the "real-world" in the classroom?', *Mathematics in School*, 39(1), 10–12.

Watson, A. (1995) 'How can I know?', *Mathematics Teaching*, 152, 42.

Watson, A. (1999) 'Paradigmatic conflicts in informal mathematics assessment as sources of social inequity', *Educational Review*, 51(2), 105–15.

Watson, A. (2002) 'Working with students on questioning to promote mathematical thinking', *Mathematics Education Review*, 15, 31–41.

Watson, A. (2006) *Raising Achievement in Secondary Mathematics*, Maidenhead: Open University Press.

Watson, A. (2007) 'Ethel Merman meets the QCA ...', *Mathematics Teaching Incorporating Micromath*, 204, 5.

Watson, A. and Mason, J. (1998) *Questions and Prompts for Mathematical Thinking*, Derby: Association of Teachers of Mathematics.

Watson, A. and Mason, J. (2005) *Mathematics as a Constructive Activity: learners generating examples*, Mahwah: Erlbaum.

Watson, A. and Mason, J. (2007) 'Taken-as-shared: a review of common assumptions about mathematical tasks in teacher education', *Journal of Mathematics Teacher Education*, 10, 205–15.

Watson, A. and Winbourne, P. (2008) *New Directions for Situated Cognition in Mathematics Education*, New York: Springer.

Watt, H.M.G., Richardson, P.W. and Pietsch, J. (2007) 'Choosing to teach in the "STEM" disciplines: characteristics and motivations of science, ICT, and mathematics teachers', in J. Watson and K. Beswick (eds) *Mathematics: essential research, essential practice—volume 2*, Proceedings of the 30th annual conference of the Mathematics Education Research Group of Australasia, Hobart, Tasmania: MERGA Inc.

Wells, D. (1997) *The Penguin Dictionary of Curious and Interesting Numbers*, London: Penguin.

Wheal, C. (2010) '£57m down the back of the sofa', 18 May, *Daily Finance*. Online. Available HTTP: <http://www.dailyfinance.co.uk/2010/05/18/57m-down-the-back-of-the-sofa/> (accessed 27 May 2011).

Whitbecka, D.A. (2000) 'Born to be a teacher: what am I doing in a college of education?', *Journal of Research in Childhood Education*, 15(1), 129–36.

Whitehead, A.N. (1962) *The Aims of Education, and other essays, etc.*, London: Ernest Benn.

Wiliam, D. (2001) 'Formative assessment in mathematics', in L. Haggarty (ed.) *Aspects of Teaching Secondary Mathematics*, London: RoutledgeFalmer.

Wiliam, D. (2009) *Assessment for Learning: why, what and how?*, London: University of London, Institute of Education.

Williams, J., Linchevski, L. and Kutscher, B. (2008) 'Situated cognition and activity theory fill the gap: the cases of integers and two-digit subtraction algorithms', in A. Watson and P. Winbourne (eds) *New Directions in Situated Cognition in Mathematics Education*, New York: Springer, pp. 153–78.

Willis, J. and Todorov, A. (2006) 'First impressions: making up your mind after a 100-ms exposure to a face', *Psychological Science*, 17(7), 592–8.

Wilson, L., Andrew, C. and Sourikova, S. (2001) 'Shape and structure in primary mathematics lessons: a comparative study in the North-East of England and St Petersburg, Russia—some implications for the daily mathematics lesson', *British Educational Research Journal*, 27(1), 29–58.

Wilson, R.J. (2002) *Four Colours Suffice: how the map problem was solved*, London: Allen Lane.

Winbourne, P. and Watson, A. (1998) 'Learning mathematics in local communities of practice', in A. Olivier and K. Newstead (eds) *Proceedings of the Twenty-Second Annual Meeting of the*

International Group for the Psychology of Mathematics Education, Vol. 4, Stellenbosch, South Africa, pp. 177–84.

Wong, J. and Waring, H.Z. (2009) '"Very good" as a teacher response', *English Language Teaching Journal*, 63(3), 195–203.

Zazkis, R. and Mamolo, A. (2011) 'Reconceptualizing knowledge at the mathematical horizon', *For the Learning of Mathematics*, 31(2), 8–13.

Index